DISTANT WITNESS

DISTANT WITNESS

Social Media, the Arab Spring and a Journalism Revolution

ANDY CARVIN
@acarvin

Published by CUNY Journalism Press
219 West 40th Street, New York, NY 10018
www.press.journalism.cuny.edu

First printing 2012

Cataloging-in-Publication data is available from the Library of Congress.
A catalog record for this book is available from the British Library.

ISBN 978-1-939293-02-2 paperback
ISBN 978-1-939293-03-9 e-book

Typeset by Lapiz Digital, Chennai, India.
Printed by BookMobile in the United States and CPI Books Ltd in the United Kingdom.
The U.S. printed edition of this book comes on Forest Stewardship Council-certified, 30% recycled paper. The printer, BookMobile, is 100% wind-powered.

For Susanne

Table of Contents

Acknowledgments

While it may be a cliché to say that this book would not have been possible without the help of countless individuals, in this particular case, it's the literal truth. By my estimate, I've interacted with at least 2,000 people as part of my online coverage of the Arab Spring. Though I'm the author of this book, every person I cite in *Distant Witness* – via Twitter, Facebook, email or face-to-face conversation – has played an important role in helping me tell this story. To each and every one of you, I thank you: *shukran jazilan.*

Of course, this doesn't allow me to get away with not thanking all the individuals who played a more hands-on role in this book. First and foremost, I owe a debt of gratitude to my wife, Susanne, who encouraged me to write this book in the first place. Without her unwavering support, patience and spot-on editing, I'd still be staring at a blank MS Word document or distracting myself with cat videos. By extension, I would like to thank my kids, Kayleigh and Sean, who put up with their daddy vanishing for hours – even days – to write this book; my parents, Bob and Nancy Carvin, for a lifetime of encouragement; my brother Eric, for showing me what it means to be a real journalist; and my mother-in-law, Mary Cornwall, who visited our home in suburban Maryland for weeks at a time to help look after the kids while I was writing.

I'd also like to thank Jeff Jarvis, who not only encouraged me to write this book, but also helped me publish it; to John Oakes of OR Books, who randomly sat next to me at a lovely conference dinner in Perugia, Italy, and first told me of plans to create a publishing house based out of the CUNY School of Journalism; and Tim Harper, who took on a hell of a lot more than he anticipated when he agreed to edit the book, and rose to the challenge of cutting me – or at least my writing – down to size.

My online work that inspired this book wouldn't have been possible without the incredible support I received from NPR, going all the way back to 2006, when Maria Thomas first recruited me. I'd like to thank Kinsey Wilson, Mark Stencel, Joel Sucherman and everyone else in NPR management for giving me the latitude to experiment; and my colleagues Kate Myers, Eyder Peralta, Wright Bryan, Ahmed Al Omran and Ellen Silva, each of whom encouraged and supported me when so many other people thought my methods were a bit nuts.

I'm also grateful to Katie Stanton and her team at Twitter. On more than one occasion, they helped get me out of tight spots when my account froze up, and were *incredibly* generous in their willingness to supply me with a copy of my entire Twitter archive. Without that archive, this book would be much, much thinner and a lot less interesting. And thanks to Burt Herman and Xavier Damman at Storify, for creating a platform that helped me weave tweets into narrative form.

I'd like to thank the entire crew at Global Voices Online – Ethan Zuckerman, Rebecca MacKinnon, and all the editors and contributors who first introduced me to the Arab blogosphere, as well as an international web of volunteers and activists around the world. If it hadn't been for those early connections, I wouldn't be doing what I'm doing today.

Lastly, I'd like to thank the journalists – professional journalists and citizen journalists alike – who put their lives on the line to cover the Arab Spring. They take risks that most of us can scarcely imagine, and we are all better informed because of them. *Stay safe, everyone.*

Foreword

By Jeff Jarvis

Whenever I arrive at a conference – I go to a lot of them – and find NPR senior strategist Andy Carvin there, I am delighted and relieved. If he attends a panel I care about, I won't have to take notes or blog what was said – or pay much attention, for that matter. Andy will reliably tweet every noteworthy thought and each shareable quote, but nothing more: just the essence of the event, live, as it happens. Andy Carvin is the maestro of the medium, Twitter's Stravinsky.

Who could have imagined that this skill could change journalism and its relationship to witnesses and the public? But then, who could have imagined that Twitter – technology reputedly devoted to discussing breakfast, dumb videos and brainless celebrities – could help change the world?

When what became the Arab Spring began, Andy brought so much to the story: his unique understanding and use of Twitter, his experience in the region, his relationships with people there, his passionate journalistic curiosity and skepticism, and especially his generous heart and spirit. He added to the story, and sometimes became the story, tweeting and retweeting up to 1,500 times a day. He helped connect witnesses and participants on the streets of Tunisia, Egypt, Bahrain, Libya, Yemen and Syria with countless others online.

Let me be clear. These were not Twitter revolutions. As one blogger in Egypt said in the thick of it, the police in the country clashed not with Twitter but with brave Egyptians. But many of the revolutionaries in these countries did take advantage of the new tools of the Net – Twitter, as well as Facebook and YouTube. They use these tools to discover one another and help organize themselves, to share information with each other, and to reveal what they saw to the rest of the world. These exchanges create a new flow of information – raw, unfiltered news – that requires no media and no mediation.

Andy Carvin adds value to that flow. He gives us a vision of what journalism can and should become. We need a new verb for what he does. He wasn't reporting from the scene. He wasn't covering the story as a foreign correspondent. He didn't write articles. He edited no one. But he performed many functions that we must teach to today's journalists – and tomorrow's.

To start with, Andy used his contacts in these countries to determine who on Twitter was where, and whose reports were reliable. In Internet terms, he discerned nodes and networks: the person he knew was a node and the people they knew were networks. Having those contacts and knowing how to build on them in an instant, from afar, will be a key journalistic skill as news breaks online. Mind you, journalists have always been expert at finding witnesses and sources, but now they have new ways to do it. Andy taught me one of his tricks: when a big story breaks – an earthquake in California, say, or a plane landing on the Hudson River in New York – Andy looks to Twitter for people who use various fleeting expletives ("WTF" and others more explicit) before the news hits wire services and TV, and before the rest of the world discovers the story. Those are probably primary witnesses.

Next, Andy confirms facts and debunks rumors – perhaps the most important journalistic skill of all. In this book, you will see many stories about tackling rumors. On the Net, as we know, misinformation travels fast. But so can corrections. Andy consistently showed skepticism. He demanded sources and confirmation. He did the hard work of journalism in public. And that's another trick he taught me: if a tweet shouts in all caps "CONFIRMED," be especially wary. Someone may be wishing it to be true.

That leads to the next of Andy's great Twitter skills: mobilizing his community to work together with him. As you'll see in these pages, he is quick to ask his Twitter followers to translate eyewitness videos; to confirm the location and timing of a demonstration in a photo; or to dig up specialized knowledge about, say, armaments used by one side or the other. He builds networks of experts.

Andy adds one more element to his style of groundbreaking journalism, one that may be controversial in some traditional quarters: humanity. As he watches and recounts – or rather, retweets – both the exhilaration and tragedy of the events he follows, Andy cannot help but be affected – and so are we, his followers and readers. It's a shared emotional experience one only rarely achieves through traditional media (think: Anderson Cooper in the flooded streets of New Orleans).

Apart from a handful of blog posts, Andy did not produce any of these amazing tales as narrative – that familiar atomic unit of news we call the story. Yet we journalists think of ourselves first and foremost as storytellers. What are we then without the story? From Andy's example, I think that is clear. He adds value. He finds witnesses and experts, gathers what is and is not known, confirms the facts and debunks the rumors, offers context and explanation, exhibits news judgment to highlight what is important, and uses the tools at hand – whether broadcast tower or printing press or Twitter account – to inform and enlighten the public. By my definition, journalism helps a community organize its knowledge so it can better organize itself. Journalists, then, must add value to that knowledge, not as gatekeepers but as facilitators.

Andy is a prototype for a new kind of journalist. He also turns out to be a masterful storyteller. He has taken all he witnessed from afar in the Arab Spring and crafted it into a dramatic, compelling, informative page-turner. He has combed his archive of more than 100,000 tweets and sifted through the rapid-fire, staccato progression of voices to find a narrative sense and create a cohesive saga.

One last observation: someone will surely ask whether there is a business model in Andy's story. Were it not for the generous support of NPR and public radio's many charitable contributors, Andy could not have worked full-time – and much more – to chronicle the revolutions and reinvent journalism. There probably is not a business model for @acarvin, Inc. But there are business lessons for the rest of the industry about the value and efficiency in collaboration with the public.

Yes, we still need reporters on the ground to ask and answer the questions. We need them to bring us perspective and context. Andy does not replace them. He and his nodes and networks of witnesses, participants and experts add to the news in ways not possible before. Journalism is not shrinking. Through Andy's example, as well as through experiments in data journalism, crowdsourcing, hyperlocal sites and innovations yet to come, journalism is growing. Andy Carvin is proof of that.

Prologue

Through the pungent haze of tear gas and smoke, they set up makeshift barricades, ripping corrugated metal off nearby rooftops to shield themselves from the firebombs. Protesters camping out at Cairo's Tahrir Square have been under assault by pro-government thugs for well over 12 hours. As dawn approaches, they're running on fumes. They struggle to repel the thugs and their Molotov cocktails – and now another fire has broken out next to the Egyptian Museum. The treasures of Egypt's 5,000-year history, along with its first real chance of democracy, are in danger of going up in smoke.

Choking on the tear gas, a young protester steps forward with the two weapons that will help determine their fate: a jagged rock and a smartphone. Gripping the phone tightly, he hurls the rock at the thugs. Before the stone even reaches its target, he's frantically tweeting again, hoping that someone – *somewhere* – will read it and bear witness.

> I've started throwing stones with the crew at the museum battle. Don't have any other choice. Viva la revolucion #jan25[1]

The pitched battles that gripped the attention of the world during the Egyptian revolution were just a taste of what we would witness over the course of 2011. The series of North African and Middle East uprisings collectively known as the Arab Spring is a flashpoint in history – perhaps the biggest upheaval of geopolitical power since the collapse of the Soviet bloc 20 years earlier.

It's also been a stunning revolution in the way breaking news is reported around the world – and who controls the news. With countless revolutionaries using the Internet as part of their protests, anyone online could gain direct access to the news, moment by moment – no filters, no spin, no delay. No longer did media outlets have a monopoly on international reporting; people on Twitter or YouTube could patch directly into the revolution of their choice.

For those of us working within mainstream media, the challenge was taking the strengths of traditional journalism and combining them with the real-time, Wild West nature of the social media landscape. Can you trust reports from so-called citizen journalists who are also actively taking part in a revolution? How do you handle the onslaught of uncensored, graphic footage circulating online that in the heyday of mass media would've never seen the light of day? As rumors spread online, do you wait for full confirmation before even mentioning them, or do you acknowledge to your audience that these rumors exist, and that you don't have all the answers yet? Is it even fair to call them an *audience* anymore? One way or another, storytelling has entered new territory.

Though it's easy to see social media as a relatively new phenomenon, it didn't come into existence overnight; it was a long, steady evolution of tools created to reflect and shape the Internet in the way that people wanted to use it. They wanted to publish travel journals and share cat videos. They wanted to collaborate on crazy projects like an encyclopedia written by the public, or free listings for local goods and services, or open-source software that no multinational company could ever control. And they wanted to get to know other people who shared their passions and interests.

The tools that came out of this dream of a better, more human Internet – Facebook, Twitter, YouTube, Wikipedia, Reddit and more – have taken on a life of their own. They're cultural drivers, tastemakers and meeting points. And somewhere along the way, people realized they could use these tools to make their lives better. For some, especially individuals living under repressive regimes, social media became a platform for organizing and dissent. From the earliest Arab political bloggers to the citizen journalists of the 2009 Iran election protests, they blazed a trail that foretold the methods used to help organize the Arab Spring.

In September 2006 – on the fifth anniversary of the 9/11 attacks – I came to NPR to experiment with these tools and explore new forms of storytelling. I wasn't part of the newsroom – I wasn't even considered a journalist by most of the staff. But over my career I'd gotten to know bloggers and online activists around the world. Those informal relationships proved invaluable in plugging me into what would become the biggest geopolitical disruption in years – and put me in a unique position to tell their stories.

My job title at NPR is Senior Strategist. It's a meaningless description in many ways, so I usually describe myself as NPR's guinea pig in residence. I'm a journalistic test pilot – I take new reporting methods for a spin, and see if they soar or crash.

I don't see the Internet as simply a place where stuff gets published or money is made. I don't even see it as a separate place that you enter and exit in and out of the "real" world. It is a living, breathing community of people who don't see a gap between their online lives and their offline ones. And if you connect the dots between the right people, amazing things can happen.

That's how I was drawn into the Arab Spring. In my previous work, as an online community organizer at the Digital Divide Network, I got to know a number of Arab bloggers and made several trips to Tunisia and other parts of the Arab world. I stayed in touch with some of them, even though they didn't have anything to do with my work at NPR. I kept track of them simply because they were a window into a world I found fascinating. No one could have anticipated that a scattering of online chatter about a fruit vendor in Tunisia would change the Arab world, journalism and my life forever.

Since the Arab Spring began, I've used social media to report remotely on uprisings in more than half a dozen countries. It started as a hobby, but soon became my calling – some might say my obsession. For months on end, seven days a week, up to 18 hours a day, I used my Twitter account to cover the revolutions as a broadcast anchor would, and worked with online volunteers all over the world to dig up new stories. Many of my sources and followers don't know what I look like, where I am in the world at any given time, or even what my full name is. To them, I'm just @acarvin, the guy on Twitter who's plugged into the Arab revolutions.

I see this book as a collection of war stories – stories that would have otherwise fallen through the cracks of history if people on the ground weren't using social media to tell them. An incredible array of individuals set aside their daily lives to fight for what they believed in. The student caught in the middle of a battle, struggling to survive the melee while towing a lost toddler. The activist standing in front of a column of military vehicles, grinding the convoy to a halt with nothing but her arms outstretched in defiance. The citizen journalist who fatefully recorded his own death while documenting the plight of his people.

Some of them succeeded beyond their wildest dreams; others didn't live long enough to see their dreams fulfilled. The one thing they had in common was their determination to use whatever tools they had to tell the world about their struggles – and to ensure that their stories wouldn't be forgotten.

The Structure of this Book

When I first began outlining *Distant Witness*, I faced a fundamental challenge: how to tell the stories of simultaneous revolutions. At the height of the Arab Spring, it wasn't unusual for me over the course of a day to intertwine the stories of dozens of people from half a dozen conflicts, from Libya to Yemen. That's the nature of major international stories when experienced through social media – when it rains, it pours. And while it makes for a thrilling real-time experience, multitasking these disparate narratives doesn't necessarily make for an easy read after the fact.

That's why I've decided to organize most of the book – the epilogue notwithstanding – by country. Rather than expecting you the reader to remember the names of 100 different characters concurrently, I've broken up their stories on a conflict-by-conflict basis. Whenever possible, I've ordered the stories chronologically. This was relatively straightforward for the uprisings in Tunisia and Egypt, since they didn't overlap other revolutions by much.

As for the other countries covered in this book – Libya, Bahrain, Yemen and Syria – their revolutions overlapped each other, sometimes in a staggered fashion, sometimes all at once. By focusing on one revolution at a time, I hope to make it easier to understand what took place – how, when, where and why. But in doing so, I sometimes hit the rewind button to tell the story of another revolution in a subsequent chapter.

I've also written the book from the perspective of what you might call a "semi-informed narrator" following breaking news amidst the fog of war – or perhaps in this case, the smog of revolution. History as it is unfolding is rarely so clear-cut as it seems in retrospect; rumors get reported as facts, and facts get reported as rumors. So rather than pretend that I knew everything while all of this was going on, you'll get to experience the stories as my Twitter followers and I did, feeling our way through the smog to find the truth.

Andy Carvin
Washington, D.C.
November 2012

Dramatis Personae

Tunisia

The Regime
Zine El Abidine Ben Ali: President of Tunisia
Leila Trabelsi: Tunisian first lady; Ben Ali's wife

The Activists
Mohamed Bouazizi: Young man who sets himself on fire in protest
Sami Ben Gharbia (@ifikra): Tunisian human rights activist, living in exile in Europe
Rafik Dammak (@rafik): Tunisian activist and engineer based in Tokyo
Mohamed Marwen Meddah (@MMM): Tunisian blogger

Egypt

The Regime
Hosni Mubarak: President of Egypt
Omar Suleiman: Mubarak's newly appointed vice president

The Activists
Alaa Abd el-Fattah (@alaa): Software developer, blogger
Manal Hasan (@manal): Alaa's wife
Mohamed El Dahshan (@TravellerW): Writer, economist
Ali Seif (@BloggerSeif): Lebanese-Canadian college student visiting Cairo
Wael Abbas (@waelabbas): Blogger
@Zeinobia: Blogger
Omar Robert Hamilton (@RiverDryFilm): British-Egyptian filmmaker
Mona Seif (@monasosh): Researcher at a local cancer lab
Mosa'ab Elshamy (@mosaaberizing): Pharmacy student and photographer
Tarek Shalaby (@tarekshalaby): Creative director, planet360 advertising agency
Nora Shalaby (@norashalaby) Egyptologist; Tarek's sister
Amr El Beleidy (@beleidy): Founder, Touringa.com
Tarek Amr (@gr33ndata): Contributor to Global Voices Online
Gigi Ibrahim (@Gsquare86): Socialist activist
Hossam Hamalawy (@3arabawy): Labor activist
Mona Eltahawy (@monaeltahawy): Egyptian-American writer and commentator
Sarah Carr (@SarahCarr): British-Egyptian blogger and writer
Wael Ghonim (@ghonim): Google executive arrested at the beginning of the revolution

Habib Haddad (@HabibH): Lebanese entrepreneur; friend of Wael Ghonim
Mahmoud Salem (@sandmonkey): Veteran blogger and political activist
Nadia El-Awady (@NadiaE): Science reporter
@Egyptocracy: Pseudonym of a female Egyptian activist
Ramy Yaacoub (@RamyYaacoub): Political analyst

Bahrain

The Regime

Hamad bin Isa Al Khalifa: King of Bahrain
Khalid Al Khalifa (@khalidalkhalifa): Foreign Minister

The Activists

Chan'ad Bahraini (@chanadbh): Blogger
Zainab Al-Khawaja (@angryarabiya): Human rights activist
Maryam Al-Khawaja (@maryamalkhawaja): Human rights activist; Zainab's sister
Abdulhadi Al-Khawaja: Human rights activist; Zainab and Maryam's father
@FroozyO: Pseudonym of Bahraini activist

The Observers

Amira Al Hussaini (@justamira): Middle East editor, Global Voices Online
Mazen Mahdi (@MazenMahdi): Freelance photographer

Libya

The Regime

Muammar Gaddafi: Libyan dictator
Khamis Gaddafi: One of Gaddafi's sons; leads a notorious military brigade

The Activists

Ghazi Gheblawi (@Gheblawi): Libyan in exile in London
Ali Tweel (@alitweel): Libyan living in Tripoli
Malik L (@LibyaSupreme): Libyan-American in Benghazi
Mohammed Nabbous: Libyan citizen journalist in Benghazi
Perditta Nabbous: Wife of Mohammed Nabbous
Niz Ben-Essa (@Niz_FGM): Pseudonym of Libyan man organizing acts of civil disobedience in Tripoli
Hamza Mousa (@Hamzamu): Egyptian doctor volunteering in Libya
Danya Bashir (@ceoDanya): Libyan student living in the UAE
DJ Meddi (@DJMeddi): Libyan-American DJ based in Georgia
Brian Conley (@baghdadbrian): Co-founder of Small World News; journalism trainer
@ShababLibya: Libyan revolutionary news service

@ChangeInLibya: Pseudonym of Libyan from Tripoli, living in Malta
@flyingbirdies: Pseudonym of Libyan in Tripoli
@Abukhit: Pseudonym of Libyan in Tripoli
@feb17voices: Group of volunteers specializing in Libyan audio
@IbnOmar2005: Pseudonym of Libyan activist
@Tripolitanian: Pseudonym of Libyan activist
@Tripoli_Latest: Underground news source in Tripoli

Yemen

The Regime
Ali Abdul Saleh: President of Yemen
Abd Rabbuh Mansur al-Hadi: Saleh's vice president
Ali Mohsen: Army general who defects to opposition

The Activists
Raja Althaibani (@RajaAlthaibani): Yemeni-American living in Sana'a, Yemen
Maria Al-Masani (@al_masani): Yemeni-Canadian intelligence expert; beauty queen contestant
Abdulkader Alguneid (@Alguneid): Physician based in Taiz, Yemen
Tawakkol Karman (@TawakkolKarman): Opposition leader and journalist
Hamza Shargabi (@ichamza): Yemeni surgeon and video blogger
Ibrahim Mothana (@imothanaYemen): Co-founder, Yemeni youth political party

The Observers
Jane Novak (@JNovak_Yemen): U.S.-based Yemen expert
Gregory D. Johnsen (@gregorydjohnsen): Yemen researcher, Princeton University
Jeb Boone (@JebBoone): Yemen-based freelance journalist
Tom Finn (@tomfinn2): Editor of the *Yemen Times*
Iona Craig (@ionacraig): Reporter for the *Times* of London

Syria

The Regime
Bashar al-Assad: President of Syria
Hafez al-Assad: Former president of Syria; Bashar's late father

The Activists
Rami Nakhla (@MalathAumran): Opposition activist
Amina Arraf: Blogger based in Damascus
Sandra Bagaria (@sade_la_bag): Amina's girlfriend in Montreal
Hamza Al-Khatib: Murdered teenage boy
Rose al Homsi (@tweets4peace): Syrian expat with family in Homs, Syria
Rami Jarrah (@AlexanderPageSY): British-Syrian activist

Basil al Sayid: Videographer; citizen journalist
Syria Pioneer: Pseudonym of a videographer; citizen journalist

The Investigators
Elizabeth Tsurkov (@Elizrael): Israeli activist and writer
Paula Brooks (@LezGetReal): Founder of the blog Lez Get Real
Liz Henry (@lizhenry): Blogger, Web developer for BlogHer.com
Jillian York (@jilliancyork): Online free speech activist, Electronic Frontier Foundation
Ali Abunimah (@AliAbunimah): Palestinian activist, co-founder of the blog Electronic Intifada
Benjamin Doherty (@bangpound): Web developer, blogger at Electronic Intifada

The Press Corps
Nicholas Kristof (@nickkristof): *New York Times* columnist
Ben Wedeman (@BenCNN): CNN Cairo bureau chief
Ian Lee (@IanInEgypt): CNN stringer
Sherine Tadros (@SherineT): Al Jazeera English reporter
Ayman Mohyeldin (@AymanM): Al Jazeera English reporter
Dan Nolan (@nolanjazeera): Al Jazeera English reporter
Evan Hill (@evanchill): Al Jazeera English reporter
Anderson Cooper (@andersoncooper): CNN host and reporter
Bel Trew (@beltrew): British freelance journalist based in Cairo
Sultan al Qassemi (@sultanalqassemi): UAE-based commentator
Hala Jaber (@HalaJaber): Correspondent for the *Sunday Times*
Sarah Raslan (@sarahraslan): *Houston Chronicle* reporter
Blake Hounshell (@blakehounshell): Managing editor, *Foreign Policy*
Ahmed Al Omran (@ahmed): Saudi blogger, production assistant at NPR
Eyder Peralta (@EyderP): Breaking news blogger, NPR
C.J. Chivers (@cjchivers): Reporter, *New York Times*
Alex Crawford (@alexcrawfordsky): Correspondent, Sky News
Lourdes Garcia-Navarro (@lourdesgnavarro): Correspondent, NPR

The Volunteers
Natasha Tynes (@NatashaTynes): Translation
Nadia Al Sheikh (@nadiaalsheikh): Translation
Samar Dahmash Jarrah: (@ArabVoicesSpeak): Translation
Shakeeb Al-Jabri (@LeShaque): Translation, analysis, sourcing
Iyad el Baghdadi (@iyad_elbaghdadi): Translation, analysis, sourcing
Nasser Weddady (@weddady): Translation, analysis, sourcing
Haris Alisic (@HarisAlisic): Munitions research
@nolesfan2011: Munitions research
@tasnimq: Translation
@ysalah: Translation

@brhone: Munitions research
@der_bluthund: Munitions research
@papakila: Munitions research
@urbanmilkmaid: Munitions research

TUNISIA

The Spark

On a bleak winter's day in a forgotten corner of North Africa, a desperate young man committed the ultimate act of defiance. It started like a normal day for him; just 26 years old and the sole breadwinner for his family, his only source of income was a humble cart he used to sell fruit around town. Earning less than $75 a week, he dreamt of saving up for a truck, and perhaps even having a permanent stall at the local produce market. For now, though, his fruit cart was all that separated him and his family from all-out destitution.[1]

As he ventured outside to sell his fruit that morning, local inspectors demanded that he pay a fine for some arbitrary infraction. Like so many other young people running a small business in this part of the world, he wasn't officially licensed; the process of receiving a license was time-consuming and prohibitively expensive for the average person. This left him at the mercy of officials and municipal police, who routinely demanded bribes or helped themselves to his fruit. This time, he refused to cooperate. A scuffle ensued, attracting municipal police. As a crowd of bystanders looked on, a female police officer reportedly slapped the young man across the face, while the inspectors confiscated his cart, electronic scale and his modest inventory of fruit crates.

The young man made an attempt to retrieve his property at the local government administrative office, but it was to no avail. His entire livelihood had been taken away from him.

At 11:30 a.m., just an hour after the confrontation began, he returned to the government office, standing outside the gates with a jug of liquid. Some say it was gasoline, others paint thinner. He reportedly yelled, "How do you expect me to make a living?" just before he poured its contents over his head.[2]

Then he lit a match.

His name was Mohamed Bouazizi, and he lived in the Tunisian town of Sidi Bou Zid. It was December 17, 2010.

Bystanders struggled to put out the fire engulfing his body. Someone had a fire extinguisher, but it was empty. Others tried water, but that only spread the flames. Eventually, they managed to douse the blaze, and he was brought to the local hospital, barely alive, 95 percent of his body covered by severe burns. Unable to cope with his injuries, doctors transported him to the next largest city, more than an hour's drive away.[3]

Word spread quickly around town. Enraged at how government officials had driven the young man to this shocking, almost unspeakable act, local residents arrived at the same government building, demanding an explanation. Many, if not all of them, had experienced similar indignities by the regime at one time or another. Despite the fact that freedom of assembly was nonexistent in Tunisia, they gathered outside the gate, jeering, whistling and raising their fists in solidarity with this gravely wounded young man, until the police eventually dispersed them.

It could have ended there – a random act of civil disobedience that no one beyond the city's borders would ever know about. But someone in that crowd had a video camera.[4]

"So . . . How are things at home?"

Half a world away from Sidi Bou Zid that very morning, I was sitting in a Washington, D.C. café with a Tunisian friend who was in town for a conference. He and I hadn't seen each other in five years, since I attended a U.N. Internet policy summit in Tunis in December 2005. It was the last time I'd been in the region. A blogger and software engineer who spoke four languages, he was typical of well-educated Tunisian twenty-somethings: multilingual and talented, but with limited opportunities for advancement in the country. He moved to Europe and got a job in the tech industry, but didn't blog much any more. Even beyond the North African nation's borders, blogging could be a dangerous pastime for a Tunisian.

After achieving its independence from France in 1956, Tunisia had known only two presidents. The country's ruler, President Zine El Abidine Ben Ali, overthrew his predecessor in the late 1970s, and then proceeded to run the country essentially as an organized crime family would. He and his wife, Leila Trabelsi, doled out the most lucrative industries to siblings, children and cousins. Citizens were forced to pay bribes for even the most mundane transactions, and government officials, from the first family on down, reaped these ill-gotten gains.[5, 6, 7]

Tunisia wasn't just a mafia state, though – it also was a police state.[8, 9] There was no free speech, no free press, no right to assembly. The Internet was heavily censored. Political opposition groups were token at best; President Ben Ali and his cronies would win re-election without legitimate challengers. Anyone who tried to

defy the system was arrested. If you were lucky, they'd release you eventually.[10]

The last time I had seen my Tunisian friend, we were backpacking across the southern part of the country. He and I were routinely hassled by police at checkpoints. When we briefly visited a family acquaintance of his, police showed up and detained the acquaintance in the back of their van for more than 30 minutes, just to intimidate us.[11] When my friend said the police ordered his acquaintance to come in for questioning the next day, I asked, "About what?" He replied, "About you."[12]

We never discussed politics. It wasn't worth the risk; too many informers, too many undercover government agents. During one of our times together at a restaurant, a pair of burly men in cheap suits sat nearby, holding up newspapers to conceal their pencils and notebooks. They barely tried to hide their note-taking;

the intimidation factor alone served as a powerful chilling effect. Even in a small café with his closest friends, sequestered in a distant corner with no other patrons or wait staff around, I would be lucky to get them to whisper more than a sentence fragment on Tunisia's suffocating human rights situation.

Now it was five years later, and we were sitting in a very different café in D.C., engaging in small talk. I truly wanted to hear his opinions on the state of affairs back in Tunisia, yet I couldn't bring myself to ask him directly. I was afraid of embarrassing him, given the uncomfortable nature of the topic. I phrased my question as obliquely as possible.

"So . . . How are things at home?"

My friend sighed, and glanced down at his coffee. He looked me in the eyes, and his face said it all.

"Some things never change," he replied, then quickly changed the subject.

Back in Sidi Bou Zid, local police had dispersed the protesters, but the public's anger simmered overnight. Riots erupted the following day as residents lashed out against years of indignities committed by the regime.[13] The Tunisian government made sure that news didn't spread through local newspapers or television, all controlled by the state.[14]

As for the Internet, video-sharing websites such as YouTube and DailyMotion were routinely blocked by the government.[15, 16] Whenever you went online, there was always the possibility that you were being watched. During my first visit to Tunisia in 2005, I went to a Tunis cybercafé to catch up on email. Directly above my computer was a garish, illuminated picture of President Ben Ali, with a brief note from the management: your Internet activities are being monitored and subject to Tunisian law.

Just because the regime blocked YouTube and other sites, it didn't mean that the Tunisian public was entirely in the dark. Far from it; in the five years since my last visit, Tunisia's overall adoption of digital technology had expanded rapidly. More than 30 percent of the country had Internet access, higher than other countries in the region.[17] And while many blogs and social media sites were routinely blocked by the regime, one particular site was noticeably not behind their firewall: Facebook.

In a country of 11 million people, approximately 2 million Tunisians were already on Facebook.[18] It was one of the few places where they could go online and interact with each other. The regime tried blocking Facebook in 2008, but that provoked such outrage that officials rescinded their decision two weeks later.[19] But the government monitored Facebook for hints of dissent, and could block pages on an individual basis.

That didn't stop Tunisians from uploading things to the network – including videos of the protests in support of Mohamed Bouazizi. The first videos from Sidi Bou Zid posted online that same day show hundreds of men and a number of women gathering in front of the government building where Bouazizi set himself on fire.[20, 21] In one video, as the camera pans to the left, you can see what appears to be a produce cart with fruit scattered around it. Surrounded by a growing crowd, an ambulance is being loaded, presumably Bouazizi himself.[22] The footage appeared on Facebook in several forms.[23, 24] Yet another video shows a crowd of hundreds of people marching on the government building.[25]

A small group of Tunisian bloggers began to circulate the video on various platforms, including Facebook and Twitter.[26] One of the first forums set up to promote the protests was a Facebook group called "Mr. President, Tunisians Are Setting Themselves On Fire."[27] In a matter of days, the group attracted more than 10,000 members, though the government blocked individual Facebook pages to censor it.[28]

Twitter, meanwhile, was far less popular in Tunisia than Facebook, but among its users were some of the most popular and influential Tunisian bloggers. The tight community of activists did their best to shame the regime, using whatever online tools at their disposal. Several of them had managed to publish a cache of U.S. State Department cables about Tunisia, acquired from WikiLeaks.[29] Now they began circulating the Bouazizi video on Twitter, creating a hashtag for it based on the name of the town: #sidibouzid.

When Twitter launched in 2006, there was no built-in mechanism for carrying on a conversation thread among a broad array of people. All you could do was subscribe to individuals involved in the discussion and do your best to keep up with it. Twitter lacked a function that would have allowed a tweet to be read by everyone interested in the topic, whether they were following each other or not. Then a Twitter user named Chris Messina proposed a simple convention, inspired by online chatroom culture: come up with a keyword that describes whatever you're talking about, then add a # sign – also known as a hash mark – in front of it.[30] Users could then search for this keyword, or *hashtag*, and follow the conversation.

The earliest tweets I've identified with the #sidibouzid hashtag were posted by Chady Neji (@Chady2009) and Taïeb Moalla (@moalla) on December 18, the day after Bouazizi set himself on fire.[31, 32] When I first came upon the hashtag, several days after the incident, I had no idea where Sidi Bou Zid was or precisely what had transpired there.

While I tried to piece together what was happening, I began to pay careful attention to the handful of Tunisian bloggers I knew on Twitter. A few I had met in person; most I'd gotten to know online. Many of us were loosely affiliated with an international blogging project launched at Harvard University known as Global Voices Online.[33] I lived near Boston when it first went online in 2005, and contributed a number of articles.[34] Global Voices also published stories by North African and Middle Eastern bloggers, many of whom had met offline at self-organized blogger conferences. As I looked at their Twitter accounts, I realized that they weren't only aware of the incident in Sidi Bou Zid; they were spreading word of it as far and wide as possible.

At the center of this group of bloggers was a Tunisian-in-exile named Sami Ben Gharbia. I'd never met him in person – he lived in the Netherlands – but had gotten to know his human rights work via his role as Global Voices' advocacy director. Sami and a small group of compatriots had created a Tunisian human rights website called Nawaat.org to gather all sorts of information as a form of online protest against the government. Photos, videos and articles embarrassing to the Tunisian regime were routinely posted on Nawaat.org. Sami and his online partners were the brains behind the Tunisia Wikileaks project, too.[35] I began to monitor the #sidibouzid hashtag over the 2010 Christmas holiday break, and discovered that they were tweeting links to dozens of photos and videos every day. Solidarity protests had spread across the country.

Increasing numbers of Tunisians began banding together to organize their own protests. In many cases, people attending a rally would document it with a video camera or smartphone, and then upload footage to Facebook. Sami and the Nawaat team gathered every fragment of protest footage they could find and posted it on their blog, which was hosted in the U.S. by the blogging service Posterous.[36] They also uploaded the materials wherever they could get away with it – other social networks, video sharing sites, community bulletin boards. The protests, which at first demanded more economic opportunities for the nation's youth, went viral both online and offline. One protest – and the footage documenting it – would catalyze more protests, inspiring nascent activists into action.

While outrage spread across Tunisia, Mohamed Bouazizi struggled to survive, having been transferred to yet another hospital. Comatose, he was unaware of the firestorm he had ignited throughout his country.

Several thousand miles away in D.C., I monitored Twitter and the Nawaat blog in astonishment. I'd encountered the regime's enforcers back in 2005 and had a basic sense of what they were capable of, yet increasing numbers of defiant Tunisians were now going out into the streets all over the country.[37] As the protests spread, the government's response became more and more violent. Several other young Tunisians killed themselves in a show of solidarity with Bouazizi.[38, 39]

I started thinking about protest movements around the world, some of them successful, some not. What exactly does it take for one of these movements to go all the way and overthrow a regime? My intuition told me to keep an eye on the protests.

A few days after Christmas, on the evening on December 28, 2010, I sent out a tweet pondering the possibilities:

> Following protests in Tunisia via #sidibouzid hashtag. Wonder what the chances of all of this leading to a "jasmine revolution." Don't know.[40]

I'd been thinking about the phrase "jasmine revolution" for a few days by then. During my visits to Tunisia, I'd seen young men strolling the streets with tiny bouquets of jasmine blossoms tucked behind their ears, while kids sold them to tourists at ridiculously marked-up rates. I had no idea if the jasmine was Tunisia's official flower, but it seemed an appropriate descriptor for a Tunisian revolution.

As New Year's Eve approached, I recognized Twitter users who were regulars on the #sidibouzid hashtag. There was Sami Ben Gharbia, of course, who went by the name @ifikra, and his group blog, @nawaat. There were a few others, including Rafik Dammak (@rafik), Riadh Guerfali (@astrubaal) and Lina Ben Mhenni (@benmhennilina), about whom I knew less. They tweeted mostly in French, but my limited language skills from high school helped me get the gist of their comments.

Then there were others offering moral support from abroad. One of them, Mona Eltahawy (@MonaEltahawy), is an Egyptian–American writer I'd seen on television from time to time. A Boston-based Mauritanian human rights activist, Nasser Weddady (@weddady), seemed to be plugged into the protest movement very closely. I also discovered a man in the UAE named Sultan Al Qassemi (@SultanAlQassemi). He was a local columnist and tweeted almost as often as I did, except that he never seemed to need any sleep.

As the protests spread, new footage got around the firewall. I struggled to interpret the full context, as I don't speak Arabic. I didn't want to bother Tunisian activists directly – they probably were too busy to notice me anyway – so I reached out to one of the Twitter users who always seemed on top of things: Nasser Weddady.

Some of my early questions revolved around how Arabic was transliterated into Latin script on Twitter. It wasn't unusual to see Arabic words with numbers mixed into them: the number 3 at the beginning or in the middle of a word, for example, as well as the numbers 2 and 7. They represented letters in the Arabic alphabet that didn't exist in English, but I didn't know which ones or how they were pronounced. I asked Nasser:

> @weddady: quick question: what sound is the 3 in Frei3a supposed to represent?[41]
>
> @weddady: is it a glottal stop? [like the sound in the middle of uh-oh][42]

Two minutes later, I heard back from him. It turned out the number 3 represented the Arabic letter *ayn*, which can only be described as a guttural noise you might make if you attempted to choke yourself while saying a vowel.

On one occasion, I received a photo of a protest sign, smeared with what appeared to be red paint to represent blood, and an Arabic phrase on it. I assumed it was a protest slogan.

> @weddady: Sorry to keep bothering you, but could you translate the words on this pic? http://flic.kr/p/99uspx thanks![43]

= perfect example of globalization.

Less than 20 seconds later, I received a response from the Tunisian activist Rafik Dammak, who happened to be following me on Twitter.

> RT @rafik: @acarvin: "mohamed amine mbarki" it is a name[44]

So it wasn't a protest slogan at all. I googled the name and quickly found two photos. One of them was of a smiling young man. The other was the same man, ashen, bloodied, lifeless, killed by Tunisia's security forces.

The new year had arrived; it was now early January 2011. Tunisia was entering its fourth week of protests. Mohamed Bouazizi died of his horrific wounds on January 4, 18 days after setting himself alight. Before Bouazizi passed away, President Ben Ali paid him a visit at the hospital. It was little more than a photo op. Ben Ali presented Bouazizi's family with a check, but an aide reportedly took the check back as soon as the cameras departed.[45] Even so, it was still astounding that Ben Ali visited at all; the president was shaken.

By then, police were routinely opening fire on activists. In one central Tunisian city, Kasserine, police killed more than 20 protesters.[46] Via the Nawaat team, I saw a video recorded at the local hospital, overrun with the dead and injured. For more than seven minutes, the video follows medical staff desperately trying to resuscitate the wounded, the ward full of stunned, wailing civilians. One after the other you see the dead protesters: a middle-aged man with several bullet holes in his chest; a younger man with a gaping mortal wound in his neck.[47] It was the first of hundreds of graphic videos I would encounter over the next year.

As government forces killed more protesters, new protests drew ever-growing crowds. Men and women, old and young, religious and secular, were all marching through Tunisia's most iconic squares and boulevards, increasingly defiant.

While a handful of major news outlets, including Al Jazeera, Reuters and France 24, kept a close eye on Tunisia, the uprising barely merited a mention in many other newsrooms. Trying to make sure NPR wasn't caught off-guard, I alerted our foreign desk editor and our breaking-news bloggers. The editor said the team would monitor the situation, and I told the bloggers I'd put together a summary of what was being documented via social media.

If I'd tried to create a social media summary just a few months earlier, it probably would have been a sloppy digital mess. Social media is ephemeral by nature – something posted one day might be next to impossible to track down again a few days later – and no one had yet created a simple, viable tool that would let you gather different types of social media materials and organize them into a compelling narrative.

Fortunately, a former AP reporter named Burt Herman had just co-founded a startup called Storify.[48] Essentially an online dashboard for organizing social media content, Storify lets you search for material on a variety of social media platforms and dig into your own collections of content. Whether a YouTube video, a Flickr photo, a Web page or a tweet, Storify gathers the pieces into a single narrative. Basically, it was one of the first storytelling tools focusing on social media content. As events in Tunisia escalated, Storify was among the best tools to document the most important content.

I had used Storify on several occasions, including the shooting of U.S. congresswoman Gabrielle Giffords that very weekend.[49] I began gathering relevant highlights from the Tunisian protests, and called my Storify collection *Sidi Bou Zid: A Jasmine Revolution In Tunisia*.[50] As the uprising surged, I had to build the story in two directions: one simply trying to keep up with the latest information, the other going back in time to trace the origins of the protests. It was the journalistic equivalent of being stuck on a busy street, swinging your head back and forth every couple of steps just to make sure you had all the information necessary to avoid getting run over.

As I dug through my prior tweets and Nawaat's online archive, I kept my eyes on the #sidibouzid hashtag. Amazingly, it remained almost entirely on topic. There's a very basic rule when it comes to hashtags: As soon as a hashtag reaches a certain level of popularity, it gets overrun with spam and irrelevant tweets. The longer a hashtag can stay even just a little under the radar, the longer you'll be able to utilize it effectively. But once it goes mainstream, it's downhill from there.

None of that had happened yet to #sidibouzid. The hashtag remained in the hands of Twitter users who really cared about what was going on. I began to bookmark every tweet I found that seemed important; some seemed potentially historic. As parallel columns of Twitter streams flowed on my desktop, I'd switch over to Storify and pull up my list of bookmarked tweets, allowing me to add them to the story without falling behind.

While incorporating new protest materials to my Storify collection, I encouraged my Twitter followers to help find more.

> Please keep sending me stuff re: #tunisia #sidibouzid #jasminerevolt; will keep working on Storify[51]

Meanwhile, whenever I hit a language roadblock, I'd ask for translation help. Rather than targeting one or two specific people, I'd throw my request to all of my followers. Not only did this increase the chances of me getting a fast response, it also let me cross-reference translations from multiple people, improving the overall accuracy.

> Arabic speakers: Can someone summarize the protest chants in this video? http://youtu.be/DTOZEJjhWHU thanks! #sidibouzid #tunisia[52]
>
> Translation RT @McRamTajouri: Crowd: We give our blood and soul for the salvation of our union http://youtu.be/DTOZEJjhWHU #sidibouzid[53]

I also called for volunteers to be on call for translation help whenever I happened to need it.

> btw, if any of you speak Arabic and want to help with my curation of #sidibouzid #tunisia content, ping me. http://bit.ly/i2PMb4 #wjchat[54]

In some cases, I was able to utilize my modest knowledge of Tunisia to make corrections to tweets and other social media. One photo being circulated claimed to show Tunisian army forces in front of the French embassy in downtown Tunis.[55] Looking at the picture, I realized it was incorrect. The background was Tunis Cathedral, not the embassy. When I mentioned it to my Twitter followers,[56] one person going by the name @Tuntweet replied.

> RT @Tuntweet: @acarvin French Embassy is opposite Catholic Cathedral.[57]

In other words, the location was correct, but the title was somewhat misleading. It wasn't an earth-shattering mistake, but it was still a useful correction, given how many people on Twitter were retweeting whatever they found, without any attempts to verify the information.

Other mistakes were more significant. One video, titled in French, "Four Dead In Six Minutes," showed protesters running away from the sound of gunfire. While it was certainly dramatic, the video itself offered no evidence that four people had been killed in six minutes. No one even appeared to be injured. That didn't mean it wasn't true, of course; it just meant the video itself shouldn't be treated as documentary evidence.[58]

There was no way I could spot each error being circulated online. Even if I could somehow magically watch every piece of footage, I didn't have the subject-matter expertise to understand everything that was happening across Tunisia. Fortunately my Twitter followers, many of whom I had never even heard of, were coming out of the woodwork, contributing their knowledge and skills to assist me. Some volunteered to monitor air traffic going in and out of Tunis, just in case they could identify a plane that might try to sneak the president and his family out of the country. Others tracked down rumors that needed to be verified or debunked. Some people alerted me to important tweets I might otherwise have missed, like this one, which warned people in French that there were snipers in the city of Gafsa near a local mosque, the national guard building and a hotel.

> RT @MarieNeigeG: Snipers à Gafsa: mosquée Sidi Ben Yaakoub/ bâtiment de la Garde Nationale/Tunisiana (ammara Karoui)/Hôtel el Maamoun #SidiBouzid[59]

The protesters were now using Twitter to share reports of sniper's nests targeting fellow activists. It was unlike anything I'd ever seen online. Their tweets were potentially saving lives.

Friday, January 14, 2011. All week I'd worked nearly nonstop, keeping up with events in Tunisia as best I could. Each day, I was online for up to 18 hours. It was all I did once I returned to work after the holidays, even though technically it had little to do with my actual day job. My usual duties of managing NPR's social media activities could wait a few days. This was too important to ignore.

NPR's breaking-news bloggers were now using my Storify collection on the NPR website;[60] our first foreign correspondent had arrived in Tunisia the prior morning, on January 13. Meanwhile, many other networks still didn't have anyone covering it. But that wasn't my problem; I just needed to keep up with events as they unfolded and hope that no one I knew in Tunisia got hurt.

That afternoon, Washington, D.C. time, tweets began to circulate a rumor that President Ben Ali and his wife were trying to flee the country. I hadn't heard anything conclusive one way or another – nor was it the first time this particular rumor had circulated – so I retweeted some of the rumors and asked my Twitter followers to help figure out what was going on.

> Anyone? MT @alexsandels: Hearing reports re: Ben Ali trying to leave on a jet to France, pilot is refusing to take off. Can anyone confirm?[61]
>
> Confirmed? RT @Nesrayne: Le commandant M. Ben Kilani refuse de décoller ac 6 Trabelsi à bord malgré les ordres, coup de feu a l aeroport[62]
>
> Did you see it yourself? RT @tom z: a 2nd now > i confirm > @zizoo: A plane just took off from the #Tunis Airport[63]

If the rumors were true, it would mean the Tunisian protesters had overthrown their head of state. That was a big if, of course. I looked at the Twitter feeds of several news outlets, as well as their raw wire feeds, and none mentioned anything about Ben Ali trying to flee the country. Why would they, though? It was still just a rumor. It wasn't the sort of thing I could post on NPR's primary Twitter account, @nprnews, without knowing it was correct. That's precisely why I used my personal Twitter account, @acarvin, rather than @nprnews. If I screwed up, it was on me, not NPR. I also presumed that my personal Twitter followers would cut me more slack and be more helpful.

Discussing these rumors in an open forum allowed me to leverage the collective knowledge of my well-informed Twitter followers. A number of them knew the region well; some were even participating in the protests. If anyone would have insight into these rumors, they would. So rather than keep quiet about the rumors,

I decided it was worth the risk to share them. I figured I might as well be transparent about the fact I didn't know what was true and ask my Twitter followers for help.

As we continued to sort out what was transpiring, Reuters sources suggested we were on the verge of some major breaking news. As new bulletins flew across the wire, I shared them with my followers.

> Reuters: "Tunisian military units on Friday surrounded the international airport " #sidibouzid[64]
>
> BREAKING: REUTERS: A MAJOR ANNOUNCEMENT TO THE TUNISIAN PEOPLE IS TO BE MADE SOON -TUNISIAN STATE TV #sidibouzid[65]

I then added, as a precaution:

> Lots of rumors flying around on Twitter that the army is in control of the country. Hopefully we'll know if true after TV broadcast.[66]

Suddenly, I heard a noise outside my house; it made me recoil in surprise.

> Just heard a helicopter over my house and I flinched. Covering #sidibouzid nonstop will do that, I guess.[67]

Twitter was going wild. Everyone monitoring the situation, including myself, was on edge. Not only was it impossible to keep up with all of the #sidibouzid tweets, my Twitter timeline was running several minutes late. The Tunisian revolution was grinding Twitter's servers to a crawl.

> Please, twitter, keep up with #sidibouzid tags, things are going down fast right now. Experiencing 5 min delays in tweets.[68]

I then started to see tweets from people monitoring Al Jazeera Arabic, including this one from an activist in Sudan:

> RT @simsimt: Aljazeera BREAKING: Ben Ali left the country and the army is taking over. http://twitpic.com/3pz12l[69]

The link he included in his tweet was a screenshot of someone's television. I assumed it was a news alert.

> Can someone translate this al jazeera graphic? http://twitpic.com/3pz12l #sidibouzid[70]

The replies came one on top of another, each saying basically the same thing, like this one from Iraqi journalist Mina Al-Orabi:

RT @AlOraibi: ALJazeera says Ben Ali has left Tunis[71]

A few moments later, I saw another urgent bulletin from Reuters:

TUNISIAN STATE TV SAYS ANTICIPATES ANNOUNCEMENT OF "HISTORIC DECISION" SATISFYING DESIRES OF PEOPLE[72]

That could be interpreted only one way: President Ben Ali was stepping down.

Shadi Hamid, a Middle East policy researcher at the Brookings Institution, watched Tunisian TV and tweeted the announcement:

RT @shadihamid: Live announcement on #Tunisia TV now: Parliamentary speaker says he is now taking over as president temporarily #sidibouzid[73]

I could barely process what was happening. The Tunisian people had demanded the fall of the regime, and their demand was being realized. It was the first successful popular uprising in the modern Arab world. And we had witnessed it online, from start to finish, not through the lens of mainstream media, but through the protesters themselves.

Egyptian-American commentator Mona Eltahawy recognized the magnitude of what we had just experienced online.

RT @monaeltahawy: Twitterverse: for real this time: you just watched a revolution happening via #Twitter! Right here! #JasminRevolt[74]

Others, such as a Moroccan lawyer who goes by @ibnkafka, reveled in the moment.

RT @ibnkafka: We are all Tunisians! We are all Mohamed Bouazizi! Sidi Bouzid capital of the Arab world! #sidibouzid[75]

An Algerian Twitter user, Aniss Bouraba, wryly mocked the ubiquitous error message Tunisians would see every time they visited a website blocked by the regime.

RT @_niss: Ben Ali 404 not found #sidibouzid #tunisie[76]

And Sami Ben Gharbia, the blogger and human rights activist who was forced into exile by the Ben Ali regime, finally got the chance to tweet what he had been dreaming for more than a decade: to return to Tunisia and his home town, Bizerte.

RT @ifikra: after 13 years in exile, next flight to. . . . #Tunisia, Bizerte Bizerte, I miss you so ! #sisibouzid[77]

At home and abroad, Tunisians rejoiced at their extraordinary achievement – one that few had thought possible. Yet among the hundreds of Tunisian tweeps savoring the moment and pondering the country's next steps, one was thinking about the implications of their revolution more broadly. It was Mohamed Marwen Meddah – @MMM – one of the bloggers I met with my friend at that Tunisian café years earlier, when we were paralyzed in our attempts to discuss politics even for a moment. That paralysis now defeated for the first time in his lifetime, he issued an online challenge:

> RT @MMM: Ok Arabs you've seen how it's done in Tunisia; Tag you're it![78]

Tag, you're it. I pictured a map of the region in my head. Egypt? The military would never let that happen. Libya? *Yeah, right.* Muammar Gaddafi would kill everyone without hesitation. And Syria? The thought was so terrifying that it wasn't even worth contemplating.

And yet @MMM's words echoed in my mind for hours that night.

Tag, you're it.

What if. . .? Could any of these countries actually pull it off? Just imagine.

I opened my Microsoft Office calendar and looked at my schedule for the rest of January and February.

Click, drag, click. I began reserving large blocks of time here and there, to discourage my colleagues from inviting me to meetings. I'd just tweeted a revolution, and didn't want to miss whatever might happen next.

What the hell had I gotten myself into?

EGYPT

The Fire Spreads

Almost immediately after the overthrow of Tunisia's dictator, the Internet was abuzz with speculation over what might happen next. Many Arabs, frustrated with their own regimes, expressed pride in the Tunisians for taking back their country. But were these ringside supporters willing to risk revolutions of their own?

It didn't take long to see if anyone would follow Tunisia's lead. On January 25, 2011, tens of thousands of protesters took to the streets and shook the heart of the Arab world – Egypt.

To many outsiders, this was a real shock. Hosni Mubarak had enjoyed dominance over the country for three decades. He seemed as steady as a pharaoh carved in rock.

But in truth, Egypt's uprising was grounded in a long history of dissent, going back at least to the 1970s. In recent years, labor unions attempted a general strike for workers rights,[1, 2] while political bloggers established themselves as independent voices critical of the government.[3]

Then in June 2010, a young man named Khaled Said was beaten to death by police in the city of Alexandria. By all accounts, he had done nothing – except upload footage he recorded of police appearing to collaborate with local drug dealers.[4, 5] Police took their revenge by grabbing Said at an Internet café and smashing in his head; they claimed the cause of death was suffocation due to swallowing a bag of hashish.[6] As photographs of Said's swollen, disfigured body circulated online, a small group of anonymous activists created a Facebook page called *We Are All Khaled Said*.[7, 8] Within weeks, more than 200,000 people joined the group, literally waiting for their marching orders.[9]

Soon after Tunisia's revolution, they received those orders. Numerous opposition groups declared their intention to hold a rally on January 25 – a not-so-subtle jab at the government, as it also happened to be National Police Day.[10] Among the organizers, activist Asmaa Mahfouz uploaded a video to YouTube, encouraging fellow Egyptians to join her:

> I, a girl, am going down to Tahrir Square, and I will stand alone. And I'll hold up a banner. Perhaps people will show some honor. Don't think you can be safe anymore. None of us are. Come down with us and demand your rights, my rights, your family's rights. I am going down on January 25th and will say no to corruption, no to this regime.[11, 12]

Building off Tunisia's momentum, Mahfouz and the other activists spread the word about the January 25 protest, using YouTube, Facebook, the Twitter hashtag #jan25, text messaging and word-of-mouth. Ten days before the event, save-the-date tweets started popping up via the #sidibouzid hashtag, spreading the protest announcement to many people who had closely followed the Tunisian revolution.[13, 14] More than 80,000 people RSVP'd via Facebook.[15, 16]

I wasn't sure if much of anything would begin that day, but it was worth being prepared. Unfortunately I knew few Egyptians. While I had gotten to know several Tunisian bloggers in person during my trips there, I'd been to Egypt once – as a backpacker 15 years earlier. So once again I turned to the Global Voices community. Ground zero for my research was a bushy-haired software developer from Cairo named Alaa.

Alaa Abd El-Fattah, known simply as @alaa on Twitter, came from a family of dissidents. His father, who had been tortured by the Egyptian government in the 1980s, founded the country's first human rights law center.[17] His aunt, Ahdaf Soueif, is a best-selling novelist.[18]

I first crossed paths with Alaa in early 2006. He had various connections with Global Voices, and I began reading the blog he published with his wife, Manal.[19] That spring, Alaa participated in a protest demanding an independent Egyptian judicial system.[20] Police broke up the protest and arrested Alaa.[21]

Global Voices community members swung into action.[22] They began to publicize his arrest far and wide, encouraging bloggers around the world to make a huge stink out of it. A blog dedicated to securing Alaa's freedom helped us keep abreast of the situation and suggested ways to shame the Egyptian government into releasing him.[23] I hadn't started working at NPR yet, and I had always been active online when it came to bloggers' free-speech rights, so I created a short video demanding his release and shared it across my various online networks.[24]

Six weeks after he was arrested, Alaa was discharged from prison.[25] I had no idea if the online campaign made an impact; I was just glad to see that he was healthy and in one piece. Eventually, Alaa and his wife left Egypt for South Africa, living in exile and continuing the struggle remotely. I met him in person years later when he came to the U.S. to speak at an Internet conference in New York. When I mentioned that I had been part of the online effort demanding his release, Alaa told me that our campaign probably kept him in prison longer. But, he added with a wry smile, it probably also saved him from being tortured.

As I began to think about how to build a network of sources in Egypt, Alaa seemed like the obvious starting point. He was well connected with bloggers and dissidents, many of whom would show up on January 25 for the first protest. I decided to follow the digital trail that might lead me to some of his closest associates: his Twitter account.

Alaa had been on Twitter for a number of years and had built a solid following. But how would I know which of his followers might be worth monitoring? I took a different approach and checked out the people *he* was following.[26]

Fortunately for my purposes, Twitter displays the list of people you follow in reverse chronological order. In other words, at the top of the list would be the most recent people you decided to follow. And anyone at the bottom of the list would represent the very first people you followed.

I clicked on the list of people that Alaa followed and scrolled further and further downward. There were hundreds of names accumulated over several years of Twitter use. When I finally reached the bottom, I found the very first people he connected with on Twitter. Not surprisingly, there was his wife, @Manal. I didn't recognize any of the others, but it seemed reasonable to surmise that he had a close connection to at least some of them. So I investigated the first dozen or so people he followed. For most, their tweets and Twitter bios made it clear that they were politically engaged in Egypt. Some talked about the protest scheduled for January 25. I began following their accounts, and then investigated the first people *they* followed on Twitter to find more activists.

Very quickly, names began to pile up – bloggers, activists, even journalists who had a history of dissent. After digging through their tweets, I could puzzle together pieces of their personalities and how they were related to each other – which ones were siblings, which ones were married, which ones were wickedly funny, which ones swore like sailors, and which ones could switch effortlessly from Arabic to English in the same tweet.

You could sometimes discern their relationships as they addressed each other online. Some discussions were curt or overly formal; perhaps these people didn't like each other. In other cases, the conversations were very informal, even intimate at times. Some people would routinely use emoticons like :-) or :p in their tweets, suggesting a certain comfort level with each other. Others would jokingly swear at each other in English. Often when someone would throw in a bit of Arabic, they'd get a reply with emoticons or text-speak like *LOL* (laughing out loud) or *LMFAO* (laughing my fucking ass off). Egyptians have a legendary sense of humor, and you could see it in spades on Twitter.

And then of course there were the retweets. Retweeting is a common activity on Twitter in which people share a tweet from someone else with their own followers. It's the Twitter equivalent of forwarding an email to a group of people. And if you pay attention to who's retweeting whom, you begin to get a sense of who they value and trust – in other words, other potential sources.

The network of Egyptian activists took shape in my head – into something like the flight route map in the back of an airline magazine. I imagined paths going from one point to another, then back again, then linking to another spot. Spokes, hubs and outliers emerged. I started to develop a sense of who in the Egyptian Twitter community was well-connected, well-informed or just popular in one way or another.

Every day I discovered more people, so I created a Twitter list dedicated to Egypt. Twitter allows you to create collections of Twitter accounts – friends, favorite athletes, politicians, whatever – and have them appear in a Twitter timeline of their own. That way, I could concentrate specifically on the people on that list rather than sorting through the noise that usually accompanies an overall Twitter timeline.

When the protests started, I hadn't reached a point where I was 100 percent comfortable regarding who on my list would be reliable and who wouldn't. But that quickly evolved as I tracked a critical mass of activists on the ground that would guide me through whatever would happen during their protests. Over 18 extraordinary days, I would be riveted to my computer, along with much of the world, watching an historic series of events unfold in a place called Tahrir Square.

The Battle for Tahrir Square

> Mubarak thugs are riding in on CAMELS AND HORSES?! What the fuck do they think this is?! The Arabian Nights v 2.0?![1]
>
> – @litfreak

On the night of February 1, Cairo was on a knife's edge. In the wake of the initial rally, police killed many protesters on January 28, leading to larger demonstrations around the country. For three days running, the Egyptian government took the dramatic step of shutting down the Internet, hoping to avoid a repeat of Tunisia.

The move backfired. Not only did protesters find ways of getting around the shutdown, it caused countless other Egyptians to leave their homes and gather with their neighbors to find out what was going on. People who might not otherwise go onto the streets were now doing just that.

As tens of thousands of protesters prepared for another night in Cairo's Tahrir Square, President Mubarak gave a speech on live television. While he acknowledged the protesters were peaceful, Mubarak said they were being exploited. He promised to step down at the end of his term later in the year.

In the early morning hours of February 2, groups of Mubarak supporters began to rally outside Tahrir. One group arrived on motorcycles chanting, "With our blood and our souls, we will defend Hosni Mubarak."[2]

Around 3 a.m. Cairo time, *New York Times* columnist Nicholas Kristof tweeted about the tension.

> RT @nickkristof: Just back from Tahrir. A bit unnerving: mob of pro-Mubarak forces running around, very aggressive, almost picking fights.[3]
>
> RT @nickkristof: Shots fired, maybe warnings. Hoping we're not seeing provocations, violence between pro- and anti-#Mubarak factions.[4]

Up the road, along the east bank of the Nile at Egyptian state TV headquarters, CNN's Ben Wedeman observed another group of Mubarak supporters itching for a confrontation.

> RT @BenCNN: Rent-a-mob outside office shouting at TV reporters "khawana! 3umala!" – "Traitors! Agents!" Regime tactics not changing. #Jan25[5]

By the time I got online the next morning, it was just past afternoon prayers in Cairo. One of the first tweets I saw came from Nick Kristof.

> RT @nickkristof: In my part of Tahrir, pro-#Mubarak mobs arrived in buses, armed with machetes, straight-razors and clubs, very menacing.[6]

Mobs brought in on buses? *Machetes and clubs?* Someone had unleashed the hounds.

As I scrolled through my Twitter streams, the situation around Tahrir came into focus. Mahmoud Salem, an internationally acclaimed Egyptian blogger, sized up the crowd.

> RT @sandmonkey: 1000 pro Mubarak demonstration is heading towards Tahrir. The military is withdrawing. This will get ugly quick[7]

Writer and economist Mohamed El Dahshan was in the middle of the confrontation.

> RT @TravellerW: INCREDIBLE standoff between pro-change and pro-Mubarak demos at Tahrir[8]

> RT @TravellerW: Real panic in tahrir. Square overun by Mubarak drmonstrstion[9]

Ali Seif, a Lebanese-Canadian college student visiting Cairo, was confronted by a Mubarak supporter.

> RT @BloggerSeif: Pro mubarak man asking me for my phone, threatening me and Lebanese here. Telling us he will attack me[10]

I went to Al Jazeera's website, hoping to find streaming live coverage. The first thing I saw was a swarm of men on horseback, some armed with batons and swords, charging one of the streets leading into Tahrir.

"It is an intense battle here," an Al Jazeera reporter said. "Honestly to God, I thought I'd never see camels charging."[11]

Did he say camels?

Mubarak thugs were making a cavalry charge – and a medieval one at that. Downtown Cairo isn't exactly an *Arabian Nights* fantasy come to life; ordinarily, the nearest camels were almost an hour away in Giza, waiting for tourists to mount them for overpriced photos in front of the pyramids.

Jewelry designer Fatma Ghaly found it surreal.

> RT @fatmaghaly: On Friday I thought we were back to the 80's no mobiles, no Internet. Today we're back to the 1200s with camels #jan25 WOW![12]

Ali Seif, the Lebanese-Canadian, described how protesters tried to protect themselves from the assault.

> RT @BloggerSeif: Horses being kicked on all side. Where the fuck is the thugs getting tear gas from[13]

A person who goes by @ArabRevolution called for reinforcements.

> RT @ArabRevolution: Everybody to Tahrir! Everybody to Tahrir! Everybody to Tahrir! Everybody to Tahrir! QUICK!! This is your last stand![14]

I had a full day of meetings ahead of me, but there was just no way I could follow through with them. The live footage of Tahrir Square showed side streets enveloped in clouds of tear gas; protesters held vinegar-soaked rags over their mouths to lessen the effects of the chemicals. And now there were swordsmen on camelback. History was unfolding before our eyes.

---

5 p.m. Cairo time. I remained glued to Al Jazeera's livestream. As I described to my Twitter followers, the situation was going from bad to worse.

> People towards the back of the crowd leading into the square throwing rocks far into the crowd. #jan25[15]
>
> One AlJaz correspondent says "at least 100 injured." "All this as the army stands aside and does nothing." #jan25[16]

Atop one roof across from Tahrir Square, a group of men smashed and ripped up parts of the roof, and then threw the heavy chunks of potentially lethal building material onto the heads of the protesters below.

> People throwing large blocks, rocks and bricks off rooftops into the crowd of protesters, ppl running out of the way. #jan25[17]
>
> About two dozen people on a roof, grabbing whatever objects they can and throwing it below. About one or two per second. #jan25[18]

Then I saw this tweet jump out of my timeline:

> BOILING WATER BEING THROWN FROM BALCONIES AROUND TAHRIR, BRICKS DROPPED DOWN #Jan25[19]

It was Ali Seif, the Lebanese-Canadian student. His timeline quickly exploded into utter panic.

RT @BloggerSeif: Pro mubarak protesters broke into square!!! Entrance broken! OMFG there's blood, omfg OmFGf[20]

RT @BloggerSeif: Screaming, crying, injured, burned, they will kill us, I swear we will die. Omfg! #Jand25[21]

RT @BloggerSeif: HOW DO WE GET OUT, SOMEONE TELL US![22]

RT @BloggerSeif: Another entrance down. . . Omg there's dead people. There's dead people. . .[23]

I continued to watch the chaos unfold on the video stream. Squadrons of pro-Mubarak thugs used their bodies as battering rams to try to penetrate the perimeter of the square, which was protected by a phalanx of protesters four or five people deep.

Ali's tweets left no doubt that his life was in danger. Whenever he stopped tweeting for several minutes, I feared the worst; each tweet could be his last. And he was just one of the tens of thousands of people around Tahrir.

After what seemed like an eternity, Ali's timeline came alive again. For the moment he was okay. He'd found a potential escape route heading northeast from Tahrir. His tweet screamed urgency:

RT @BloggerSeif: PEOPLE LEAVE TAHRIR VIA OMAR MAKRAM, SEMIRAMIS THEN VIA NILE! #jan25[24]

Thank God. My pounding heart finally began to slow down. It was a convoluted route, going clockwise several blocks beyond the perimeter of Tahrir, until reaching the Intercontinental Semiramis Hotel. Beyond the hotel is the east bank of the Nile. As long as he didn't go north from there along the riverbank, he'd probably be safe.

Then he piped in again:

RT @BloggerSeif: '(omg I have someones child, I have a child. 2 yrs max, green eyes, says his name mahmoud. Tweet it for me #jan25[25]

A child?!? There could be hundreds of thousands of people in the vicinity of Tahrir Square. Many of them brought their families to the protest rallies. And now they were all under siege by countless armed thugs.

How on earth would Ali reunite the boy with his parents? At least he tweeted a description of him. Hopefully someone in Tahrir would notice the tweet and help reunite the boy with his family.

But what about all the others trapped there?

It was just shy of 5:30 p.m. in Cairo. Only another hour or so of daylight remained; the battle continued to rage. In Tahrir, protesters chiseled roads, sidewalks, walls – whatever they could find to arm themselves with makeshift projectiles. Up the road toward the Egyptian Museum, government thugs were doing the same.

Al Jazeera managed to keep its live video feed up and running. I continued to do my best and narrate it for my Twitter followers.

> Men and women near center of the square are tearing apart roads, making brickbats to protect themselves. #jan25[26]

Attention shifted toward the Egyptian Museum. Just a few hundred meters north of Tahrir, it was a base for Mubarak supporters most of the day, and now a band of protesters arriving from Tahrir was trying to push them further back.

Suddenly, I heard multiple popping sounds.

> You can hear shots being fired. Can't tell if they're warning shots. Maybe the military. #jan25[27]

Probably not, though. The Egyptian army remained on the sidelines, loitering like confused bystanders rather than protecting civilians. Al Jazeera quoted one officer: "We have no orders, we aren't going to do anything."[28] Their impotence gave Mubarak's thugs carte blanche to wreak havoc.

Ben Wedeman's tweets carried a sense of foreboding. He knew Cairo better than almost any Western reporter – he had lived there for many years – so his words carried added weight.

> RT @BenCNN: Just got out of Tahrir. Very ugly. Something is being cooked up here. Tienanmen 2? Is this stability? #Egypt #Jan25[29]
>
> RT @BenCNN: I was not injured. Harassed? Yes. Appears the pro-government "demonstrators" have been given instructions to target press.[30]

Al Jazeera reporters faced perhaps the gravest danger. The Mubarak regime blamed the network for fomenting the uprising; who knew what its henchmen were capable of doing to their journalists? Two Al Jazeera reporters, Sherine Tadros and Ayman Mohyeldin, filed their tweets by dictating them over the phone. It was certainly safer than standing in the middle of a street while typing.

> RT @SherineT: right in middle of clashes. I've been hit in the face. huge stampedes. Rocks flying. Crazy atmosphere. #egypt #jan25[31]
>
> RT @SherineT: right in the middle of the clashes. my cameraman is bloodied. utter CHAOS right now! #egypt #jan25 (tweeting via friend)[32]

> RT @AymanM: I am ok but keeping a low profile for safety reasons #Egypt #jan25 (via phone call)[33]

Nearby, CNN's Anderson Cooper and his production team were assaulted.

> RT @AndersonCooper: Got roughed up by thugs in pro-mubarak crowd..punched and kicked repeatedly. Had to escape. Safe now[34]

> RT @AndersonCooper: Thanks for tweets of concern..I'm sore and head hurts but fine. Neil and mary anne are bruised but ok too. Thanks #jan25[35]

While Western journalists took shelter, Ali Seif, the Lebanese-Canadian, continued to alert people about the lost toddler. No more than 20 minutes had passed since his prior tweets. He'd also found another escape route, northeast toward Abdeen Square.

> RT @BloggerSeif: He doesn't know his parensts naems, he's 2 yrs max. . . . rushdi calling ppl to come our way to omar makram[36]

> RT @BloggerSeif: May god take your souls if this childs parents are dead, may mubarak die. Mubarak your a murderer. . . .[37]

> RT @BloggerSeif: We want to live, we have to get out. Carrying child. . . Rushdi bleeding, abdeen [square] is open! #jan25[38]

Back at Tahrir, British-Egyptian filmmaker Omar Robert Hamilton mobilized with other protesters to block government thugs from breaking into the square. Hamilton, also known as @RiverDryFilm, was one of the first to observe online that many of the pro-Mubarak thugs were actually employees of the regime rather than mere counter-protesters.

> RT @RiverDryFilm: Mubarak supporters have been caught and their IDs confiscated – they are always members of the security forces. #jan25[39]

The protesters were up against a rent-a-mob.

---

6 p.m. Cairo time; just past sunset. Ali Seif continued his escape with the toddler and a small band of friends. Now they tried to exit via their original route toward the Semiramis Hotel.

> RT @BloggerSeif: Heading back towards mogama, will say we are lost tourists, and the child is my brother. Rushdi will back us up.[40]

> RT @BloggerSeif: Just outside tahrir now. . . There will be a massacre in the square now. Something burning, dunno what building. #Jan25[41]

Fighting was breaking out everywhere, noted Omar Robert Hamilton.

> RT @RiverDryFilm: The stand-off is over, Tahrir is a battleground again. #jan25[42]

Near the Egyptian Museum, Mubarak thugs were now throwing Molotov cocktails. The Egyptian blogger known as Zeinobia expressed her concern that they'd set the museum on fire.

> RT @Zeinobia: Mubarak thugs are throwing Molotov on the Egyptian museum save it I beg it now[43]

Between Tahrir and the museum, adjacent to the local Hardee's restaurant, volunteers offered medical assistance to the injured. Blogger Wael Abbas spread word to his many Egyptian Twitter followers:

> RT @WaelAbbas: makeshift clinic to treat wounded on corner of Tahrir near the Hardy's-NEED SUPPLIES URGENTLY #Jan25[44]

> RT @WaelAbbas: Volunteers needed in El Kasr El Eieny 2 organise donations & receive injured ppl call Omneya & Jihan[45]

Mona Seif, a young researcher at a local cancer lab volunteering at the field clinic, called for reinforcements. There just weren't enough protesters to prevent the square from falling.

> RT @monasosh: Every1 who is in other areas should take 2 the streets and protest! Ppl in tahrir cannot hold their ground agnst all thugs[46]

Nearby, Cairo journalist Ethar El Katatny received word that a local hospital several kilometers northeast of Tahrir was prepared to treat the wounded.

> RT @etharkamel: Doctor in Demerdash just told me that the hospital is now receiving patients from tahrir w/ the worst kind of burns. #jan25[47]

Of course, this assumed wounded protesters could get there. For now, as CNN stringer Ian Lee noted, their situation appeared grave.

> RT @IanInEgypt: Tahrir Square is now the anti-Mubarak protesters' Alamo. #jan25 #egypt[48]

On the Al Jazeera stream, an eyewitness phoned in to describe the scene at the field clinic. She sounded terrified. There were hundreds of injured, many of them unconscious. Thugs were throwing stones at them, and they lacked medicine. "There are broken arms, many injuries, and we have no supplies."[49]

At the end of the call, the Al Jazeera host identified the eyewitness as Mona Seif – @Monasosh – the lab worker who was helping organize the makeshift clinic.

---

7 p.m. Cairo time. Tahrir was getting dark. As the final prayer of the day approached, protesters steeled themselves for a very long night. Respites from the violence were intermittent. The skirmish line between Tahrir and the Egyptian Museum shifted back and forth. Economist Mohamed El Dahshan had a direct view of the fighting.

> RT @TravellerW: I am seeing – not reporting, seeing – Mubarak ppl throwing, molotov cocktails on demonstrators, and on shops. #Egypt #jan25[50]

The gasoline bombs appeared to emanate from the opposing line, suggesting that Mubarak supporters were launching them. Omar Robert Hamilton tweeted:

> RT @RiverDryFilm: This is getting really scary. I don't know what else to say. The men at the front are so brave. #jan25[51]

Hundreds of heavily armed soldiers had been ordered to stay out of the fray, but some couldn't take it any more.

Blogger Wael Abbas offered a chilling story:

> RT @WaelAbbas: Eyewitness: Tank commander put a pistol in his mouth to commit suicide, his soldiers stopped him & burst out crying #Jan25[52]

The people trapped in Tahrir, meanwhile, were determined to hold it.

Saeed Kazim, an engineer using the name @SailorRipley, implored them to maintain the perimeter and evacuate anyone who couldn't defend themselves. Hundreds, if not thousands of families were trapped with their children.

> RT @SailorRipley: Hold the square, but get the children out. Save the weak, and defend with your strong. Hold the square.[53]

Once again, Ali Seif tweeted an update. He still had the boy that had been separated from his parents.

> RT @BloggerSeif: Other than bruises, unable to stand, starved, and panic, were all fine. Feeling betrayed, all of us are.[54]

> RT @BloggerSeif: B4 I go, I want to say I will see the reuniting thing, if childs fam isn't there, he stays with us.[55]

> RT @BloggerSeif: he was sitting there, no one around him. We couldn't leave him[56]

Around the same time, I saw tweets from people on the front lines, half a mile north of Tahrir. Among them was Mosa'ab Elshamy, an Egyptian pharmacy student. He and a group of protesters were on the move, trying to force the Mubarak supporters further away from Tahrir. They had to defend themselves, but at least one of them was deeply troubled by it.

> RT @mosaaberizing: Saw one of the stone throwers crying and asking God to forgive him. "Its only coz they beat us first." he said. #Jan25[57]

> RT @mosaaberizing: We got hold of some roofs and are bombarding them from above. Slowly pushing them behind. #Jan25[58]

Just a few yards from Mosa'ab, his friend Tarek Shalaby had joined the battle.

> RT @TarekShalaby: I've started throwing stones with the crew at the museum battle. Don't have any other choice. Viva la revolucion. #jan25[59]

---

8 p.m., Cairo time. As protesters improved their security perimeter around Tahrir, they captured more opponents. One after another, they reported their prisoners were carrying government employee IDs. Gigi Ibrahim took a picture of one of them being taken away.

> RT @Gsquare86: We r getting the thugs one by one and confiscating their I.D.s that say 'police' http://yfrog.com/gyh5vxaaj[60]

In the blurry picture, a group of men escort another man in a yellow shirt, presumably the thug they'd captured. One of them appears to be talking to him as they walk quickly.

Activists assembled their prisoners inside the Sadat metro station, inside the perimeter of the square. At one point, a protester named Mustafa Ahmed tweeted in Arabic:

> RT @tafatefo: I am sitting on a thug.[61]

10:30 p.m. While protesters had pushed back the pro-Mubarak mob by the Egyptian Museum, they struggled to hold the line. Mosa'ab Elshamy, the pharmacy student, was in the thick of it.

RT @mosaaberizing: Very tense near musuem. We're still blocking them but fatigue & injuries slowly catching up with us. More people needed.[62]

RT @mosaaberizing: Worth noting that the tanks in Tahrir were abandoned by the army soldiers. If we could only start them up :) #Jan25[63]

RT @mosaaberizing: We did start a truck, though, which wasn't entirely broken. This shall be interesting. #Jan25[64]

Al Jazeera's Evan Hill tweeted a play-by-play of the melee.

RT @evanchill: The pro-Mubarak crowd has mounted several charges against the advancing Tahrirites, but they never get w/in 75 ft.[65]

RT @evanchill: Protesters at museum look like they outnumber Mubarak supporters. They have formed a staggered wall of angled metal shields[66]

RT @evanchill: Tahrir protesters open the barricade, allow men with metal shields to advance on pro-Mubarak crowd. #jan25[67]

RT @evanchill: The Mubarak crowd at the Egyptian museum is melting away. #jan25[68]

The momentum began to shift; the protesters had deployed reinforcements. Omar Robert Hamilton cheered:

RT @RiverDryFilm: They've pushed as far as 6th October bridge! #jan25[69]

Evan Hill then added:

RT @evanchill: Tahrir protesters are beating on metal barricades in unison, in celebration. (shades of the movie Zulu) #jan25[70]

Shades of the movie Zulu. I was almost speechless. I could barely manage a tweet.

Wow. Wow.[71]

With each incoming tweet, the better I could visualize the situation on the ground. Even though I had access to Al Jazeera's feed, it was showing only a couple of hotspots in a combat zone stretching more than a mile along the Nile. The people tweeting from Tahrir had their own extraordinary perspective – but it was limited to each's immediate field of view. There was no way for them to report on what was going on everywhere.

I imagined myself flying over Tahrir in a helicopter, looking down at the field of battle. It was all coming together in my mind – a situational awareness I probably couldn't have achieved on the ground.

---

11 p.m. Cairo time. While protesters successfully pushed Mubarak's supporters beyond the Egyptian Museum, the battle shifted to the 6th of October Bridge, which crosses the Nile about a mile northwest of Tahrir. The bridge connects to the east bank of the Nile via a tangle of overpasses. Each overpass became a new fortification, a new platform for bombarding the enemy.

Mosa'ab the pharmacy student remained confident.

> RT @mosaaberizing: Despite the blood & pain, spirits here are sky-high. People singing the anthem waving flags while throwing stones. #Jan25[72]

Back at Tahrir, things heated up again as armed Mubarak supporters occupied the streets radiating from the square. The Al Jazeera livestream was very dark, with just a few street lights giving a hint of an outline to frenetic figures in shadowy form.

Suddenly, fireballs ignited the sky, crashing like misdirected fireworks into sheets of metal.

A Molotov cocktail battle had begun. I had never seen anything like it.

> Molotov cocktails flying; one just crashed into a building wall. Another spot in the middle of the road on fire. There goes another. #jan25[73]
>
> Wall of people four or five thick. Ones in front throwing molotovs into the darkness. Other sides has large planks as shields. #jan25[74]
>
> Molotov just crashed in front of a guy, set his coat on fire. Looked like he removed it quickly enough; still might've been burned. #jan25[75]

Most of the Molotov cocktails seemed to originate from the pro-Mubarak side, though occasionally from the protesters as well. A person would run forward, arch his shoulder and let the bottle fly, creating a damp trail of fire before shattering into a blossom of flame on one of the corrugated metal roof sheets the protesters used as shields. Sometimes, a Molotov cocktail would blow up in their hands as they tried to dispatch it. Twice I saw men attempt to throw a bottle at protesters and become engulfed in flames. People were burning themselves alive on live TV.

A huge wave of people moved forward, as if someone had ordered a charge. Evan Hill described the scene.

> RT @evanchill: Jaw-dropping: the Tahrir protesters have broken out completely and rushed the Mubarak crowd. #jan25[76]

> RT @evanchill: Mubarak protesters in complete retreat. This is incredible. Spectators running from their position. Barricades being moved[77]

The thugs' front lines were collapsing everywhere at once.

Back at the 6th of October Bridge, Mosa'ab Elshamy celebrated his squad's successes.

> RT @mosaaberizing: YES! We've pushed them away from the musuem! They're running like rats. #Tahrir #Jan25[78]

> RT @mosaaberizing: The musuem battle was the toughest today. Took over 8 hrs Huge win. #Tahrir #Jan25[79]

But was it over? Didn't seem like it. On Al Jazeera, I saw more Molotov cocktails soaring through the air. Some of Mubarak's most strident supporters had no intention of leaving the field.

> Looks like there's still a battle line; saw another molotov fly. And another. #jan25[80]

> The Battle of Tahrir Square continues. Opposing lines have drawn closer; molotovs lobbed every few seconds. #jan25[81]

Al Jazeera's Evan Hill still had a prime view.

> RT @evanchill: The protesters have massed behind a new line of barricades and are exchanging molotovs w/ the remnants of the pro-Mub crowd.[82]

Then I saw a series of tweets from Alaa Abd El-Fattah. He was the first Egyptian dissident I'd gotten to know online, five years earlier. In the days leading up to January 25, it was Alaa's tweets that helped me start the process of identifying which protesters were connected to each other.

Alaa had moved to South Africa, but returned to Egypt right before the battle. And the entire day, he hadn't tweeted. For a guy who's a Twitter regular, and one of the leading voices of resistance online, it was very troubling.

Just before midnight, he broke his silence.

> RT @alaa: Am ok, lousy at throwing rocks but did my part anyway i doubt i threw a single one that landed in target no injuries so far #Jan25[83]

> RT @alaa: Tahrir square is resiliant, will not be defeated, but outside protest hotspots morales are very low. #Jan25[84]

> RT @alaa: We never had the need to defend ourselves like this before. Came as shock after 4 peaceful days #Jan25[85]

Even though I had to be careful about maintaining professional distance from the protesters, I couldn't help but feel relieved for him.

Midnight in Cairo. Some protesters had been fighting all day – as had Mubarak's people. While the numbers in Tahrir remained strong, pro-government forces had thinned out somewhat. Were they done for the night or taking a break? And were they expecting reinforcements of their own?

Mosa'ab Elshamy tweeted an update from his position near the 6th of October Bridge.

> RT @mosaaberizing: Conflicts still going on under October bridge but seems a matter of time before they go home. #Jan25 #Tahrir[86]

> RT @mosaaberizing: Soldiers back to their tanks (M60 for those asking about the type) now after the musuem area became safe. #Jan25[87]

As ridiculous as it seems when compared to the protesters and the journalists in Cairo, I too needed a break. Amazingly, people were tweeting me just to say they were praying for my safety. They didn't realize I was 4,000 miles away from the action.

"Thanks but don't worry," I told one of them. "I'm not there right now. But all the other journalists and Egyptians could use your prayers."[88]

Trying to maintain a semblance of a domestic routine – even on chaotic days like this – I left the office, cooked dinner, gave the kids a bath, and read stories to my daughter before putting her to bed. Hopefully Tahrir would remain peaceful as well.

> RT @mosaaberizing: We're about 10,000 at the musuem area now. People getting ready for new thug waves. #Jan25 #Tahrir[89]

Around 2:30 a.m. Cairo time, Mosa'ab Elshamy's tweet snapped me out of my naïve hope that things would be over by now. I caught up by reading the tweets that accumulated over the prior 90 minutes, but there were so many I could barely go back half an hour. A tweet from CNN's Ben Wedeman stood out:

> RT @BenCNN: Almost 2 AM in Cairo, clashes in Tahrir have been going on for 12 hours. Government onslaught continues. Stability? #Jan25[90]

The battle continued, but not as intensely. It gave some of the protesters a few moments to reflect. Among them were some of Mosa'ab's friends—Amr El Beleidy, Tarek Shalaby and Hazem Zohny—who were back in the center of Tahrir. Amr wrote:

> RT @beleidy: 3 injuries to my group of friends were 1 rock to the lip, 2 stitches, one rock to the head, moltov burns on the hand/forearm[91]
>
> RT @beleidy: If protesters succeed in removing the pres it will set a powerful precedent to those after him, we can remove you if u mess up[92]

As for Tarek Shalaby:

> RT @tarekshalaby: Resting at Bansyon el horreyya while @hazemzohny n @beleidy look for a safe exit (unlikely). Will return to battle soon[93]

Bansyon el Horreya, or The Freedom Motel, is what Tarek affectionately called his small orange-and-gray tent at the very center of Tahrir Square.

Hazem was more pessimistic.

> RT @hazemzohny: The sense of citizen unity fostered over the past week is being ripped apart by these pro and anti mub clashes #Jan25[94]
>
> RT @hazemzohny: Worried ppl rnt realising that mubarak had no qualms killing at least 300 ppl just to stay in power a few more months #Jan25[95]

Northeast of Tahrir, Mosa'ab's group was dealing with some of the prisoners they'd captured.

> RT @mosaaberizing: Arrested a few of the thugs at Abd El Meneim Reyad sq. Receiving a proper beating now while being escorted to their mates[96]

Caught somewhere in between, Al Jazeera's Evan Hill found a brief moment to laugh at his predicament.

> RT @evanchill: Even on the front lines of a revolt, an egyptian tells me the lie that I speak arabic well[97]

Mona Seif kept tweeting while working at the medical clinic.

> RT @monasosh: Ppl r using the car ruins & rubbish around them 2 create shields to advance. I feel as if reporting on a battlefield[98]

"You are," I told her.[99]

RT @monasosh: I can hear gun shots close to the museum #Jan25[100]

4 a.m., Cairo time. Mona's tweet reminded me how battles often come in waves. Just when you think it's over, it's not. Up on the front line, Mosa'ab Elshamy was still at it, a smartphone in one hand and a rock in the other.

> RT @mosaaberizing: 1000s of thugs bombarding us with molotov & stones from bridge. We're keeping our high lines and defending well. #jan25[101]
>
> RT @mosaaberizing: Tired/injured protesters leave. New ones keep coming to October bridge. #Tahrir #Jan25[102]
>
> RT @mosaaberizing: Sigh, tired thugs leaving, new ones coming. #jan25[103]

Fighting also continued on the Qasr al Nil Bridge, as Mona Seif noted:

> RT @monasosh: Some1 among the thugs on bridge had a riffle, took his time & aimed, 3 wounded, 1 dead, army to intervening #Jan25[104]

Once again it appeared that protesters were making progress, especially around the bridge. Mosa'ab tweeted:

> RT @mosaaberizing: Many retreating. Just a few of them left on the bridge now. Still throwing molotov. #Tahrir[105]

Evan Hill witnessed the thrust.

> RT @evanchill: Anti govt supporters are advancing from here, they've taken the bridge[106]

Cairo-based British journalist Bel Trew documented what was going on in her neighborhood east of Tahrir.

> RT @BelTrew: Confirmed reports that live ammunition is being used by pro-mubarak mob – this is definitely state sponsored.[107]
>
> RT @BelTrew: Hearing a lot of gunshots – machine gun fire in downtown and in the square. Very worried. #Tahrir #jan25 #Egypt[108]

> RT @BelTrew: Extremely worried, we can hear machine gun fire a lot of it. A FUCKING LOT OF IT. GOD SAVE THEM please god please.[109]

After more than six hours of lost contact, Ali Seif finally reappeared in my twitter stream. I had assumed he was going to keep a low profile for the rest of the night. But his tweets echoed Bel's concern that Mubarak thugs were firing live ammunition.

> RT @BloggerSeif: We have no neighbourhood watches here tonight, ppl inside homes #Jan25[110]

> RT @BloggerSeif: Choppers, ambulances all over. If you couldn't guess, our location is close to Tahrir. They are shooting to kill #Jan25[111]

CNN's Ben Wedeman pointed out that the shooting was as bad as it had been all night:

> RT @BenCNN: More gunfire from #Tahrir, more than we've heard yet. #Jan25 #Egypt[112]

> RT @BenCNN: Witness in #Tahrir says pro-democracy people being shot at from rooftops, several dead. #Egypt #Jan25[113]

Bel Trew was now extremely upset.

> RT @BelTrew: I feel sick. I need to calm down. Another person has been killed by the Mubarak thugs. Live fire. #Jan25[114]

Mona Seif was still at the clinic, assisting the wounded.

> RT @monasosh: Another ambulance moving speedly wt wounded protesters #Jan25[115]

> RT @monasosh: My friend called me from frontline, another protester is shot dead right infront of her #Jan25[116]

> RT @monasosh: 2 of my friends confirm another one is shot through the head, dead. My friend called me crying #Jan25 this is awful[117]

And then my Twitter account ground to a halt.

I gave it a few moments and tried again. Nothing. As the worst gunfire of the night continued around Tahrir, I couldn't get my account to work. It was as if I were in the middle of anchoring a live broadcast that suddenly went mute. I'd been sent to Twitter jail.

Twitter, it turns out, doles out tweet quotas to users. If you tweet too many times in a given period, it temporarily suspends you. The idea is to discourage spammers, but now it was preventing me from covering one of the most dramatic days of the Egyptian revolution. No wonder: I was probably approaching my 1,000th tweet of the night.

I emailed Katie Stanton, an executive I knew at Twitter. She quickly returned my email after alerting Twitter engineers. My tweets would continue to be sluggish for a while, she said, but I had been "whitelisted." This meant I could tweet without fear of being shut down again.

Thank you, @KatieS.

---

6 a.m., Cairo time. Hints of dawn shone from the east. Tweets from Tahrir became less frequent, less frantic. Despite having been attacked by well-armed thugs for almost 18 hours, protesters still controlled the square. The siege had been broken. For all intents and purposes, the protesters had won. Skirmishes continued at a few hotspots, but Tahrir remained theirs. Alaa Abd El-Fattah, getting back to his more talkative online self, tried to sum up the experience, including his own doubts throughout the night.

> RT @alaa: I can't believe the bravery and determnation of revolutionaries. I abandoned post thinking this was impossible to win #Jan25[118]
>
> RT @alaa: It required rushing en mass under barrage of fire from above and in face of live ammo #Jan25[119]
>
> RT @alaa: At some stage found an elderly univ prof throwing rocks next to me had to drag him away by force #Jan25[120]

Al Jazeera's Evan Hill finally left the front lines for a well-earned rest.

> RT @evanchill: Made it back safe. Soldier tried to confiscate my camera. I convinced him to just take the battery & the memory was hidden.[121]
>
> RT @evanchill: suffice to say tonight was the Battle of Tahrir, and the protesters won. Cairo is changed. #jan25[122]

Apart from a brief respite with my family, I had tweeted almost nonstop for around 14 hours, providing my own form of anchor coverage for my Twitter community. How many tweets did I post? More than 1,400 of them, apparently. I offered my gratitude to Katie Stanton and her team at Twitter for clearing the path for my account:

> Thanks to @KatieS and the engineering team at Twitter for taking the time out of their evening to help get my account working again. #jan25[123]

My hands were numb; I felt the eye strain spreading to my sinuses. Looking around stung my corneas – I probably had barely blinked all day.

But what the hell was I complaining about? I had been sitting *in front of a computer*. I got to cook dinner and put my kids to bed. My experience paled in comparison to everyone at Tahrir Square.

On Al Jazeera, they replayed an interview with Mona Seif. When I first heard her many hours earlier, I thought she sounded terrified. Now I heard something else. Determination. Defiance. The need to bear witness and tell the world what was happening.

I then saw a tweet from Egyptian-American commentator @MonaEltahawy congratulating Mona Seif on her role during the battle. She also made a reference to Mona's brother. It was @alaa. I was stunned.

> I had no idea @alaa and @monasosh were siblings. So we've literally watched a family tweet a battle today. Extraordinary.[124]

Back on the Qasr al Nil Bridge, pharmacy student Mosa'ab Elshamy fought in one of the final skirmishes, dividing his time between throwing rocks and tweeting. Did this kid ever need sleep? Oh wait – he's a college student.

After a while, his tweets started to sound downright slap-happy from exhaustion.

> RT @mosaaberizing: A group of them actually got bored of fighting and is just taunting us from the bridge. Kids. . . #Tahrir[125]

> RT @mosaaberizing: Only molotov & stones with them now, and they suck at both. #jan25[126]

> RT @mosaaberizing: I kid you not. A group of us are practicing baseball with the stones they're throwing. Bats and all. Fun revolution :)[127]

Despite his obvious adrenaline rush mixing with a generous dose of fatigue, Mosa'ab paused for a moment to reflect on the scene, just as the morning call to prayer began.

> RT @mosaaberizing: Sunrise in Cairo. Blood spilled in Tahrir more noticed now. All over the place. #Jan25[128]

> RT @BenCNN: State-run Nile TV reports 4 dead, 829 wounded in battle of #Tahrir Square. Expect more upward revisions. #Egypt #Jan25.[129]

Ben Wedemen tweeted the latest casualty numbers as a new day dawned on Cairo. Beyond Tahrir Square, the museum and the bridges, it was as if nothing had happened. Traffic flowed as usual – or perhaps more accurately, didn't flow as usual – while shopkeepers readied their storefronts for business.

But in this one-mile stretch along the east bank of the Nile, the stench and detritus of battle was everywhere. Overturned cars. Haphazard piles of sheet metal. Streets with large pockets of concrete chiseled away. Torched palm trees. And thousands of dazed people, trying to comprehend how they managed to survive 18 hours of hell.

It was past 1:30 a.m. at my house outside Washington, D.C. I tweeted a goodnight message to everyone.

> Okay, folks, I need to wind down for at least a few hours. Everyone stay safe; I'll be back online in the morning D.C. time. #jan25[130]

Afterward, I realized that I still didn't know the status of Ali Seif and the little boy he rescued. I dug through his Twitter timeline to see if I had missed anything. I did the same for every person he had spent time with over the course of the battle. I even looked at the people he replied to over the course of the night, to see if they might've said anything. I couldn't message Ali privately, because he wasn't following me on Twitter.

As I was ready to give up hope, I looked at his tweets again. And there it was, right in front of me the whole time.

> RT @BloggerSeif: Tried to sleep but child's parents came to get him. What a beautiful mother and father. Cairo is wild![131]

I was overjoyed. Cairo *is* indeed wild.

Knowing that many of my Twitter followers were also worried for the boy, I sent out an additional tweet.

> One last thing before I call it a night – the 2-yr-old boy rescued by @bloggerseif was reunited with his family later that evening. #jan25[132]

The siege at Tahrir Square was over; the protesters held their ground.

As the sun rose over Tahrir, a group of activists resisted their bodies' need for sleep and began to chant.

Mosa'ab Elshamy, his tour of duty now complete, translated their shouts:

> *The people want to take down the system.*
>
> *The people want to take down the president.*
>
> *The people want to put the president on trial.*
>
> *The people want to hang the criminal.*[133]

As they chanted, the crowd of activists expanded, larger and larger.

It was a new day in Cairo – and time to initiate another protest rally.

The People Demand

Two weeks into the protests, the Egyptian uprising reached an impasse. While activists succeeded in securing Tahrir Square and could still attract crowds by the tens of thousands – even hundreds of thousands – the government's position hadn't really budged. Many protesters worried they would cave before Mubarak did.

That was all before the reappearance of Wael Ghonim.

Ghonim, a Dubai-based Google executive who had secretly helped launch the *We Are All Khaled Said* Facebook page, was taken into police custody in the first days of the revolution. He wrote in his last tweet prior to arrest:

> RT @ghonim: Pray for #Egypt. Very worried as it seems that government is planning a war crime tomorrow against people. We are all ready to die #Jan25[1]

For almost two weeks, no one heard from him, and activists feared the worst.

> RT @MMM: Help is needed. My friend Wael Ghonim @ghonim from Google is missing in Egypt since #Jan25. Spread the word & help locate him[2]

> RT @Sandmonkey: It's an outrage that Wael @Ghonim is still missing. Our hearts are with you. #jan25[3]

> RT @Zeinobia: Where is Wael Ghonim , you bastards?[4]

Then on February 7, a rumor claimed that Ghonim had been released and was with fellow protesters.

> RT @nadaauf: Wael Ghoneim is here! Wael Ghoneim is here! #tahrir #jan25[5]

However, his closest friends and family had yet to receive word that he had indeed been released. Until they did, I remained cautious.

Several Arabic language news channels, including Al Jazeera and Alarabiya, were now reporting he had been released.[6] There was also much confusion about official confirmation.

> RT @habibh: State Department confirms to WSJ Wael @Ghonim has been released. Family still waiting for him[7]

> RT @NYT_JenPreston: I talked to State Dept. It is not confirmed that @ghonim's been released. Too many conflicting reports.[8]

While we awaited more details, I received an angry tweet from one of my Twitter followers. He was unfollowing me because I talked too much about Egypt. Yes, this wasn't a topic I dwelled on prior to the Tunisian revolution, but this was too important to ignore. As far as I was concerned, that was his problem, not mine.

> Just had my first follower publicly say they're unfollowing me due to too much Egypt coverage. Sorry, but I'm in for the long haul. #jan25[9]

That tweet got me thinking, though. Things had moved so fast in Tunisia and Egypt, I hadn't spent much time pondering how long I was going to keep this up. In all honesty, I hadn't done much work related to my official job at NPR for several weeks; thankfully no one seemed to notice. As long as this went on, I wanted to keep tweeting. But what if this was the beginning of something much bigger than Tunisia or Egypt?

Then I saw a tweet from Wael Ghonim's Twitter account, quoted by his friend Habib Haddad.

> RT @habibh: @Ghonim just tweeted "Freedom is a bless that deserves fighting for it. #Jan25" Good to have you back buddy!!!![10]

I direct-messaged Habib to get more details. He told me he had just spoken with Ghonim's wife. "She talked to him," Habib reported. "He is safe and sound, resting with his parents."

Soon, new photos of Ghonim circulated on Twitter; he looked exhausted, but was otherwise healthy.[11] Perhaps most importantly, he looked well enough to talk. The night of his release, he agreed to an interview on Dream TV, an Egyptian independent news channel.

Ghonim's TV appearance captured the attention of the entire nation. Overwhelmed with emotion, he broke down and cried while discussing the deaths of protesters, describing them as the real heroes of the revolution.

Nasser Weddady, who had been so helpful to me during the Tunisian revolution, captured some of the highlights of Ghonim's interview.

> RT @weddady: This talk show is playing out as an emotional H-Bomb being dropped on Mubarak. #Jan25[12]
>
> RT @weddady: Wael @Ghonim breaks out in tears when show host shows pictures of the youth protesters who were killed by the regime #Jan25[13]

> RT @weddady: Wael @Ghonim apologizes to the mothers of the killed, and says it's government's fault. WALKS OFF SET #JAn25[14]

The political impact of the interview seemed clear to me.

> The Egyptian govt didn't want @ghonim to act as the leader of #jan25. They're probably realizing now they just turned him into it.[15]

Ben Wedemen of CNN watched the interview back in Cairo.

> RT @bencnn: the wael @ghonim interview on DreamTV: Earthshaking. #Jan25 #Egypt #tahrir[16]

Ghonim's powerful TV interview re-energized the protesters. Twitter and Facebook exploded with calls for Egyptians to return to the streets. Though no one individual could claim to be the leader of the uprising, as far as the media was concerned, Ghonim had become its poster child.

The next day, as word spread that Wael Ghonim would soon visit Tahrir Square, hundreds of thousands of people left their homes to hear him speak.

> RT @Ghonim: Tahrir Square is blocked. We are trying to get there now. Egyptians are making history. #Jan25[17]

CNN's Ivan Watson and Ben Wedeman sized up the crowd.

> RT @ivanCNN: The crowd in Tahrir Square is HUGE today. More people than I've ever seen. Full from the north end all the way to the Egyptian Museum #Egypt[18]

> MT @bencnn: Lots of people in #Tahrir for first time today? Reasons: curious, @Ghonim interview. tired of staying at home. #Jan25[19]

People from all walks of life came out of the woodwork. The protesters had regained the initiative, as observed by documentary maker Omar Robert Hamilton, pharmacy student Mosa'ab Elshamy and economist Mohamed El Dahshan.

> RT @RiverDryFilm: From Ray Bans to Botox to Versace veils to full niqabs, Tahrir is hosting everyone equally. #jan25 #egypt[20]

> RT @mosaaberizing: Heard someone speaking on the phone: "State TV says we're 5000? That's just the people queuing for the bathroom, honey"[21]

> RT @TravellerW: Yesterday it felt like #Tahrir was gearing up for war. Today it really feels like we've won. #Egypt #jan25[22]

The revolution had been rejuvenated. And President Mubarak would have no choice but to address the nation.

The next day, February 10, Egyptian military leaders issued a statement called *Communiqué Number One* – code words often used in the region when a coup was in process. Many people assumed that the statement would proclaim the overthrow of Mubarak. Instead it said that a core group of officers known as the Supreme Council of the Armed Forces (SCAF) had met, and would continue to meet, to study options for keeping Egypt and its people safe.[23]

Several hours later, word leaked that Mubarak would make a speech to the nation. For the hundreds of thousands of people in Tahrir Square, not to mention the millions watching remotely, it was widely assumed that this would be a resignation speech.

Political activists Ramy Yaacoub and Mahmoud Salem (@SandMonkey) could barely contain their enthusiasm.

> RT @RamyYaacoub: OnPhoneW/ The incredible @SandMonkey: ". . . Hey dude . . . Its happening" #Egypt #Jan25[24]

Back in the U.S., Fox News reported Hosni Mubarak would indeed resign.

> RT @foxnews: Fox News confirms #Mubarak will step down shortly, transfer power to a joint military council #jan25[25]

Nasser Weddady heard similar reports from his contacts.

> RT @weddady: Again: my sources tell me that Hosni is leaving within 24h #Jan25 decision was taken 6 hours ago.[26]

"We'll see," I wrote back.[27] I wasn't going to pass judgment until I heard what Mubarak had to say.

When Mubarak finally went on air late evening Cairo time, I was participating in a panel discussion with several other journalists at the *New York Times* headquarters. Because of all the delays, no one knew exactly when he would begin speaking, so we monitored Twitter and the news networks as best we could during the forum. When Mubarak suddenly appeared on TV, everything came to a halt; I knelt in front of the director's chair I had been sitting on onstage to use it as a makeshift desk so I could live-tweet Mubarak's remarks.

The first part of Mubarak's speech sounded like he was leading up to his resignation.

> Mubarak: your demands are lawful and legitimate[28]
>
> Mubarak: mistakes are likely in any regime though it's important to admit to mistakes and punish those responsible[29]

As he spoke, his tone began to change. This was no resignation speech.

> Mubarak: I cannot and will not accept being dictated orders from the outside, no matter what the source is[30]
>
> Mubarak: i announced in very plain words I won't run in the next election.[31]
>
> Mubarak: . . . until the power is handed over in september in a fair, free election[32]
>
> Mubarak: there will be a steering committee. Two committees with independent and transparent jurists, legal profesionals[33]
>
> Mubarak: egypt will live on until I hand over the trust and the banner. It is my homeland of my birth and death.[34]
>
> Mubarak: i will not separate from the soil until I am buried underneath[35]

On TV, we watched thousands of people in Tahrir Square raising their shoes in the air to express their contempt for the president. Some even threw their footwear at a giant projection screen.

> RT @SultanAlQassemi: WOW. Al Jazeera is showing furious protesters in Meydan Tahrir. They are certainly disappointed. This may turn ugly.[36]
>
> RT @RiverDryFilm: Fucking prick. #jan25 #egypt[37]
>
> RT @Sandmonkey: People are going crazy in the street. We are joining them. #jan25[38]

For Cairo's exhausted protesters, this was perhaps their most agonizing moment. Tweet after tweet, you could taste their fear and disgust. Mubarak would never leave, it seemed, and they'd probably die trying to oust him. As Egyptian science reporter Nadia El-Awady tweeted, "No one is expecting anything less than a blood bath tomorrow."[39]

Friday, February 11. I was at a New York hotel and needed to check out before noon. The first tweet I saw came from media critic Jeff Jarvis.

> RT @jeffjarvis: @acarvin this is your alarm clock[40]

"I'm up, I'm up….." I wrote back.[41]

Back in Cairo, the crowds appeared to reach into the multiple hundreds of thousands. Tahrir was getting so jammed that protesters were forced to spread out to other locations – including the state TV building, known as Maspero, about a mile north of Tahrir.

> RT @RiverDryFilm: Filling up fast outside state TV building. Barbed wire looking flimsy #jan25 #egypt[42]

> RT @mosaaberizing: The barricades at State TV were totally blocked but starting to open up under pressure. Thousands joining. #Jan25 #Maspero[43]

> RT @bencnn: MASSIVE crowd outside State TV. . .must be 10,000 plus and still growing. #Tahrir #Egypt #Jan25[44]

> RT @monasosh: Infront of TV building, BIG CROWD RT @justimage: Army general on other side crying and shaking hands with protesters. #jan25[45]

Nadia El-Awady and Mahmoud Salem were about six miles northeast of Tahrir in the Heliopolis neighborhood, not far from President Mubarak's official residence.

> RT @NadiaE: Army not threatening thousands gathered at presidential palace. If this continues they have my respect for that #jan25 #egypt[46]

> RT @Sandmonkey: People are peacefull but very angry. This is interesting. #jan25[47]

Socialist activist Gigi Ibrahim uploaded a photo that showed a human wave filling Tahrir.

> RT @Gsquare86: My eyes tear-up as I'm hearing millions chanting "yaskoot yaskoot [down with, down with] Hosni Mubarak" at once #Tahrir http://yfrog.com/h3q53baj[48]

According to labor activist Hossam Hamalawy, protesters were attempting to interfere with helicopters hovering over the square.

> RT @3arabawy: protesters in Tahrir r flying kites on high altitudes to harass the military helicopter :D #jan25[49]

Mona Seif noted protest rallies forming all over the city.

> RT @monasosh: Amazing! Anywhere in downtown u find scattered crowds holding Anti mubarak slogand. A month ago this was an unimaginable dream[50]

Wael Ghonim, meanwhile, took advantage of his newfound influence by issuing a Twitter-length open letter to Mubarak.

> RT @Ghonim: Dear President Mubarak your dignity is no longer important, the blood of Egyptians is. Please leave the country NOW. #Jan25[51]

Back in the U.S., Nasser Weddady was on CNN discussing the standoff between Mubarak and the protesters.

> Nasser @Weddady on CNN: Twitter and FB have become the news agencies for people on the ground in Egypt. #jan25[52]

> @weddady on CNN: I was named after Gamel abdel Nasser, who essentially started this regime. It's proven to be an absolute failure. #jan25[53]

Then Egyptian blogger @Zeinobia, monitoring state television, tweeted that the government would soon release another statement.[54] Back in my hotel room, I multitasked feverishly while keeping an eye on the clock.

> Hope these statements come out in the next 65 mins; need to check out of hotel then. Otherwise will go mobile again. #jan25[55]

> Listening to CNN and AlJaz simultaneously. Good thing I have two ears. Three would be better. #jan25 #callingDrMoreau[56]

My hotel TV switched to a live feed of Egyptian state television. Hosni Mubarak's recently appointed vice president, Omar Suleiman, made a statement so brief I was able to tweet the entire translation of it:

> Breaking! Suleiman: Mubarak has decided to wave the office of the president and have the supreme council run the affairs of the country.[57]

I had to re-read several times it to make sure I understood what had just happened, but it was all there: Mubarak had resigned.

The TV then switched to a live shot of Tahrir. It was absolute mayhem.

> Crowd in Tahrir explode with joy #jan25[58]

The reaction among my Twitter contacts, many of whom were in Cairo, was one of complete shock.

> RT @mosaaberizing: IT HAPPENED?![59]
>
> RT @monaeltahawy: Is he gone?? Seriously?! Good riddance #Mubarak! Now the regime can follow him too! Yalla #Egypt! #Jan25[60]
>
> RT @monasosh: Shit! Ppl are going crazy, screaming and running, Mubarak jas stepped down #Jan25[61]
>
> RT @Egyptocracy: Fireworks, confetti and the national anthem over and over again. Presidential Palace. #Egypt #Jan25[62]
>
> RT @NadiaE: ululation at pres palace! He resigned![63]
>
> RT @TravellerW: Egypt, the Middle East, the World will never be the same. From #Tahrir square – CONGRATULATIONS, FREE #EGYPT! #jan25[64]
>
> RT @SultanAlQassemi: UNBELIEVABLE. THE EGYPTIANS REALLY DID IT.[65]

Blogger @Zeinobia was flooded with emotion.

> RT @Zeinobia: Hosni Mubarak has stepped down !! Do you hear me ya world ya people !!? #Egypt #Jan25[66]
>
> RT @Zeinobia: We have an ex-president[67]

Mosa'ab Elshamy, the pharmacy student who withstood the onslaught of Molotov cocktails during the battle for Tahrir Square, gave credit where credit was due.

> RT @mosaaberizing: Tears filling Tahrir![68]
>
> RT @mosaaberizing: Don't forget the 300+ martyrs who sacrificed their lives for this moment to come true. The real heroes of #Jan25[69]

Mona Seif, meanwhile, soaked in the moment.

> RT @monasosh: Ppl are screaming " long live the revolution" we finally got rid of him #Jan25[70]
>
> RT @monasosh: Some random man pointed at me and said this is Egypt's smile. I love this country #Jan25[71]
>
> RT @monasosh: Today we fulfilled our promise to those who died #Jan25 #KhaledSaid[72]

In Dubai, intrepid tweeter Sultan Al Qassemi congratulated the revolutionaries.

> RT @sultanalqassemi: 85 Million Arabs are free from a 30 year old dictatorship. This is truly a great and historic moment for humanity.[73]

> RT @SultanAlQassemi: A million congratulations to Egyptians. You are the heroes of the Arab World. #Jan25[74]

> RT @SultanAlQassemi This one's for you Khaled Saeed & for the countless victims of this brutal dictator.[75]

And Egyptian protester Sarah Naguib gave perhaps the best advice of the day.

> RT @Sarahngb: EGYPTIANS ACROSS THE WORLD. LEAVE YOUR COMPUTERS AND GO OUT CELEBRATE #Egypt #jan25[76]

Back at my hotel, I kept hitting the retweet button as dozens of people I'd gotten to know over the previous 18 days expressed pride in their stunning accomplishment. Almost no one had thought it was possible they would be able to force out Mubarak, let alone do it in less than three weeks.

I began thinking about the Arabic word for Egypt – *Masr* – and tweeted:

> Extraordinary. Simply extraordinary. The students become the Masr. #jan25[77]

As I sat back and watched the celebrations from afar, I began to contemplate what the protesters had achieved. For 18 days, thousands stood their ground in Tahrir Square and across Egypt. Hundreds of them died in the process. And they accomplished their primary goal: overthrowing President Mubarak. Yes, I was merely a distant witness to these events, but a witness nonetheless, and it had moved me profoundly:

> Tunisia's revolution took four weeks. Egypt: 17 days. Who's next and how much time do they have? #jan25[78]

> Somewhere, Khaled Said is smiling. And Mohamed Bouazizi. And MLK, for that matter. #jan25[79]

> Yes, social media played a role in #jan25. But don't call this the Twitter or FB revolution. Real people protested and died. It's theirs.[80]

> "Brothers and sisters don't you cry / There'll be good times by & by / Pharaoh's army got drownded / O, Mary, don't you weep" #jan25[81]

And somewhere on Twitter, an anonymous person with a fake Mubarak account tweeted:

RT @HosniMobarak: You're welcome. #Egypt #Jan25[82]

The next morning, I slept in. When I finally looked at Twitter, something was different. The names were all the same, but many images were unfamiliar. Then it dawned on me. During their 18-day revolution, many protesters used inspirational symbols as their personal avatars – Egyptian flags, raised fists and the like. Now those symbols were gone and replaced with something quite different: portrait photos.

For the first time, I saw their faces. They were so young, so proud. And they were safe now: safe enough to show their real selves online. It was like meeting them all over again.

revealed themselves.

Arrested Development

Egypt's euphoria was short-lived. After Mubarak's resignation, the Supreme Council of the Armed Forces (SCAF) took over the country and slowly began planning elections. The vast majority of protesters went home – back to school, back to work. But Tahrir Square did not empty. A core group of activists planned to remain until all of their revolutionary goals were met, including the transition to a democratically elected government.

These activists didn't trust SCAF. The army had arrested many protesters and tried them in military courts, only exacerbating the tensions. On the second Friday in April, they held another mass rally in Tahrir, protesting the slow pace of SCAF's transition plan. Some announced they would protest until President Mubarak was put on trial.[1] Relations between the protesters and the general public also began to fray; many Egyptians simply wanted everyone to go home and give SCAF the time they needed to complete the government transition.

On May 15, three months after the fall of Mubarak, protesters came out in force to commemorate Nakba Day. Nakba, Arabic for "catastrophe," is the word used to describe the displacement of hundreds of thousands of Palestinians after Israel declared independence. Activists across the Arab world scheduled protests against Israel for that day.

Not surprisingly, I knew some of the people planning to attend the Nakba event in Cairo – a rally in front of the Israeli embassy in the suburb of Giza, southwest of downtown. Some went to document the protests, while others participated more directly.[2] Mosa'ab Elshamy and Gigi Ibrahim were among the most prolific tweeters that day.

> RT @mosaaberizing: Heading to the Israeli embassy protest. It doesn't feel quite enough but oh well..[3]
>
> RT @Gsquare86: I am in a march heading to #Israeli embassy in #Cairo#Nakba coming from nile ferry[4]

At first, the protesters were allowed to go about their business in front of the embassy. As the day wore on, though, riot police known as the Central Security Force arrived on the scene. It was a recipe for chaos.

> RT @mosaaberizing: Large group of CSF troops just arrived at the embassy. Met with angry chants.[5]

The riot police began firing tear gas into the crowd.

RT @mosaaberizing: Protestors are dispersed across the bridge, can't estimate numbers but it's big enough to attract street vendors and their carts.[6]

RT @Gsquare86: The peaceful protesters at the #IsraeliEmbassy in#Cairo are doing nothing to the embassy, why are they firing tear gas and shooting in air?[7]

RT @3arabawy: shit shit tear gas showers[8]

Some angry protesters fought back; others set small fires in the streets. Riot police responded with gunfire, causing numerous injuries. Protester Nora Shalaby, a professional Egyptologist, was caught in the thick of it.

RT @norashalaby: Still firing tear gas mostly in direction towards murad st.[9]

RT @norashalaby: Fuck its been awhile since I smelt this shit![10]

RT @norashalaby: Loud shots being fired in the air. Not sure what is being fired[11]

Gigi Ibrahim tried to reason with one of the police.

RT @Gsquare86: I talked with the police officer who was shooting at protesters saying why !!! Aren't these ur brothers and sisters[12]

RT @Gsquare86: They are drenching the area with tear gas ..we can't breath[13]

In the midst of the fracas, Mosa'ab Elshamy remained calm. I imagined this was nothing compared to the action he'd seen in Tahrir Square.

RT @mosaaberizing: Typical push n retreat game in here. Don't know where this is going but protesters are pretty resilient against police violence.[14]

RT @mosaaberizing: Protesters say their only demand now is taking down the Israeli flag off the embassy. Chanting "peaceful".[15]

In her nearby home, science reporter Nadia El-Awady despaired at what she felt was the fracturing of the revolution.

RT @NadiaE: My son's school is 3 blocks from israeli embassy. He has a final tomorrow. What do I do??[16]

RT @NadiaE: Sick to my stomach – literally – about what's happening in Egypt.[17]

RT @NadiaE: And egypt army and police killing protesters is fixing a wrong with a worse wrong[18]

RT @NadiaE: One of the scariest things in the world is to have a front row seat to your country descending into chaos[19]

Activist Mostafa Hossein (@moftasa) noted the similarities to January 28, the date of one of the most violent crackdowns during the revolution, but wondered aloud if their motivations for protesting had changed.

RT @moftasa: Well everyone tweeting its like the 28 again . . . it is. And it is not the bloody tear gas that we crave it's the adrenaline.[20]

Tarek Shalaby, Nora's brother, had been out of town, but plunged in as soon as he learned about the furor around the Israeli embassy.

RT @tarekshalaby: Just arrived to Cairo and came straight to Giza. . . .[21]

RT @tarekshalaby: Finally got by the Four Seasons and parked. Smells like tear gas – takes me back..[22]

RT @tarekshalaby: Met a group of young men (medic volunteers) gave us cotton to block nose from tear gas[23]

Not far from Tarek, Mosa'ab took photos as the protesters marched back toward the embassy.

RT @mosaaberizing: Protesters gathering en route to the embassy http://twitpic.com/4y7v3f[24]

RT @mosaaberizing: Lights have been cut off some streets near the embassy. More tear gas.[25]

Tarek eventually met up with Mosa'ab and started streaming live videos on his phone, documenting the march. The situation remained extremely tense.

RT @tarekshalaby: Israel embassy, Giza – LIVE at http://bambuser.com/v/1658990[26]

RT @tarekshalaby: Young men just dropped to the ground in front of me. Prolly just temporary breathing problem. . .[27]

The protesters were struggling to remain assembled. Each time they tried moving forward, police forced them back. It was probably a matter of time before they were completely dispersed.

Suddenly, Tarek tweeted:

> RT @tarekshalaby: Shit! We've been ambushed! Army coming from other side. Ran into side street. . .[28]

And then, nothing.

Gigi Ibrahim was among the first to worry about what might be happening to Tarek.

> RT @Gsquare86: is @tarekshalaby ok ..he was tweeting and now his phone is off[29]

I was worried, too. Like Mosa'ab, Tarek was often at the front lines in the battles for Tahrir. And now riot police had apparently ambushed the two of them.

A few moments later, I was relieved when Tarek's face reappeared in my Twitter timeline. The tweet contained an automated message:

> RT @tarekshalaby: Israel embassy, Giza – tear gas – LIVE at http://bambuser.com/v/1659053[30]

It was the same message Tarek's phone sent out every time he began a new livestream. I clicked on the link and soon heard yelling and gunfire. My Twitter followers needed to watch this.

> Turn this on NOW. RT @tarekshalaby: Israel embassy, Giza – tear gas – LIVE at http://bit.ly/mI1sb6[31]

The video quality was terrible. For a moment it looked like several people were being forced to the ground. I saw a flash of pavement, then the underside of the car. I couldn't tell if Tarek was hiding, or had been shoved to the ground next to the vehicle.

Another person watching the livestream was Yemeni-American Raja Althaibani, who was in Yemen's capital, Sana'a.

> RT @RajaAlthaibani: TARIQ I HEAR GUNSHOTS! STAY UNDER THE CAR! DONT MOVE! @tarekshalaby #EGYPT #CAIRO #ISRAEL[32]
>
> RT @RajaAlthaibani: @tarekshalaby Are you okay? I'm watching ur livefeed! Stay low and hide until they're gone![33]

I begged my Twitter followers to help decipher what was happening to Tarek.

> Someone please go to the livestream and translate in real time, PLEASE! http://bit.ly/mI1sb6[34]

The livestream continued. Tarek was still down on the ground next to the car. Immediately to his left, I saw another man on the ground, as if he was about to crawl on all fours. As far as I could tell, it wasn't Mosa'ab. A shadowy figure stood over him, barking out commands.

Assuming the man on all fours was under arrest, it seemed very unlikely that Tarek had managed to hide under the car. They were just too close to each other to not be noticed by police. Tarek, and presumably Mosa'ab, too, were probably down on the ground, but the police had no idea his phone was streaming live video.

For a moment, I heard whispering; I believed it was Tarek trying to communicate with us. He was live-streaming his own arrest. I cursed myself for not speaking Egyptian Arabic.

A policeman then lifted the man on the ground in front of Tarek. The officer appeared to be taking him away. Suddenly, Tarek's camera phone trundled out of focus, then went black. The audio, however, kept rolling. I was pretty sure I heard someone say the word "camera."

There's still nothing but black. The audio was somewhat muffled, but you could hear arguing, yelling – and then a shockingly loud volley of machine gun fire.[35]

> OK, this is getting terrifying. #egypt[36]

Someone barked out more commands; other police yelled at other arrested protesters. More gunfire, then the sounds of a scuffle. I heard a shuffling noise, as if the phone's mic was rubbing against fabric. Someone started shooting again.

Out of nowhere, I heard the tinny sound of a ringtone – a cheery tune that stood in bizarre contrast to what was happening to Tarek and the protesters.

> And all of a sudden the shooting stops and now I hear cheezy music. Cell phone ringing? Jesus, @tarekshalaby, are you ok? #egypt[37]

The stream continued live for several more minutes and then stopped.

> The livestream just went dead. Oh God. #egypt[38]
>
> I think we just listened to @mosaaberizing and @tarekshalaby getting arrested. Don't know for sure but they've gone silent.[39]

Tarek's sister Nora asked if anyone knew what was going on.

> RT @norashalaby: I think @tarekshalaby is cornered by army and is livestreaming from phone in his pocket. Anyone near him?[40]

I wrote back:

> @norashalaby His stream just went dead. Scrambling to find out anything I can. #egypt[41]

Mona Seif was equally worried:

> RT @Monasosh: From @mosaaberizing tweets, looks like Army cracked down and arrested protesters !!!! anyone else there?[42]

I replied to Mona, as well as to Nora and Gigi Ibrahim:

> @monasosh @norashalaby @Gsquare86 Here is the stream. There are gun shots, lots of yelling, don't understand Arabic. http://bit.ly/kJVE3c[43]

By now, a number of my Twitter followers were reviewing the video to translate the altercation.

> RT @AmrAlzain: @acarvin voice saying "get up, hands behind your head"[44]
>
> RT @Lastarabianman: @acarvin seems like a police or army officer saying go collect the mother fuckers. . .on your knees. . . .follow orders. . . .[45]
>
> RT @Pacinthe: @acarvin Prior to that, commands to get on their knees, get in line, listen to orders. . . .[46]
>
> RT @RajaAlthaibani: @acarvin Soldier:"get up from here! Listen to what I'm saying!"[47]

One person I had never heard of, who went by @ysalah, tweeted the most detailed account of the exchange.

> RT @ysalah: @acarvin he just said "why are some people looking up?" = they're face down on the ground[48]
>
> RT @ysalah: @acarvin all that talking you hear is them cussing at protesters..[49]
>
> RT @ysalah: @acarvin more cussing, distant yelling – "i was on my way home" – yelling – they start walking – "look straight ahead!" – walking, silence[50]
>
> RT @ysalah: @acarvin "this son of a bitch thinks he'll liberate palestine"[51]
>
> RT @ysalah: @acarvin commotion "on your stomach" – "sir i work at a hotel" – "what are you doing here?" – "i work at a hotel & i was on my way home[52]

> RT @ysalah: @acarvin tarek: we're surrounded army "hands on ur head, ev1 on their knees!" fire "do as i say!" "get up!" fire "stand up" "get back down"[53]

Another person going by the alias @mxbw observed something I had completely missed while watching the live video.

> RT @mxbw: @acarvin hah the cheesy music was the super mario theme[54]

"Jeez," I responded, laughing to myself. "I was so amped up I didn't even recognize it."[55]

I watched the video two more times, trying to decipher whatever I could. Now that @mxbw had mentioned it, I thought more about why we heard that ring tone so loudly. I doubted it was Tarek's – his phone probably wouldn't ring while streaming simultaneously – so it must have been very close to another mobile phone. But whose phone?

Aha.

> Listening to it again I think @Tarekshalaby's phone was in a security officer's pocket! Could be why we hear ringtone, phone vibration.[56]

The arresting officer had been so clueless about Tarek's livestream that he didn't even check the phone before putting it in his own pocket. Thanks to him, thousands of people around the world got to witness Tarek's arrest.

Later that night, Mosa'ab and Tarek's siblings tweeted updates about their status.

> RT @abdallahelshamy: My brother @mosaaberizing just called me on the phone and said he's detained in a csf truck in front of Modyryet Amn ElGiza[57]

> RT @norashalaby: Confirmed. Friend called from scene and said that @tarekshalaby has been arrested by the army[58]

I went back to look at Mosa'ab's most recent tweets. He kept his sense of humor even up to the moments before his arrest.

> Funny even when chased. RT @mosaaberizing: I was tweeting from under a tree & a bird shit fell on the mobile's screen. What does that mean?[59]

Sarah Naguib replied:

> RT @Sarahngb: @acarvin @mosaaberizing :(and I told him it means he should go home. He was about to leave.[60]

The scope of the melee became apparent after the protesters dispersed. Al Jazeera English producer Adam Makary reported that at least 120 of them had been injured.[61] Hala Jaber, correspondent for the *Sunday Times*, offered a grim assessment.

> RT @HalaJaber: #egypt This latest turn of events is xtremely bad & can only spell further trouble. What happened 2 the g8 solidarity displayed during Revol[62]

Mahmoud Salem summed up the mood of the activists.

> RT @Sandmonkey: What a fuckin mess.. what a fuckin mess..what a fuckin mess. . .[63]

Tarek Shalaby and Mosa'ab Elshamy were among the lucky ones. Tarek's sister was allowed to visit them the next day, and she reported they were in good health. Friends and supporters rallied in Tahrir Square, demanding their release.[64] After several days, they each went before a military court. Tarek was found not guilty on all charges; Mosa'ab was acquitted on all counts except one minor charge.[65] Both were then released from prison.[66, 67]

More than 12,000 Egyptian civilians received military trials in the weeks and months following Mubarak's resignation. Many were beaten and left languishing in prison.

In the wake of SCAF coming to power, Mona Seif and a small group of activists formed a campaign called No To Military Trials For Civilians, or #NoMilTrials on Twitter. As they explained on their website, "Minors have been sent to adult prisons. Death sentences have been handed down. This is not the freedom that we fought and died for."[68]

More than a year would pass before Egypt held presidential elections. The three moderate candidates running in the primary canceled each other out. The runoff of the top two candidates was a liberal protester's nightmare: Mubarak's former prime minister and a Muslim Brotherhood leader. In the final vote, the Muslim Brotherhood candidate won.

Was this the freedom they fought and died for?

BAHRAIN

U Cant Break Us

A woman stands alone, arms raised high, her fingers on each hand displaying the V for Victory. She's cloaked in the traditional black gown and headscarf worn by many Bahraini Shia women. Tear gas shells have filled the air with an acrid mist. She is blocking a convoy of police vehicles dispatched to arrest protesters. The riot police don't know how to react. They are trained for urban fighting, mass disturbances, but not this – one woman, alone, defiant. They threaten her, curse her, but dare not touch her. They need to find a female officer to take her down. In the meantime, this woman – known online as @angryarabiya – has given her fellow protesters the time they needed to retreat.

While the world's collective attention focused on Tahrir Square and the fall of President Mubarak, other activists across the region were mobilizing. Tunisia and Egypt had captured the imagination of the Arab world, and many people felt this was their opportunity to break the yoke of their own repressive governments.

Learning from the experiences of Tunisia and Egypt, these activists began to adopt similar tactics: creating Facebook pages, identifying ways of accessing the Internet if their government tried to shut it down, and so on. Among the most overt tactics they adopted was creating hashtags to identify the launch date for their uprisings, just as the Egyptians had used #jan25. Bahrain rallied around #Feb14. Libyans chose #feb17. Algeria was to kick off two days later – #feb19. Morocco would use #feb20. Activists in Yemen, Syria, Jordan and Oman were also planning to man the barricades.

Country by country, dissidents came out of the woodwork and declared online: *save the date – rsvp.* It didn't seem to matter that declaring a start date would alert the authorities. By now, a critical mass of aspiring protesters had set aside their fears. *If Tunisia and Egypt could do it, we can do it too.*

Though I had no idea how I would attempt to cover multiple uprisings, I prepared as best I could. This still wasn't my official job, and I had been neglecting my duties for more than a month.

Then an NPR executive strolled by my cubicle. He leaned over the dividing wall and paused for a moment.

"I don't completely understand what you're doing," he said. "But please keep doing it."

I spent the rest of February selecting which countries I would tackle. Among them was Bahrain.

Bahrain, a small island nation off the coast of Saudi Arabia, had a reputation in the West of being reform-minded. Beneath the surface, though, tensions simmered between the government, dominated by a Sunni royal family, and the Shia majority of the population. Shia activists had long accused the government of giving preferential treatment to Sunnis: better jobs, higher positions in the government and more investments in local infrastructure. Opposition members and free speech activists were often jailed, even tortured.[1, 2] A series of protests in the 1990s led to government concessions, culminating in a "national action charter" that led to several political reforms.[3, 4, 5, 6]

Now, opposition groups announced they would begin a series of protests on February 14 – the tenth anniversary of the national action charter vote. A Facebook page announcing the protests quickly reached more than 14,000 members, while the #Feb14 hashtag made the rounds on Twitter.[7]

Like their Egyptian counterparts, the Bahraini protesters occupied a central location: an enormous traffic circle known as Pearl Roundabout. Locally, it was called Lulu Roundabout, "lulu" being Arabic for "pearl." Numerous Bahrainis began to use #lulu as a secondary hashtag.

The initial protests were civil, celebratory, even family-oriented affairs. Thousands of people gathered at Lulu waving flags, singing patriotic songs and giving uplifting speeches. It wasn't solely a Shia crowd, either: many Sunnis attended the rallies, supporting more political reforms.

The Bahraini government, though, was clearly on edge. Riot police patrolled the perimeter of Pearl Roundabout and Shia villages. Many police were mercenaries brought in from South Asia. These forces commanded smaller salaries than Bahraini citizens and were less likely to hesitate to act against the local populace.

By February 16, the protesters had settled into a routine: tens of thousands of Bahrainis marched the streets to rally at Lulu each day, while a subset of them spent the night there with their families. Government forces monitored the situation, but maintained a healthy distance.

That night, I was scheduled to give a talk about social media and journalism to Georgetown University graduate students. The class was meeting in downtown D.C., so I decided to grab some dinner at Zaytinya, a local Turkish restaurant. It was happy hour, and the bar was jammed, so I retreated to a dining table and casually checked Twitter. By all appearances, the situation in Bahrain hadn't changed.

After paying the bill, I joined the long line for the men's room. I pulled up Twitter on my phone, just to kill time.

I never made it inside the bathroom. It was 3 a.m. Bahrain time, and Lulu was under attack.

Blogger Chan'ad Bahraini, whom I had tracked down by following the #feb14 hashtag, reported:

> RT @chanadbh: RIGHT NOW: Riot police are firing at protesters at Pearl Roundabout #Bahrain Follow @maryamalkhawaja[8]

I quickly replied, asking for confirmation, then checked the torrent of tweets coming from Maryam Al-Khawaja (@maryamalkhawaja), a young woman from a family of prominent Shia human rights activists. Her tweets were chilling.

> RT @maryamalkhawaja: I see them on the bridge, hundreds of them[9]
>
> RT @maryamalkhawaja: They're shooting at us[10]
>
> RT @maryamalkhawaja: People are chanting "we demand the fall of the regime"[11]
>
> RT @maryamalkhawaja: There are wounded, area is surrounded[12]
>
> RT @maryamalkhawaja: Women are running carrying their children[13]
>
> RT @maryamalkhawaja: they're shooting repeatedly non stop[14]

I sent off a quick tweet to see if I could find out what exactly the police were using as ammunition.

> @maryamalkhawaja live ammo? Tear gas? Are u safe? #bahrain[15]

A few moments later, @chanadbh replied.

> RT @chanadbh: @acarvin To clarify. The exact nature of the "firing" is not confirmed. Definitely tear gas. Not sure what else[16]

Within minutes, many other Bahrainis alerted their Twitter followers. One, using the pseudonym @FroozyO, offered a dramatic account.

> RT @FroozyO: We can't escape. . .we can't escape. We're stuck. We can't see anything. Tear gas everywhere[17]
>
> RT @FroozyO: Thounsands of women and children were sleeping and we've been attacked. Its 3:23 am here now in Manama[18]
>
> RT @FroozyO: They're shooting rubber bullets. . .there's tear gas everywhere we can't see$ please help some bone[19]

Amira Al Hussaini (@justamira), a Global Voices editor based in Bahrain, was at home, not far from the traffic circle.

> RT @JustAmira: @acarvin @chanadbh @maryamalkhawaja YES CONFIRMED SPOKE TO PEOPLE THERE[20]
>
> RT @JustAmira: I can hear the choppers here – far away from pearl roundabout. One part of me tells me to go and see with my own eyes to believe #Feb14[21]

One after another, Bahraini protesters described what was happening.

> RT @Moaweya: Tear gases being throw at people in #lulu #bahrain http://yfrog.com/h371itrj #now[22]

> RT @hhusaini: I still hear gunshots! #lulu #bahrain[23]

> RT @lailaalbeiti: There is an ambulance at Pearl roundabout,inshallah kheir ya rab [God willing it'll be okay, Oh, God] #lulu #bahrain[24]

> RT @Moaweya: Kids and women are running everywhere and very scared in #lulu #bahrain[25]

> RT @tariqal: HOLY SHIT – as I was heading out, around 200 riot police pulled up heading towards pearl!!!!!!! #Bahrain #Lulu #Feb14.[26]

> RT @Ali_Fareed: Sure wait till 3 a.m., PPL would be asleep, all international news agencies would be running reruns & other programs.. #Bahrain[27]

> RT @nehayoo: Protesters are chanting: is this reforming? Attacking at 3 a.m.?[28]

> RT @MohmdAshoor: I don't give a fuck what was said and done, YOU DO NOT ATTACK UNARMED CIVILIANS WITH WOMEN & CHILDREN AT 3 FUCKING AM!!!!![29]

> RT @bahrain14feb: Help us!!!!! #Bahrain #feb14 #lulu[30]

The blogger known as @emoodz was almost at a loss for words.

> RT @emoodz: They did it.. They did it.. They did it.. #bahrain #feb14 #lulu[31]

Maryam Al-Khawaja's sister Zainab, who went by @angryarabiya on Twitter, frantically searched for her.

> RT @angryarabiya: Saw more than 30 riot police jeep, lookin 4 my sis desperatly. She was sleepin there![32]

> RT @angryarabiya: They've been attacked, while chanting peaceful peaceful. On my way there now #bahrain #lulu #feb14[33]

I had recently started following @angryarabiya, before Mubarak resigned in Egypt. She avidly followed regional politics, and never hesitated to share her opinions. Now the Arab Spring was playing out right in front of her. Over the next two years she would become one of the symbols of resistance in Bahrain.

---

everyone is a journalist - but someone needs to compose and compile.

I have no idea how long I stood outside the men's room at the Turkish restaurant. At least a dozen other guys cut in front of me while I stared at my phone, oblivious. While the attack on Lulu was in some ways similar to the battle in Egypt's Tahrir Square, I had a very different reaction to it. The attack had come out of nowhere, without warning. Men, women and children spending another peaceful night sleeping there were now under fire, some possibly dead. I felt their surprise, their fear, their panic. I was profoundly shaken.

My visit to the Georgetown class was a blur. I was amped; I talked almost nonstop, pulling up Bahrain tweets for the students. I answered questions, but can't remember what we talked about. My mind was 7,000 miles away.

After class, my phone battery was nearly dead. I found a chair not far from a power outlet. Plugging in, I plugged myself back into Bahrain. For the first time since the Arab revolutions began, I felt really scared for my contacts. Few photos or videos were coming out of Lulu, so I could only read tweets, one after another. They were just text, but extraordinarily vivid, like reading a novel. But these weren't fictional characters – they were real people I felt I knew, and they might not survive the night.

It was nearly dawn in Bahrain. Riot police were still breaking up protesters, and @angryarabiya lived up to her Twitter name, defiant as ever.

> RT @angryarabiya: I'd give up my life n my 1 year old daughters life be4 I let this gov continue oppressing us. She won't grow up oppressed like this! #feb14[34]
>
> RT @angryarabiya: [King] Alkhalifa u have signed ur death certificate. This is the end for u. We will all die martyrs rather than let u stay! #bahrain #feb14[35]
>
> RT @angryarabiya: Are we not humanbeings, don't we deserve to live with freedom and rights. Why do they kill us like animals? #bahrain #feb14 #lula[36]
>
> RT @angryarabiya: Crowds much bigger now, 500 ppl or more. A little boy is throwing up, looks very scared. #bahrain #lulu #feb14[37]

A little boy is throwing up. I felt sick to my stomach. My own son was in bed, just a few miles away, perfectly safe and sound. And yet I couldn't get the image out of my head: my little boy, standing in front of me, throwing up again and again, shaking with terror. Even now, the thought of it rattles me.

I had to clear my head. Yet no matter how upset I was, my fear paled in comparison to what the protesters were going through in Bahrain. Who was I to bitch about being upset while thousands of people were actually getting shot at? I began to feel guilty about it. But I couldn't shake the feeling that I had somehow experienced the attack with them, much more so than during the protests in Tunisia and Egypt. I kept it to myself; I didn't think anyone would understand.

Over the coming weeks, the Bahrain government escalated its crackdown on protesters. Police fired assault rifles into crowds, killing dozens. The deaths emboldened the protesters, with some calling for the death of the king. Mediation attempts failed. The government declared a state of emergency and invited military forces from Saudi Arabia to help crush the revolt. Soon, the protesters were scattered, Lulu Roundabout secured. The activists' momentum evaporated.

On April 9, nearly two months after the first protests, Zainab Al-Khawaja went online in the middle of the night. As a mother who was nursing her one-year-old daughter, it wasn't unusual for her to be up and tweeting at odd hours. But this was different.

> RT @angryarabiya: THEY JUST CAME! They took my dad, my dads blood is still on the stairs! They hit my dad so much! They beat him and he cudnt breath[38]
>
> RT @angryarabiya: they broke the doors, all wearing masks. They took my father and husband and brother in law.[39]
>
> RT @angryarabiya: they beat up my other brother in law mohammed almaskati, and then threw him in a room and told him not to come out[40]
>
> RT @angryarabiya: we knew they were coming, they had gone to my fathers apartment first and taken my cousin who lives in the same building[41]
>
> RT @angryarabiya: we all changed and my father told us to stay calm when they come, he told us not to interfere if they take him so they dont hurt us[42]
>
> RT @angryarabiya: we heard door of the building being broken, then the door of the apartment. my father went straight to the door, they started shouting[43]
>
> RT @angryarabiya: they held my father from his neck & started dragging him down the steps. they lay him on the floor between the steps & started beating him[44]
>
> RT @angryarabiya: He was covering his face while more than 5 men were beating him at the same time, I heard him say he cant breath[45]
>
> RT @angryarabiya: I said "he will go with you, you dont need to beat him" that when I saw my husband & brothers in law being dragged down[46]
>
> RT @angryarabiya: One of them grabbed me form my shirt and started dragging me up the stairs, my mum was begging him to let me go[47]
>
> RT @angryarabiya: then they locked the doors on us, and took the men to the lower apartment, lay them on the ground and started beating them[48]

> RT @angryarabiya: When they unlocked the door, I ran down & saw drops of blood on stairs. My fathers blood, my brave heroic fathers blood[49]
>
> RT @angryarabiya: I will go sit with my mum, she keeps saying be prepared for the worse. If any1 can do anything for my dad, husband & brother in law, plz do[50]
>
> RT @angryarabiya: My father is Human Rights activist Abdulhadi Alkhawaja, my husband is Wafi Almajed, and my brother in law is Hussain Ahmed Hussain.[51]
>
> RT @angryarabiya: Alkhalifa [the royal family], YOU CANT BREAK US, U CANT BREAK US. WE WILL ALWAYS STAND STRONG AGAINST YOU.[52]

As word of the arrests spread, I tweeted Bahrain's foreign minister, Khalid al-Khalifa.

> @khalidalkhalifa: Could I get a comment from you on the arrest of Abdulhadi Alkhawaja? Reports are that he was severely beaten. Thank you.[53]

Sixteen hours later, he responded.

> RT @khalidalkhalifa: @acarvin re question on the arrest of alkhawaja. Yes he was arrested for charges to be brought against him legally. He violently resisted the arrest and had to be subdued[54]

I alerted my followers.

> #Bahrain foreign minister @khalidalkhalifa replies to my question about the arrest of Abdulhadi Alkhawaja last night: http://bit.ly/h2txWB[55]

A few minutes later, Zainab responded angrily. She CCed the foreign minister on every tweet.

> RT @angryarabiya: @khalidalkhalifa You are a liar Khalid Alkhalifa, My father NEVER resisted arrest.[56]
>
> RT @angryarabiya: @khalidalkhalifa Infact before they arrived my father told us to let them take him away and be calm and patient[57]
>
> RT @angryarabiya: @khalidalkhalifa they beat him and he never raised his hand once, not once. I was watching them.[58]
>
> RT @angryarabiya: @khalidalkhalifa if u have "legal" charges against my father then u need an arrest warrant[59]

While some people might have been paralyzed by the arrest of their father, husband and brother-in-law, Zainab's resolve strengthened, both online and offline.

> RT @angryarabiya: I will start a hunger strike to demand the release of my family starting 6pm #Bahrain time. Hoping my next meal will be with them[60]

Two days after the arrests, Zainab Al-Khawaja announced she was going on a hunger strike. She published an open letter to President Obama on her blog.[61]

> RT @angryarabiya: announcing my hunger strike in a letter to #Obama: http://angryarabiya.blogspot.com/2011/04/letter-to-president-obama.html #bahrain[62]

> RT @angryarabiya: My hunger strike has officially begun, I thank every1 who said they'll join me, is spreading the word or is praying for my ppl & my family[63]

While members of Bahrain's opposition generally supported her hunger strike, she received scathing comments from other Bahrainis who continued their allegiance to the royal family. At times these comments felt more like teenage cyber-bullying than a political dispute.

> RT @TheDivineThaj: LOL @angryarabiya is going on a hunger strike. & we care because? I'm not the one who's going to end up looking like a decomposed dead body[64]

> RT @TheDivineThaj: Or. . . she could be on a liquid diet. Its healthy, requires no food, & she can shed a few pounds. Bikini season? You go girl @angryarabiya.[65]

> RT @hassanmushaima: – @angryarabia I thought she was angry because of Politics, turns out she's FAT![66]

> RT @TheDivineThaj: Gotta shed the baby weight mushi[67]

> RT @TheDivineThaj: @angryarabiya I make delicious deserts. Ill send u. We can forget about your bitchyness and binge & play dress up *yay*[68]

> RT @SarahYJA: Hunger strikes #MoreEmptyThreats.. Pfft didnt they say #ReadytoDie? Why all the fuss now? Hey @angryarabiya Guess wot? NO ONE CARES![69]

Someone even created a fake Twitter account – @hangryarabiya – to mock her hunger strike.

> RT @hangryarabiya: Who needs food when you got attention?[70]

Not all the replies to her were childish; some were simply blunt criticism.

> RT @mariamalk: AngryArabiya is old enough 2take responsibility 4 the things she says and hold her own @i_Strive_[71]
>
> RT @RashidAlghatam: @angryarabiya Your father applauded the economic damage done to Bahrain, as a private business man i am against that mentality[72]
>
> RT @dilmunstar: thats why @angryarabiya needs 2 stop d fast.Why punish a new born child? Is the baby's life less important?#bahrain[73]

The attacks on Zainab were part of a larger trend in Bahrain that I hadn't seen in either Tunisia or Egypt. The Bahrain government and its supporters were just as sophisticated as the opposition when it came to social media. Protesters in the other Arab uprisings dominated social networks, not the governments or their supporters. In Bahrain, though, we had a country where people across the political spectrum went online to continue their battles.

I started receiving attacks, too – from the Bahraini opposition. They chided me for documenting the bullying of @angryarabiya. To me, it seemed perfectly natural to retweet the pro-government perspective, because this was a new dynamic we hadn't witnessed yet. To others, though, my retweets seemed like a betrayal of their cause, because they assumed my retweets were tantamount to endorsements of the views they contained. For example, this tweet by @miasarah captured the sentiment of a number of Twitter users that day.

> RT @miasarah: terribly disappointed that @acarvin gave into twitter gossip.[74]

It became clear that I had to explain my reasoning for retweeting things that were critical, even insulting to the opposition.

> Look, folks: it's not my job to show the Bahrain situation from just one point of view. Don't expect me to be a mouthpiece.[75]
>
> And so far, Bahrain has been one of the few countries where people for AND against the protests are online. I won't ignore one side.[76]
>
> And besides, by showing the attacks that people are making on @angryarabiya, it shows how ugly and divided the situation is.[77]
>
> I think it's important that people see how some are reacting to her hunger strike. Should I pretend it's not happening?[78]

> The battles taking place over politics in the mideast don't just happen in squares and roundabouts. They also happen online. Hence my tweets[79]

Interestingly, one person who came out to defend my retweets of people bullying Zainab was Zainab herself.

> RT @angryarabiya: no hard feelings, I understand that u were only trying to show wats being said[80]

Over the course of the next week, Zainab's tweets became fewer and fewer. On day three of the hunger strike, she wrote:

> RT @angryarabiya: to every1 who is supporting me, ur words give me strength. I'm sorry if I dont get a chance to reply to each of your wonderful tweets[81]

Her sister Maryam often published updates on her behalf.

> RT @maryamalkhawaja: @angryarabiya's health is deteriorating, she cannot stay awake for long hours at a time and has difficulty moving #bahrain #feb14[82]

> RT @maryamalkhawaja: @angryarabiya's younger sister who is a nurse is with her. She only drinks water every two hours #bahrain #Feb14[83]

Every couple of days, Zainab managed a tweet or two.

> RT @angryarabiya: Hello to my Twitter family & frnds, wanted to let u know I'm still ok. Not feelin hungry, but dizzy & weak & having alot of pain[84]

> RT @angryarabiya: becuz I'm 2 weak to pray, & no longer able to speak to media, & my family is pressuring me, I will be drinking 1 glass of sugar water a day[85]

> RT @angryarabiya: thank u all for ur support & sorry I've been too weak to come online. I send u all love from Bahrain[86]

> RT @angryarabiya: I cudnt sleep becuz of the pain last night, cant sit, cant sleep, & 2 dizzy to stand. So trying to do 5 minutes of each[87]

After 10 days, Zainab ended the strike.[88] When she finally went back online, she focused on a heartbreaking phone call with her father in prison.

> RT @angryarabiya: My father just called. . . & my heart is bleeding for him. He could barely speak, I asked him how he was, he replied [in Arabic, "It's such an ordeal"][89]

> RT @angryarabiya: My father said his trial will b tomorrow at 8 a.m. in military court. "baba are you ok" & he gave me same reply ["It's such an ordeal"][90]

> RT @angryarabiya: never in my life have I heard my father speak of his pain, he's always strong. To hear those words, to hear his voice like that kills me[91]

Not long after Zainab's hunger strike, her father was sentenced to life in prison for his role in the protests. His sentence received relatively little coverage; the world's attention had turned to other countries in the region engaged in their own uprisings. The government had successfully cracked down on the protests, even razing the monument at the center of Lulu Roundabout to the ground. It would take much larger acts of civil disobedience to renew attention to their cause.

For the next six months, news trickled out of Bahrain in fits and starts. Activists such as Zainab Al-Khawaja continued their protests, even though they had generally become smaller and more isolated events, sometimes just a handful of people participating. Then one day in late November 2011, word began to spread that Zainab had been arrested. I'd heard earlier that she would participate in a mourners' protest in the town of A'ali, in response to recent deaths of two protesters run over by police vehicles.

Initially the details were scant.

> RT @BahrainOnline: #Bahrain now zainab alkhawaja @angryarabiya is protesting now next to police jeep in a,ali after they attack the protesters via @saidyousif[92]

Zainab's sister Maryam then confirmed that she had been arrested.

> RT @MARYAMALKHAWAJA: Urgent: Arrest of @angryarabiya now #bahrain #feb14 #arabspring[93]

Numerous Bahrainis retweeted a photo from @Mo7ammedMirza.[94] The text was in Arabic, and translated roughly as "Another photo of Zainab Al-Khawaja before arrest, standing face-to-face."

The photo clearly identified Zainab and a convoy of security vehicles – at least six of them. She's in the middle of the road, stopping them in their tracks. Her back to the camera, she's dressed in a traditional *abaya*, covering her body in a black gown. Her arms are in the air, making V for victory gestures with each hand. A policeman with an automatic rifle paces toward her right, uncertain. It was an extraordinary image: Zainab was using her own body to prevent police forces from advancing toward escaping protesters.

Soon, people began circulating a video of the incident.[95] The air is hazy with tear gas; horns are honking. The camera pulls back to show that the caravan of police vehicles is longer than the six cars seen in the initial photo. Zainab turns toward the protesters, holding her hands in the same V for Victory gesture. Several protesters surge closer to her, one wearing a Bahraini flag. You can hear some of them chanting *Allahu Akbar* – God is great! – in Arabic. Zainab then turns back to the police.

Her arrest didn't last long; within a few hours she was back online, tweeting about the experience.

> Hi all, first of all I hope there were no serious injuries after the attack today by riot police on the mourners in Aali #Bahrain[96]
>
> I have been thinking for awhile about our protests, and tweeting that we shud be sitting peacefully infront of police, not running #Bahrain[97]
>
> Today I didn't run, and as police ran towards me shooting at the protesters, I remained on my knees holding up a Bahraini flag #Bahrain[98]
>
> I expected to get injured with the amount of shooting, but I didn't and within seconds I was surrounded by riot police #Bahrain[99]
>
> I was already infront of them but I stood up and held up my hands in victory sign. and I started shouting Yasqot Hamad [down with the king] #Bahrain[100]
>
> So they all got out of their jeeps, some came towards me wanting to beat me but again were prevented from hitting me #Bahrain[101]
>
> The riot police wanted to arrest me but because they had orders not to touch me were waiting for the female police to arrive #Bahrain[102]
>
> 1 of police car was trying to go arnd me & i didn't move, he said "u know we can just run u over" I said "It wudnt be the 1st time" #Bahrain[103]
>
> Then a police woman arrived and started dragging me to a civilian car. I sat on the ground & refused to move #Bahrain[104]
>
> I was on the ground, and raised both my hands in sign of victory. The police woman dragged me to the car #Bahrain[105]
>
> then an officer told the police to bring their cars arnd, he said "rioters are probably filming u from 4 directions now" #Bahrain[106]

> The officer said to me "You got what u wanted, get in the car now!" I said "I got what I wanted? . . . Why? Did the regime fall?" #Bahrain[107]
>
> I wish the world cared abt every single innocent Bahraini, I wish the gov feared to be exposed when they attack any protester #Bahrain[108]
>
> They might have changed their mind abt arresting me, to avoid being exposed. But I will expose their crimes every single day #Bahrain[109]
>
> The real brave protesters are the ones who are unknown and unprotected and yet choose to face the riot police #Bahrain[110]

Zainab sent out more than 50 tweets detailing her protest and arrest.[111] Her supporters retweeted them far and wide. A minor incident with a small group of opposition activists resulted in a widely publicized embarrassment for the government, and a boon for Zainab, whose bravery – or recklessness, depending on your point of view – captured the imagination of people across the Internet.

Less than three weeks later, Zainab was arrested again.

Leah McElrath, a woman in New York who had been active in supporting the Bahrain opposition online, reported:

> RT @alphaleah: #BAHRAIN : HEADS UP – numerous sources reporting Zainab AlKhawaja aka @angryarabiya has been arrested.[112]

Within a few minutes, though, Zainab's sister Maryam confirmed her arrest.

> RT @MARYAMALKHAWAJA: Pic of Zainab Alkhawaja @angryarabiya being arrested she is now in budaiya police station http://t.co/gti1XFqt #Bahrain #Feb14 #arabspring[113]

Maryam's tweet linked to a blurry photo. The picture shows a person on the ground, along the perimeter of a traffic circle, flat on her back. Two police officers, at least one a woman, squat down in front of her.

Maryam shared a link to a video claiming to show her sister being dragged away by government mercenaries.[114] The video appears to have been recorded from a building on the far side of the traffic circle. You can barely make out a woman in a headscarf, apparently being arrested.[115]

A few moments later, Boston-based activist Nasser Weddady tweeted out a link to a dramatic photo.

> RT @weddady: All u need to know about #Bahrain's civil rights struggle: powerful image of Zainab Al-Khawaja handcuffed & dragged on ground #FreeZainab pic.twitter.com/TqTAV7kK[116]

The picture, much clearer and closer, shows a female police officer dragging Zainab by the handcuffs, flat on her back and refusing to cooperate.

More photos streamed in from Bahraini photojournalist Mazen Mahdi (@mazenmahdi). Zainab and several other women had been staging a sit-in. When police ordered them to leave, Zainab refused.

In one photo taken by Mazen, Zainab sits with two women, holding tissues over their mouths after apparently being tear-gassed.[117, 118] In another, Zainab is handcuffed, cross-legged in the grass. She raises her cuffed hands in a plaintive motion as the angry policewoman leans down, waving a menacing hand at her.[119, 120] A third photo shows her being dragged away by the policewoman, her legs flailing.[121, 122]

As Mazen shared his photos, I saw tweets from Bahrain government supporters claiming that Zainab had been arrested for smacking a police officer. I reached out to Mazen to find out if he saw anything like this happen.

> @MazenMahdi I've seen some people tweet that @angryarabiya slapped a police officer prior to arrest. Can you confirm this?[123]
>
> RT @MazenMahdi: At no time did @angryarabiya hit anyone .. She took the hits and stood her ground I was there @acarvin[124]
>
> RT @MazenMahdi: The assault charge is like for the screaming @angryarabiya did and refusal to vacate roundabout @acarvin[125]

More footage spread across Twitter. One video clip, apparently shot from that same building across the street, shows police firing multiple tear gas rounds toward the women.[126, 127] Another video captured most of Zainab's arrest. In the three-minute clip, the policewoman leans down to place handcuffs on her, and she raises her hands in compliance. The officer, clearly angry, paces back and forth, then rushes over again, wagging her finger at her.

A second policewoman appears and grabs Zainab by the handcuffs, then by her sweater, knocking her over. The officer starts to drag her by the handcuffs, but Zainab turns over onto her back, trying to slow her down. Both policewomen then drag her across the traffic circle, several feet at a time, slapping her along the way.

When they reach the pavement, they lift her by the arms and feet and toss her to the asphalt in a hammock-like rocking motion, as you would throw a corpse into a mass grave. One of the policewomen then punches Zainab in the face.

Within a matter of hours, the story of her arrest appeared on the homepage of the BBC and other news organizations.[128] Zainab was released from prison several days later.

In February 2012, almost exactly a year after the Bahrain protests began, Zainab's father Abdulhadi went on a hunger strike of his own. In an open letter to the foreign minister of Denmark, he wrote:

> I have no regrets that I had to pay a price for my work to promote human rights. It is a serious business to address issues such as corruption, inequality and discrimination in order to promote the interests of members of the ruling family, and documenting arbitrary detention and torture by the brutal National Security Apparatus. . . .
>
> . . .I [have] been severely beaten, arbitrarily detained, held in solitary confinement and subjected to torture for more than two months, brought before a military court on charges faked by the National Security Apparatus, such as "instigating hatred against the regime!" and "planning to overthrow it!" and eventually sentenced to life imprisonment, a sentence which I have been serving to date.[129]

At first, the hunger strike received little attention. He continued to drink small amounts of liquids, stretching out the length of his hunger strike for more than two months. By late March 2012, Amnesty International declared him a Prisoner of Conscience;[130] news organizations began to take the hunger strike more seriously.

A few days after the Amnesty International announcement, Zainab attempted to visit her father in prison. It was the 57th day of his strike. She and her family had been granted visits in the past, but now that his condition was so poor, government officials refused them any access.

Zainab wasn't deterred. That night, she stood outside the prison walls, alone, demanding to see him. In a video that was released a few hours later, you can hear her screaming, "Father! Father!" in Arabic:

> *Abaaaaaaa!!! Aaaabaaaaaaa!!!*[131]

Her screams echo into the night, hopeless, futile, heartbreaking.

Soon after the video was recorded, Zainab was arrested yet again. The government claimed she had slapped a police officer.[132]

Even as I write this in late 2012, nearly two years after the start of Bahrain uprising, the saga continues to play out. Zainab Al-Khawaja has been in and out of prison for various acts of civil disobedience. Another Bahraini court reaffirmed her father's life sentence, despite the international attention drawn to his case by his spring 2012 hunger strike, which ended when he was force-fed by government authorities. Zainab's husband and brother-in-law received lighter sentences.

In so many ways, the story of Bahrain and the Al-Khawaja family is the perfect illustration of how news dramas play out on Twitter. There is no clear-cut ending to this story. You can't tie a bow on it, publish it and call it a day; *the Twitter stream is the story*. It is an ongoing narrative – a struggle – where the status of protesters ebbs and flows, with each success and setback captured live online.

For now, the Bahrain government has the upper hand. Yet it is not unusual for thousands of protesters to return to the streets of Manama, the capital, demanding more reforms and the release of political prisoners. And every so often, you can see these protesters wearing paper masks – masks of the faces of the imprisoned Al-Khawaja family.

Feedly?
organized by #.

LIBYA

Long Shot

Of all the fledgling revolutions that hatched in February 2011, Libya's seemed least likely to succeed. The country's notoriously despotic leader, Muammar Gaddafi,[1] had maintained his grip on power for 42 years. To get a sense of that timespan, imagine if Richard Nixon were still U.S. president in 2011.

For more than four decades, Gaddafi pillaged the country's vast oil wealth, enriching his family while neglecting Libya's infrastructure. He ruled as a cult of personality, on par with no other country save perhaps North Korea.

Gaddafi was also a survivor, a shape-shifter who adjusted to whatever the times dictated. In the 1980s, he was America's Public Enemy No. 1, branded a terrorist by President Reagan but revered in much of the Arab world as the ultimate underdog. In the 1990s, Gaddafi styled himself as crown prince of Africa, determined to unite the continent with him as its leader. Then in the 2000s, he became the pragmatist, cooperating with Western governments by giving up WMDs in exchange for lucrative oil contracts.

No matter what guise Gaddafi took, millions of Libya's citizens reviled him. Nearly everyone in Libya has a relative or a friend who had been tortured, imprisoned or killed by the regime. They lived in fear of Gaddafi, as well as each other, not knowing who was an informant and who wasn't.

By early February 2011, word began to spread online: Libya's revolution would commence February 17.[2, 3, 4, 5, 6] It was a bold, even reckless, decision to publicize it; Gaddafi's secret police could have easily hunted down the organizers before the protests even got off the ground. But that didn't happen; the mere thought of revolution was just too ludicrous for Gaddafi to take seriously. He was their leader, their father; no one would dare challenge his rule. In fact, there were reports that Gaddafi would try to co-opt the uprising and turn up at a protest to proclaim himself a lifelong revolutionary.[7]

I wanted to prepare for whatever might happen in Libya, but I faced one particular obstacle: I didn't know, nor had I ever met, any Libyans. And the Internet didn't seem like it would be a great place to track down many Libyans. Unlike Bahrain, where nearly four out of five people were online, not even one in five Libyans used the Internet.[8]

Once again, I was able to turn to my fellow tweeps, some of whom introduced me to Libyans on Twitter. Mona Eltahawy recommended following Ghazi Gheblawi (@Gheblawi), a Libyan in exile in London.[9] In the days leading up to February 17, @Gheblawi documented the brief detention of Fathi Tarbel, a prominent Libyan lawyer.[10] Tarbel and other Libyans were so eager to get their revolution under way that they started to protest at least two days before the official launch date.

Ghazi Gheblawi's tweets also led me to a Twitter contact that would be absolutely indispensible for the next nine months. The account was called @ShababLibya, which means "Libyan youth" in Arabic. I didn't know who was behind it – or how many people, for that matter. By February 16th, @ShababLibya was already posting incessantly, claiming that deadly protests had erupted across the eastern coast of the country, including in the cities of Benghazi, Derna and Al-Bayda.

> MT @ShababLibya: there are a handful of deaths in #benghazi & #beida nobody knows exactly due to lack of indy news agencies present #libya[11]

@ShababLibya also started sharing links to videos they claimed were from the scene of the first protests. I asked my followers to review the videos and help verify them.

> Has anyone been able to verify this video claiming to show Libyan protesters getting shot at, one of them hit? http://bit.ly/gIQqiK #libya[12]

> Another video reportedly from #Libya. Arabic speakers: can you translate and/or recognize Libyan accents? http://bit.ly/gkR2X1[13]

I quickly got a reply from a Twitter account that was new to me: @ChangeInLibya.

> RT @ChangeInLibya: Definitely from Libya. Probably benghazi. They shout slogans against gaddafi and guy says "see this martyr blood?"[14]

Another Twitter user going by the name @LibyaSupreme reached out to me with what he claimed was evidence of attacks on protesters.

> RT @LibyaSupreme: @acarvin Have footage of Libya protests and violence. Pls reply. #libya #feb17[15]

I wrote back to him and received a quick response.

> @LibyaSupreme have you posted it anywhere? Interested in seeing it.[16]

> RT @LibyaSupreme: @acarvin Yes from tonight. It was filmed in albayda by contacts[17]

I wasn't precisely sure where Al-Bayda was,[18] apart from in the east of the country. But this was the first video I'd seen that seemed to have direct evidence of it being filmed in Libya.

> Video appearing to show bonfires, defaced billboard of Ghadafi. Date not yet known. http://ow.ly/3XU40 #libya #albadya #feb17[19]

It was the early hours of February 17, and by all accounts, Libyan forces were attacking protesters in multiple cities. But this was much more difficult to cover than protests in other countries. Libya was so cut off from the rest of the world, it was hard to understand what might be true or false. There weren't any Western reporters in the country, and Gaddafi was already beginning to shut off Internet access. We had to rely on the words of the handful of people circulating information they claimed was from Libya.

The @ShababLibya account was probably the most prolific I'd found so far, but I didn't know who they were or whether they were trustworthy. At times they appeared to contradict themselves.

> RT @ShababLibya: Confirmed Reports from #Benghazi, 6 people killed today in the city #Libya[20]

"Confirmed how?" I asked.

> RT @ShababLibya: death toll unconfirmed, 6 dead today in Benghazi, drs not allowed to contact any media, we need help #Libya #feb17[21]

The person running the @ChangeInLibya account was also circulating new footage.

> RT @ChangeInLibya: hooded man risking DEATH to protect brothers in #benghazi, where is media? http://tinyurl.com/6gauyj6[22]

I asked my followers if anyone could translate.[23] @ChangeInLibya wrote back:

> RT @ChangeInLibya: @acarvin Here they come, gaddafi's revolutionary guard and supporters (he repeats it 3 or 4 times). They're shooting people[24]

But @ShababLibya continued to be the greatest challenge, making one claim after another. I didn't know the user's sources or methods; he or she was too busy tweeting to notice my pleas. Yet those tweets seemed the most detailed of any account I was following at that point in time, a potentially important source.

> Confirmed how? Pls more details RT @ChangeInLibya: killing people while praying and death toll just today is 19 CONFIRMED. god help us#libya[25]

Despite my initial concerns, @ShababLibya seemed to have the most consistent sources of video footage. By all accounts, the violence was getting worse.

> Harrowing, graphic video apparently showing protester shot dead in Benghazi. Can anyone verify/translate? http://youtu.be/ptcgEPszQW8 #libya[26]

> Protesters heard chanting "Libya Libya!" At least one shot, possibly dead. Cameraman notices blood on his hands. http://youtu.be/ptcgEPszQW8[27]

Other contacts began to reply to my requests for translation help. Natasha Tynes, a Jordanian journalist I know in D.C., sent me a quick summary.

> RT @NatashaTynes: It is saying "A man was killed by the police." http://youtu.be/ptcgEPszQW8[28]

My Twitter timeline was now filling up with new videos faster than I could watch them. I did my best to skim, and requested help from my followers.

> Could someone who speaks Arabic pls listen to the video and translate a summary of the conversations? http://on.fb.me/es7iQ1 #libya[29]

Another woman, Nadia Al Sheikh, tweeted back a series of translations.

> RT @nadiaalsheikh: @acarvin it's a demonstration that took place yhis eve at bengazi next to al majouri & calling for the youth of Libya to help them[30]

> RT @nadiaalsheikh: @acarvin youth of tarablus [Tripoli] help us in [the neighborhood of] Fashloum as we are few & surrounded by police[31]

Every time I saw a new video, I checked to see where it was posted. If from Facebook, I'd subscribe to the user or group that uploaded it; if from YouTube, I'd subscribe to the channel. That way, I wouldn't have to rely solely on videos suggested via Twitter. Instead, I could return to Facebook and YouTube periodically in search for new footage, such as this extended clip of marching protesters:

> Another video reportedly from Libya. 9 mins long. Protest chants (please translate!) tires set on fire. http://bit.ly/enjm5q #feb17[32]

This time, I got translations from two different people, and they corroborated each other.

> RT @nadiaalsheikh: The main two chants are Praising God" La Ilaha Illa Allah and" the people want the regime to change"[33]

> RT @ArabVoicesSpeak: chants god is great,people want to bring down the regime[34]

I was getting overwhelmed. I kept retweeting whatever information I could find, but had to keep reminding my readers that the situation was volatile.

> This info come out of Libya is very fluid and unverified. Please consider this when reading/seeing related tweets.[35]

There was still very little Libya coverage coming out of the Western media. One of the first to report on it, not surprisingly, was Al Jazeera English. As the news anchor described the situation, I noted that I recognized the footage.

> AlJaz showing clips of the videos I shared before, believed to be from Benghazi, Libya. Ppl reportedly shot, police station torched. #feb17[36]

Soon afterward, I discovered a dramatic photo of a Libyan woman dressed in a black hijab.[37] Her head tilted downward, she held a green protest sign with these words:

WE WILL NOT SURRENDER
WE WILL WIN OR WE WILL DIE
THIS IS NOT THE END!
YOU WILL FIGHT US + YOU
WILL FIGHT THE GENERATIONS
THAT FOLLOW US UNTIL
LIBYA IS FREE!

I had to share it with my followers.

> Woman with Libyan protest sign. Powerful pic. http://bit.ly/fCOQJL #libya #feb17[38]

I then received a reply from one of my followers.

> RT @Zero: Not just a sign – Libya's flag is all green. It's essentially a flag she wrote on.[39]

It hadn't even occurred to me. She wasn't holding a protest sign. She had defaced the flag adopted by Muammar Gaddafi after he became dictator. It was a potentially life-threatening act of defiance.

I couldn't help but think of the risks these Libyans were taking, both offline and online. While there had been violent crackdowns in Tunisia, Egypt and Bahrain, Libya seemed to on the edge of a precipice. If Gaddafi did go down, he'd go down fighting; it was entirely possible that he would try to take his entire country with him.

One night that week, just before going offline after a long day of tweeting, I sent out a tweet directed to all the citizen journalists, protesters and civilians caught in the middle of the fighting:

"Stay safe, everyone."

Over the course of 2011, I would end countless nights tweeting that same mantra.

By the third week of February, Twitter was awash with new footage claiming to be from Libya, mostly from Benghazi and the restive east of the country. Tripoli was a tougher nut to crack. Gaddafi still controlled the communications infrastructure in the western part of Libya, including Tripoli, and could shut it down whenever he wanted, or use it to trace anyone posting footage documenting the government crackdown.

Among the few brave enough to tweet from Tripoli were a trio of people who appeared to know each other: @alitweel, @abukhit and @flyingbirdies. Only one – @alitweel – appeared to be using his real name, Ali Tweel. Their Twitter avatars didn't give many hints, either. While @abukhit's avatar appeared to be a Mr. Spock-like closeup of his right eye,[40] the other two used symbols as their pictures. For @alitweel, it was a mesmerizing animated image of a circle rotating within another circle;[41] for @flyingbirdies, a handicraft stitching of a blue Twitter bird flying over three flowers.[42] Even with this limited information, there was something about the tone of their tweets, not to mention the level of detail they offered, that rang authentic.

Initially, they spent much of their time on Twitter relaying their own experiences, as well as occasional second-hand information from friends and family. Their tweets picked up steam as violence escalated against protesters in Tripoli, where Gaddafi was determined to crush the resistance.

> RT @flyingbirdies: Gunshot can be heard now. #Tripoli #Libya[43]

> RT @AliTweel: in my area we had 6 young unarmed non-protestors killed because of random gunfire! can you imagine the chaos? #libya[44]

These and other tweets matched initial reports coming from other sources. One of them, @feb17voices, was a U.S.-based citizen journalism project that contacted friends and family in Libya and recorded interviews with them. A producer for the NPR show *On The Media* was a member of the team, so I had a fair amount of confidence in their reporting.

> RT @feb17voices: EYEWITNESS: Army helicopters flying into #Tripoli and mercenaries are everywhere. People in a state of extreme fear. #Libya #Feb17[45]

Similar reports soon appeared on Al Jazeera English. I retweeted their claims but cautioned that nothing was confirmed yet.

> AJE: Reports of huge march in Tripoli, live ammo and aircraft weaponry used against them, NOT CONFIRMED, but horrifying if true. #libya[46]

Ali Tweel continued to tweet his own eyewitness reports, but cautioned other Twitter users to be more judicious when it came to retweeting unconfirmed information.

> RT @AliTweel: Gunfire on the west side.[47]
>
> RT @AliTweel: There is no tanks in ben ashur please double check your sources[48]
>
> RT @AliTweel: Guys stop spreading news as you recieve it!! There is no aircraft bombing in tripoli we can not seet it we only hear antiaircraft guns[49]

The next day, the three of them picked up where they left off amid the chaos around Tripoli, including the eastern suburbs of Tajoura and Souq Al Juma. By all accounts, Gaddafi was regaining control of the capital using overwhelming force, firing high-caliber weapons at civilians.

> RT @AliTweel: Woman in tajoura killed by the 14.5" bullets, she was observing from her house window, her head exploded. No photos just imagine.[50]
>
> RT @AliTweel: . . .i dont think i'm better than my brothers who died by machineguns, so i will take my chances and fight here until reporters take over.[51]
>
> RT @AliTweel: Dear followers i don't deny that i'm afraid that one of the regime agents might look for me, and this could lead to dark places, but.[52]
>
> @AliTweel: That's it!! Im going out! Will come back with photos hopfully.[53]

Four hours later, Ali returned from his reconnaissance outing. From everything he and his friends were tweeting, it seemed that pro-Gaddafi forces had the upper hand.

> RT @AliTweel: the gunfire now sounds like rain.[54]
>
> RT @flyingbirdies: Gunfire more & more #Tripoli #Libya[55]

> RT @AliTweel: I can not see any voice but the voices of the [pro] regime protesters, they are huge marching in the street, protected by the police.[56]

> RT @AliTweel: that's why I think tripoli lost the battle to the regime. I don't know what about tomorrow.[57]

> RT @AliTweel: In #Tripoli I have 2 friends lost in action since 3 days, please pray for them. Feb17[58]

The protests weren't even a week old, yet some estimates suggested that as many as 400 people had been killed.[59] Gaddafi was using all the military tools at his disposal to suppress the uprising. Gruesome footage showed the remains of people who appeared to have been killed by heavy weapons intended for targeting tanks and airplanes, not human beings. One series of graphic photos documented the remains of two men. They were literally blown to pieces.[60]

Amidst this horrifying footage, I found a video showing a toddler being readied for surgery. On a bloodstained gurney, the injured boy lay quietly while two men prepped him prior to going into the operation room. He was already sedated, and didn't seem too badly injured. His left arm twitched a bit while they cleaned his wounds. One of the men gently patted the boy's tummy with a gloved hand, as if to let the unconscious child know that everything was going to be okay.[61]

Relieved to see footage of someone who had made it to the hospital in one piece, I tweeted it.

> Video of a wounded child being treated. Not graphic, but upsetting nonetheless. http://bit.ly/gPmbex #libya[62]

Twenty minutes later, I received a reply.

> RT @freelibyatoday: i think you will find the child was dead – they were funeral washing[63]

I felt like I had been kicked in the stomach; I thought I might vomit.

Frantic, I went back and watched the video again. They were washing the toddler from head to toe – as Muslims do prior to burial. I replayed the part where his arm twitched. One of the men had actually moved it while washing him. The boy wasn't unconscious; he was lifeless. And in the background you can hear at least one man sobbing.

How could I have been so stupid?

I quickly apologized to everyone on Twitter.

> Dear God, I'm sorry i thought he was moving. RIP[64]

> I was so wrong- the child is dead and they are washing him. So sorry for suggesting otherwise http://bit.ly/gPmbex #libya[65]

I was deeply ashamed of my mistake. In my haste to post the video I hadn't noticed what should have been obvious if I had considered the cultural context. If I had bothered to spend just one moment having the title of the video translated, I would have known he was dead. But I didn't. In my rush to tweet, I couldn't tell the difference between life and death.

And I truly thought I saw him twitch.

As Gaddafi forces continued to reassert their control over Tripoli, @Abukhit tweeted a series of troubling messages from his home in the suburb of Souq Al Juma. Fighting had apparently erupted right outside his window.

> RT @Abukhit: oh . . . god gun shots[66]

> RT @Abukhit: bomb guys i heard bomb alot of gun shot please[67] help

> RT @Abukhit: a gun shot on my house[68]

> RT @Abukhit: i need to upload i need to upload i can't upload even a picture . . .[69]

> RT @Abukhit: http://twitpic.com/43lf80[70]

He had managed to upload a photo, which showed a yellow wall with an arched window at the bottom. Just to the upper right of the window, there was an irregularly shaped area of chipped paint, at the center of which was a small bullet hole.

> RT @Abukhit: one of the people had AK47 and shoot back the merciners [mercenaries] i think one of them is down . . .(in front of my eyes)[71]

> RT @Abukhit: guys i'm keeping my self in safe area . . .[72]

> RT @Abukhit: and if i died i don't care i did my prayer[73]

I did my prayer. He really thought he was going to die. His next tweet, though, was even more chilling.

> RT @Abukhit: guys i'm risking my family if some one saw my video . . . what do u think[74]

While bullets were flying in and around his home, @Abukhit was asking us to debate the merits of uploading the video he had just recorded. My first thought was, of course, please upload it. We need to see exactly what's going on. But this was footage from inside his home. If any Gaddafi supporter or agent recognized that particular neighborhood in Souq Al Juma, they could easily triangulate it to @Abukhit's residence.

I imagined myself in the same situation. If the U.S. government were hunting protesters outside my home, would I upload footage of it? The journalist in me wouldn't hesitate. The father in me, however, would shudder in fear at the consequences.

I honestly didn't know what to tell him. Before I could reply, though, he made his decision.

> RT @Abukhit: i'll send the video and allah be with me[75]
>
> RT @Abukhit: Allah help me . . . http://twitpic.com/43lxpd[76]

I clicked the link and found his video. Only 13 seconds long, it begins with the camera inside his home, approaching a window. As the camera's aperture adjusts to the outside light, I see a residential Tripoli neighborhood. He's filming from at least two or three stories above the ground floor; you can see the rooftops of smaller homes next door, as well as taller whitewashed buildings across the street. Several palm trees dot the neighborhood, their fronds gracefully swaying in the breeze.

On the street below are two men, one standing by a car and the other walking down the road. One appears to have a rifle.

And then gunfire erupts. *Bam, bam bam bam, bam bam!*

The camera suddenly pulls back, reflexively ducking away from the bullets. Everything goes black due to the underexposure of the home's interior, but for a brief moment the aperture adjusts again, revealing several coffee mugs hanging on hooks along the wall. The camera then pushes back to the window, showing the same two men in the distance.

Bam bam!

The video ends. By all signs, @Abukhit was telling the truth: a firefight was taking place right outside his family's home.

While @Abukhit kept his head low, Ali Tweel and @flyingbirdies chimed in, lamenting the fact that they couldn't upload footage from their phones.

> RT: @AliTweel: I can't describe how I feel now, I want gprs in my damn phone so i can go out![77]
>
> RT @flyingbirdies: me too. I want to use geotag on my iphone too[78]

Geotag?!? The thought made me queasy. Geotagging allows a smartphone user to mark tweets, photos or other media with their exact latitude and longitude, right down to their precise location. While using geotagging would certainly assist people like me when it comes to verifying whether someone was actually in Tripoli,

I couldn't help but imagine what would happen to @Abukhit if he geotagged his tweets.

> RT @Abukhit: i see guns with people . . . . shots r everywhere . . .[79]
>
> RT @Abukhit: my cam is full i need to empty it[80]
>
> RT @Abukhit: ohgos[81]
>
> RT @Abukhit: boomb[82]
>
> RT @Abukhit: i have to go off now to think about my life . . .[83]

His twitter stream went quiet. There was little to do except pray for his safety and tell the world what was happening to him.

While @Abukhit and his family took shelter in their home, @flyingbirdies reported that Libyan state TV was broadcasting a speech by Muammar Gaddafi at Tripoli's Green Square.

> RT @flyingbirdies: Gadaffi appears in Green square now. from alsaraya Elhamra . Libyan State TV #Libya[84]

My Twitter contacts around the region began to translate, including Abdullah AlAthba in Qatar and Ramy Yaacoub in Cairo.

> RT @Abdulla_AlAthba: #Gaddafi: ppl, be ready to dance, and be happy, We are stronger than bad tv chans, Look to us USA, EU and Arab, look to people around me![85]

> RT @RamyYaacoub: Gaddafi #Libya: The revolution that made Libya leader of the third world, in fact the entire world[86]
>
> RT @RamyYaacoub: Gaddafi #Libya: "Here is Gaddafi between the masses"[87]
>
> RT @Abdulla_AlAthba: #Gaddafi: Our revolutionary forced Italy to apology and pay to us![88]
>
> RT @Abdulla_AlAthba: #Gaddafi: We will get into war and we will win, will defeat all these foreign agents, like what happened with Italy.[89]
>
> RT @Abdulla_AlAthba: #Gaddafi: Youth, dance and enjoy the honorable life, I'm just one of you, dance and sing and play![90]

His speech was clearly intended to incite his supporters and demoralize the protesters. But was it live? It certainly was in Gaddafi's interest to do it live, as a way to remind Libyans he still had a stranglehold on Tripoli. But if it'd been taped on a previous day, that might suggest his hold on the capital was more tenuous, as there'd be no way to know if he was still in the city.

I asked my Twitter followers for assistance.

> Gaddafi appears to be live. Can anyone confirm?[91]

@Echo2Zs looked up the time of sunset in Tripoli for that day.

> RT @Echo2Zs: @acarvin Looks like it is, sunset is momentarily, sky looks consistent.[92]

A few moments later, the anchor on Al Jazeera English noted that the clock in the square matched the actual time in Tripoli.[93] Some of my Twitter followers, though, were skeptical.

> RT @FoxTare19: @acarvin Could this have been filmed yesterday, or the day before, and then shown now to fool everyone it is live?[94]

It was certainly possible, I told him. But @flyingbirdies, who was actually in Tripoli, was sure that it was live because of the current weather.

> RT @flyingbirdies: Gadaffi speech was Live & no doubt. it was sunset time. also cloudy weather with strong wind now. #Libya #Tripoli[95]

And Syrian Twitter user Shakeeb Al-Jabri noted:

> RT @LeShaque: It's 99% live, the horizon matches the data I have on the position of the sun in Tripoli now[96]

"Astronomy as news confirmation," I replied, marveling at the concept.[97] Twitter users were opening their entire bag of tricks to authenticate what was going on in Tripoli, in ways that likely would've never occurred to me.

While the situation in Tripoli continued to deteriorate, I kept close tabs on fighting in the east of the country, where protesters were gaining control of Benghazi and other cities. @ShababLibya appeared to have the greatest range of sources in that part of the country, and my confidence grew as more of their footage appeared to be authentic.

Then they shared this link:

> RT @ShababLibya: please watch live feed: http://www.livestream.com/libya17feb #feb17 #libya[98]

Again, less than 30 seconds later:

> RT @ShababLibya: http://bit.ly/ikvas5 WATCH THIS LIVESTREAM FROM BENGHAZI #libya[99]

It was a live video feed. How anyone in Benghazi could be doing it was completely beyond me – Gaddafi had throttled most of the Internet access in the eastern part of the country. But there it was, reportedly live from the city's courthouse. I googled for some images of the building, and they seemed to be a match.

On screen, a young man was describing the situation in Benghazi. The footage was poorly shot, and at times difficult to make out. I tried to live-tweet a summary of it, but couldn't get much beyond saying, "Unclear exactly what's going on here."[100] He spoke English with a British-influenced accent, and had short-cropped hair suggesting he was balding prematurely. I guessed he was around 30 years old.

While I struggled to keep up with the video, I was drawn to the livestream's chatroom. People were posting dozens of messages each minute in Arabic, English and a handful of other languages. Some were claiming this town or another had been liberated, or under fire from Gaddafi forces. Others asked for help getting a hold of family members. A surprising number posted Libyan phone numbers in hopes someone would track down their relatives. Some just exclaimed *Allahu Akbar* – God is Great.

While watching the stream, I received a Twitter direct message from a contact in Europe who was monitoring the situation in Benghazi.

> This livestream is so crazy! Have you seen the chat there? It's unfreakingbelievable[101]

Unfreakingbelievable, yes. But who was the young man on the livestream – and how on earth was he getting away with it?

As word of the livestream began to spread, news organizations attempted to track down the Libyan who was hosting it. One of the first to conduct an interview with the mysterious young man from Benghazi was CNN International. It was definitely the guy – same hair, same accent – and he was saying each word loudly and precisely, to ensure that he would be heard.

> We are peaceful people! They are killing unarmed civilians. We are peaceful people. . . Put pressure on Gaddafi. Tell Gaddafi to leave. We want him to leave Libya. . . Ask him to stop killing us. I mean, I don't understand how you people can just watch us getting killed and not putting any pressure on him. That's the minimum we can ask.

> We just want to live free. . .We want our human rights. Our *basic* human rights. We want to be free. . .Long live Libya. *Long live Free Libya!*[102]

The CNN anchor, Ralitsa Vassileva, then asked the young man, "What will happen next?"

"I can't assure you that I'm gonna be alive in five minutes, Ralitsa," he replied.

"What are you most afraid of? What will happen next?" she continued.

"I'm not afraid to die; I'm afraid to lose the battle," he said. "That's why I want the media to see what's going on."[103]

I'm not afraid to die; I'm afraid to lose the battle.

I needed to find out who this guy was.

Despite all of Gaddafi's efforts to put a stranglehold on the country, this Libyan was somehow patching together live video from Benghazi. It was almost like a wartime version of C-SPAN. Many times I'd turn it on and see four multiple camera angles appearing on a split screen, as if it were security camera footage. And whenever it was live, dozens of people shared the latest information with each other in its chatroom. The stream had become an audiovisual nerve center, connecting Benghazi with the rest of the world.

Over the course of that first week, I'd managed to get the Skype names of several people in Libya. I started by tracking down Libyan Americans in Atlanta, Chicago, Kentucky and elsewhere. They suggested names, Skype contacts and phone numbers of English speakers in Benghazi. None of the Libyan Americans seemed to know who the young man from Benghazi was, though they put me in touch with people in Libya who might.

The morning after that CNN interview, almost as soon as I opened my laptop, I received a Skype text from one of these new sources in Benghazi.[104]

"Are you there?" his message read.

"Yep, I'm here," I replied a few moments later.

"Do you know of the livestream that is up? from Benghazi? I have his number. He told me only to give it to journalist."

"Cool, great, I'll take it," I responded.

He sent me the number.

"Please only keep this to yourself," he said.

"Will do," I replied. "Do you know his name?"

"Mohammed Nabbous."

"Thanks for everything – you've been tremendously helpful. It's been a real struggle for us to track down folks that are reachable in Libya this week."

"Hey np [no problem] It is the least I can do. I feel so helpless."

My contact then disconnected from Skype. But now I had a name to go with the face I saw on CNN and that extraordinary livestream: Mohammed Nabbous. I had no idea at the time how much he would impact my life over the next two years.

A Candle Loses Nothing

> Hello? Sound check, sound check, sound check.
> Hello? Check.
> Sound check, everybody?
> OK.
> I would like to say that I think we are being bombed right now.[1]

March 19, 5 a.m. Libya time. Opposition forces had reached a very dangerous crossroads, an existential threat to their entire revolution. After several weeks of combat successes, their militias were getting pushed further and further back toward their stronghold in Benghazi. This wasn't an orderly, tactical retreat; it was one panicked rout after another.

In western Libya, Gaddafi solidified his control of Tripoli. Remaining opposition had been crushed. And in early March, my three closest sources in Tripoli – @alitweel, @Abukhit and @flyingbirdies – all vanished without a trace when the government shut down local Internet access.[2] I didn't know if the three of them were safe or captured, alive or dead.

The U.N. Security Council passed a resolution in support of military intervention if Gaddafi didn't agree to enforce a ceasefire.[3] Libya's foreign minister stated the country would abide by it.[4]

It was just before 8 p.m. in Washington, D.C. I'd been online for 15 hours, monitoring the deteriorating situation among the opposition forces. I needed a break. My mother-in-law was visiting, so I wrested myself offline for a couple of hours to go on a date with my wife.

After a relaxing night out, just before going to bed, I checked Twitter. My timeline was full of Libyans reporting Gaddafi forces were bracing for NATO attacks on Tripoli as fighting advanced toward the outskirts of Benghazi. Libyan expat @IbnOmar2005, in contact with people across the country, tweeted:

> RT @IbnOmar2005: Contacts near m3etiga [Tripoli's air force base] and main airport told me they are waiting for the "3eris" [No Fly Zone bombing] to start. Sounded real scary[5]

> RT @IbnOmar2005: Mo in #benghazi: heavy artillery heard in #benghazi, windows were shaking. #libya[6]

Mo in Benghazi. The livestream created by Mohammed Nabbous had just reached its one-month anniversary. Over the course of those weeks, I became a regular at the livestream's chatroom, hanging out with Mo and his volunteers to keep up with the latest news from Libya. He and I weren't in direct contact with each other very often, but I felt like I had become a member of his livestream community.

I loaded the livestream page. Mo materialized onscreen, stress in his voice.

> I can hear really big bangs around our area. . .I think we're being bombed big-time.[7]

Gaddafi forces were pushing opposition forces out of Ajdabiya, a mere two hours' drive south of Benghazi. Soon they would reach the rebel stronghold.

On the livestream, Mo sat at a desk in his southern Benghazi apartment, his oversized headphones cupping his ears as usual. He looked exhausted; I wondered how long it'd been since he'd had a chance to bathe, eat, sleep, even use the toilet.

> I am trying to call people to check what's going on but Benghazi is being bombed right now and not so many people know because I think most of the people has gone asleep; I don't know what's wrong.[8]

Mo said Benghazi was under attack. Supporters of Libya's revolution feared such an assault; Gaddafi had threatened to destroy the entire city, including its civilian population. Some news organizations pulled staff out of the city, driving east toward Egypt as fast as they could. Mo, in a section of the city that would likely face the first wave of attacks, refused to leave.

The audio of the stream was comprised of Mo's voice, the scratchy sound of people talking to him over the phone, and occasional chatter behind the camera. I couldn't detect explosions, but Mo was clearly agitated by something taking place outside his apartment.

> I mean, this can't be nothing. I am sure of what I have heard. I don't know how many people couldn't have heard that; I don't know. Right now it's calm again but I don't know.[9]

He paused for a moment, lowering his head and rubbing his eyes.

> Give me any numbers; I would just like to call any numbers, just [so] you know what's going on. I don't know how people can't hear this. I mean I hear it very well in my bedroom.[10]

A longer pause, another eye rub. Mo looked terrible.

> My eyes hurt.

> People will actually wake up and see what's happening. They are asleep; they don't know what's happening.[11]

Mo continued contacting people on the phone and through Skype. His devices beeped nonstop. He sometimes had three connections running at once. Members of his chatroom typed as fast as they could, supplying him more phone numbers, while others translated Mo's conversations from Arabic.

Something undoubtedly was going on near Benghazi, but Mo was still struggling to paint a clear picture. He let out a long, audible sigh and vented.

> I wish I had a wireless connection so I could take my – you know – camera and just go around while you can watch at the same time. But that's – *how can he bomb Benghazi, for God's sake?!?*[12]

A female voice with a British accent suddenly appeared out of nowhere; she must've been connected to Mo over Skype. You could hear the exasperation in her voice. "I don't know, Mohammed," she said.[13]

Losing patience after countless hours of streaming, he took out his frustrations on her.

> *What do you mean you don't know?* What about the U.N.? What about these people, what they said? If he's gonna bomb into Benghazi, it's going to be a big disaster. *He's going to kill a lot of people.*[14]

A few moments later, something caught Mo's attention.

> It's shaking the windows in here. Oh my God. This is loud. I wish I had a very super mic for you to hear. I'm gonna call the guys again. Hang on a second.[15]
>
> This was about 10 bombs right now, in turns, you know? While I'm talking to you right now. . .There it is again.
>
> OK, the windows are really shaking right now. And that's again. When I say "that's again," that's bombing.
>
> *Allahu Akbar, Allahu Akbar, Allahu Akbar. . .*[16]

The stress oozed from pores on Mo's forehead. Praying to God's greatness for strength would undoubtedly worry some people watching the stream or participating in the chatroom. I was certainly concerned.

Mo made more phone calls, searching for whatever information he could gather. Then his ears perked up again. Uttering the first half of another prayer, the *shahada* – "There is no God but God" – he pointed out each explosion in the distance, increasing in frequency.

> *La illaha illahallah, Allahu Akbar.* There's – that's another one. That's another one. That's another one. That's another one. That's another one.
>
> I'm not kidding. I'm not – *that's another one.* I'm not making this up people – so many bombing is happening right now.[17]

People in the chatroom urged him and his wife to move to a safer location. Mo responded in English, increasingly frustrated.

> Where am I gonna move? Where? He's bombing *everywhere.* It doesn't matter if I'm staying here – that's another one – or if I'm going anywhere else. That's another one. And it's getting closer, guys, it's getting really closer to here to the house.
>
> OK, the windows are shaking big time – big time. Another four right now, together. That's another two.[18]

Mo couldn't stand not knowing what was going on so close to his city, his family, his home.

> I don't think I should be sitting here any more. I'm just gonna try to go and find what's going on, OK? You can't see anything from my windows, guys. I'm from a village area. It's useless.

The British women connected via Skype piped in again. Her tone had changed; she was now pleading with him.

"Mo, get out."

Mo was furious.

> *Get out?!? Go where?!?* Don't tell me to go out. . .*I have nowhere to go,* this is *my* city. *It's not going to matter anymore!* It's not gonna matter.[19]

I didn't like what he was implying. I recalled his words from one month earlier, during one of his first TV interviews: *I'm not afraid to die; I'm afraid to lose the battle.* I had the sense he thought both fears were about to come to fruition. He seemed almost paralyzed, hopeless, even helpless. Yet within a few moments, his body language changed to something quite different: resolve.

> OK, it's really getting closer. I'll get dressed.[20]

Mo took off his headphones and walked away from his laptop. The stream continued to broadcast, though, and I heard him arguing off-camera, presumably with his wife Perditta, who was six months pregnant with their first child.

> I'm going to get to the end of this! That's where I'm going. I need to see for myself. . .I don't know what's happening. . .I'll try to do something. I don't know what I'm gonna do exactly, but, but I'll try.[21]

Mo reappeared in front of his laptop.

> Okay. . .everyone, I'm back. I will connect my wife's mobile – I will connect it here. And I'll be reporting to you from the field, okay?[22]
>
> Hello? Hello, everybody, hello? Hello? Hello? Hello? Can you hear me now? Check, check, check, check. Sound check.[23]

His voice during the sound check sounded tinny, distant. He was talking over his mobile phone, which was on the line with Perditta's phone. Somehow he managed to jerry-rig it to the livestream.

Mo was going to venture outside into the darkness and report live over his phone.

Numerous people in the chatroom confirmed his audio was coming through, but they weren't happy with Mo leaving the relatively safe confines of his apartment.

> pilotdebby: Mo you have to be careful
> Moam84: be carefull mo plzzzz
> pilotdebby: Do ot go out there
> Moam84: we are with you mo
> 000DM: mo place your cam outside your window and get back in
> hayleytaipari: STAY WHERE You will survive
> pilotdebby: Do not go out on the street
> oakice: Go to a basement someplace without windows. Somebody tell him.
> hababbi: LET HIS WIFE STOP HIM
> Marwouantounsi: Stop giving him advise he know what he is doing
> fatcowxlive: guys calm down
> fatcowxlive: He is not going or about to dye[24]

In his car, Mo couldn't access the chatroom to read their pleas. He was in broadcast mode only: all he could do was drive and report.

Mo's phone didn't have video streaming capability, so there wasn't much to see on his livestream except the backdrop of where he had been sitting a few minutes earlier. Then for a brief moment, a pretty young woman in a headscarf with striking blue eyes appeared on screen, fiddling with some equipment.

Was that his wife Perditta?

Mo's voice resurfaced.

> Okay, okay. Now I'm in the car right now. I will try to get to the Hawari area [a neighborhood along the southern outskirts of Benghazi] from here. It's not that far. It's just five or 10 minutes away.[25]

I alerted my followers that Mo was hitting the road.

> Mo is streaming from his phone driving around Benghazi reporting on explosions nearby: http://www.livestream.com/libya17feb[26]

His phone connection was awful. I could barely make out what he was saying. I didn't know if he was wearing a headset or had simply dumped the phone in his lap while he was driving. However he was managing it, he kept on talking.

> Oh shit – this road is blocked. I'm gonna have to go back. One second... The road is blocked.[27]

According to Mo, the streets of Hawari were practically deserted, except for random groups of militiamen setting up checkpoints.

> I should try to be taking videos right now. Okay. I'm gonna keep you here and [shoot] video, okay? Let me just get the camera. How to do it?[28]

How to do *what* exactly? Apparently Mo was determined to record video on his camera. I envisioned him speeding down the back roads of suburban Benghazi, one hand on the wheel and the other balancing a camera, his mobile phone bouncing in his lap. I couldn't help but admire his stubbornness.

Despite the explosions Mo had heard from his apartment, nothing seemed to be happening anywhere, except for those ever-expanding opposition militia roadblocks. Even with so little to report, Mo felt the need to talk, like a broadcast anchor trying to avoid dead airtime during a lull in a breaking story.

> Sam, if anything happens I won't hang up, because the phone, it's between my legs. I'm holding the camera in my hand. Hold on. . .I'll hold the phone as well but I won't be able to hear what's going on on the phone. . .[29]

On and on he went. And who was Sam? One of his volunteers? There were so many people in the chatroom it was difficult to track them all, but I didn't see anyone named Sam.

Meanwhile, chatroom members began to worry about his wife's safety. Using Mo's chat handle FulanWeladFulan, she kept up a brave face, but her concern was palpable.

FulanWeladFulan: AH this is frstrating he cant hear me :-(
Moam84: sis stay strong we are with you ((hugs))
FulanWeladFulan: we need the world what Gerdaffi[30] is doing here, but obviously the bombing is not close to MO, its still LOUD here, but right now its less than before
FulanWeladFulan: world to know*[31]

Mo finally reached the neighborhood where shelling had been reported. The local militiamen recognized him at a checkpoint and let him pass.

It was approaching 12:30 a.m. my time, just before dawn in Benghazi. And to think I had almost gone to sleep a couple of hours earlier.

> The funny thing is that I was about to go to bed and checked Twitter one last time. So here we are.[32]

As Mo pieced together new information – still pretty thin on the ground – he kept talking.

> This is where they told me where the bombs came from. That's the side of Suluq, which is toward Ajdabiya, from the north side. . .It came from all the way in the back, and hit there, behind these buildings. And they're not sure what bomb was it.[33]

This was supposedly ground zero for the assault everyone feared on Benghazi, but Mo couldn't find any tangible evidence of it. Militiamen said they didn't know what was going on. Some denied that any attack had happened in the first place, perhaps to prevent panic spreading across the city.

Mo had also mentioned a town called Suluq. I tried searching for it on Google Maps, but couldn't find it. In the chatroom, I asked for help.

andycarvin: where is Suluq in relation to Benghazi?[34]

Everyone in the chatroom talked over each other. The moderators struggled to keep the discussion focused.

bintlibya2011: hes telling him where he heard it
abdulghani: please stop please stop please stop
Libiya7urra: please,I'm Libyan lives in USA,is everything OK in Benghazi
Bensrieti: I just came out from fuwayhat have you heard anything?
FreeBenghazi: WE HAVE TO LEAVE CHAT OPEN UNLESS WE'RE TRANSLATING
Moam84: PPL BEHAVE[35]

Soon enough, they spotted my question.

> tellmemo: Andy, Suluq is far to the south of B.
> plemochoe: acarvin, Suluq south a little east even
> bint_benghazi: Soloq is 50 miles from Benghazi
> Moam84: WE WILL HELP YOU GET ANSWERS
> tellmemo: Andy, 31°40′07″N 20°15′01″E سلوق Suluq[36]

I copied and pasted the latitude and longitude into Google Maps. Bingo.[37] I easily located Suluq, but @bint_benghazi's math was a little off. Looking at the map, I was pretty sure she meant 50 kilometers from Benghazi, rather than 50 miles. Probably no more than an hour's drive. Someone else in the chat chimed in, confirming my suspicions.

> loenkelley: acarvin 34 miles 55 km[38]

The geography came into focus. When Mo talked about an attack from Suluq, he was referring to the *road* from Suluq rather than the town itself. That would explain why explosions were occurring near Benghazi – Gaddafi forces were somewhere between the two cities, much closer than I imagined.

Mo continued his drive around southern Benghazi. Despite little to report, he wouldn't stop talking. If he paused even for a few moments, I'd feel a knot twisting in my gut.

Just keep talking, Mo.

Without concrete evidence of the attack he could hear from his home, Mo began to vent against the United Nations.

> I don't know what the U.N. are doing exactly. Are they waiting for more casualties?. . . *For God's sake. . .* How much should we pay before someone does something? How much – *I want a freaking wireless camera right now!* If something goes wrong I want this to be on tape. People should be seeing if anything goes wrong.
>
> *Allahu Akbar*
>
> *Allahu Akbar*
>
> *Allahu Akbar*
>
> *Allahu Akbar*
>
> *Allahu Akbar*
>
> *Allahu Akbar*[39]

My fears for his safety increased. *Mo, please go home and call it a night.*

He continued:

> Nobody knows what's happening, and that's wrong. We *should* know. We should be informed of what's happening. We can't just be left in the dark like this.
>
> Okay. Right now I'm gonna head home. . .I know that we'll survive this night.[40]

Thank God. Get back home to your wife and unborn child, for Christ's sake.

An engine went silent. Mo opened the car door and went inside, still talking into his phone.

> My family is upset because I went alone.[41]

Ya think? I tried to picture the look my wife might give me if I ever tried pulling a stunt like that.

Mo returned to his laptop. The young woman I assumed was Perditta appeared briefly. Behind them, I noticed a framed photo. A wedding photo? It certainly looked like Mo, dressed to the nines, and it appeared to be her as well. She asked him about the explosions; I tweeted their conversation, and threw in a thought of my own.

> Mo's wife: there was a lot of shooting in our area.
> Mo: "It must be our guys shooting back."
> Question: false alarm?[42]

Mo put on his headphones.

> Hi everybody. I'm sorry I left like this, but I just had to find out what's going on. . .Okay, we can hear the bombing again.[43]

Mo tilted his head down, as he often did while staring at his laptop screen to catch up with the rapid-fire conversations in the chatroom. So many people there had been worried sick about his safety.

> Don't worry, don't worry. Don't worry, everybody Skyping me – they were worried about me.
>
> Listen – I always tell my wife that I'm a devil, so nothing's gonna happen to me, okay?
>
> I'm not meant to die easily, so. . .Don't worry about that.
>
> I'm sure I'm being saved for a bigger. . .[44]

His voice trailed off, then he changed the subject.

> Okay, let me take this video for you right now. . .[45]

It would take time for Mo to connect his video camera into the live feed, and it didn't sound like he'd gotten useful footage. I figured this was my chance to sleep for a few hours. I glanced at the clock; it was just after 1 a.m. One last tweet for the night:

> OK folks, I need to sign off and get some sleep soon. My wife promised to wake me later in case anything major happens. Stay safe, everyone.[46]

Especially you, Mo, I thought to myself. *Stay home – and please don't do anything stupid.*

March 19, 7 a.m. Washington, D.C. time.

I had managed five hours of sleep, yet I still felt completely wired from watching Mo's reporting in the wee hours of the morning. Once I got a cup of coffee brewing, I opened my laptop. Mo's video channel was still on my browser, so I refreshed the page to load the most recent video. It was now late morning in Benghazi, and the clip showed what appeared to be daylight footage of a residential neighborhood that suffered some damage overnight.

I checked in with my tweeps, linking to the livestream.

> Just got up. What's Mo streaming right now? Is that bomb damage in Benghazi? http://bit.ly/ikvas5[47]

As people replied, I watched the video. It was recorded in an upscale Benghazi neighborhood known as Hai al Dollar – *Dollar,* as in, you needed dollars to afford to live there.

The stream showed Mo walking past heavily damaged cars into someone's home.

> I wanna show you inside this guy's house, he wants me to see and show you, how everything is down from the glass, and here as well. And that's some of the – Oh my God, *oh my God.* You should be able to see this. Everything has fallen down, even the aluminum, everything is down, everything is broken in his house.[48]

His voice rose to a higher pitch as he became angry.

> This was aimed *at civilians! The U.N. should act!* I mean, what if this family was sleeping in this room?!?

> . . .A guy was sleeping in this bed just earlier this morning when this happened. As you can see, I mean, the glass and everything was broken from here. Thank God this guy wasn't even injured.[49]

Mo rummaged through the debris. You could hear the clinking of twisted metal and the crunching of what had until this morning had been a family's possessions. Mo held up a large piece of rocket shrapnel.

> These are the shells. I'm speechless; as you can see what happened to this guy here.[50]

He explored the damaged property. Several more cars outside the house were burnt to a crisp, and the home's windows were blown out. He said nothing about casualties.

"These are civilians," Mo said, exasperated. "This is still happening."[51]

Someone off-camera told him to look around the other side of the house. There was damage everywhere.

> The other side is more damaged? Oh my God, as you can see, these little metal rounded things. And if someone had been in here, they would be in pieces. *In pieces.*[52]

Mo turned a corner and headed down a hallway, acknowledging the owner of the house and his neighbors.

> Thank everybody; thank you so much for this.[53]

The stream suddenly froze on the last frame of the video: an ornate china cabinet that curiously survived the rocket attack intact.

A female voice with a vaguely American accent – the woman I assumed was Perditta – then said over the stream, "Check, check. Ok, I'll put Mo on now. Bye."[54]

I went to the stream archive and began working my way through other videos posted earlier that morning. Then I received a confusing message from an American volunteer who was regularly in touch with Mo's team in Benghazi.

"Did you hear anything about Mo being hurt earlier today?" she said. "I heard he got shot at."[55]

I had no idea what she was talking about.

> Oh my God, *Oh my God*, look at those. This is actually blood; we've had casualties in here, you can see. This is blood, you can see right now.[56]

The next video was recorded in the same neighborhood. Mo looked perfectly fine. *Thank God for that.* Unfortunately, this particular area sustained several casualties. Mo maneuvered his camera to show a large hole in a roof, a clear blue sky shining through it. He pivoted the camera toward a bed; I saw two small, bloodied pillows. Children's pillows.

> Gaddafi has attacked here in Benghazi city. And as you can see, look what happened. These were two missiles inside of Benghazi city right now. . .*This is the blood of kids:* one of them is five, the other is four months old. And these were actually attacked today. And as you can see, we can see the sky out of this hole, it happened right here, in the roof of this room.
>
> I mean, *these are civilians!* I don't know. . .I mean, what is this? You can see. . .*Who would do such a thing?*
>
> . . .They're taking us to the roof to show what happened, the damage. Oh my God. . .Look at this, look at this, *look at this* – this is here in Benghazi city. Look, look, look at this. I mean, what can you call this? Isn't this attacking civilians? This is the hole of the bedroom we were in right now. And these are the pillows and the blood inside the. . . *I can't believe this.*

Mo paused, composed himself, and sighed deeply.

> Oh, I don't know what to say any more. I am coming back home.[57]

Mo's video of the damaged house ended, but there was audio afterward. The woman I assumed to be Perditta began to talk into the microphone, off camera.

> Ok, I'm pretty sure everyone heard what was going on, what Mohammed was saying on his trip to the Dollar area. And as he said it's very important that all of you contact everyone you know, let them watch the video that he is going to post once he arrives home. So please everyone – I know you've already Twittered and already put it on Facebook. So try to get as many people as you can to watch this, because this is important. This is proof that Gaddafi is actually attacking Benghazi civilians. He's not attacking any military grounds, he's not attacking the airport – he's attacking civilians. Please, people, try to get as much as you can to watch this. We need the world to see this. It's very important.
>
> Once Mohammed comes back home, he will put the video and. . .It won't take hours for Mo to return; it'll take a maximum, 15 minutes. . . .we need the world to see this. . .

> Ok, I'm gonna hang up right now and wait for Mo to come home. And hopefully he'll be here very, very soon. See you guys, *inshallah khair* [God willing, everything will be okay]. Bye bye.[58]

While I had slept, Mo found what he was looking for – tangible evidence that Gaddafi had violated the ceasefire and attacked a civilian neighborhood. Mo's footage would soon appear on television screens around the world.

I received a Skype message from another contact.

> Have you heard anything about Mo? His stream went dead this morning. Ppl worried he's hurt.[59]

It didn't go dead, I thought to myself. I've been watching it since I woke up. Yes, his videos often cut off abruptly, but I wouldn't exactly call that "going dead."

I looked up at my TV; Al Jazeera was playing the very footage I'd just finished watching.

Nice work, Mo.

As the Al Jazeera host discussed Mo's footage, I received a Twitter direct message from a colleague who was also covering Libya. The words sent a chill up my spine.

> There's a rumor that Mo has been shot in the head by a sniper. I'm in touch with the sister of a guy on the Benghazi media team; unconfirmed[60]

Before I could reply, an email arrived from one of Mo's volunteers.

> We don't know if this is true, so please do not retweet. Hamzamu has tweeted that Mo was shot by a sniper and is in the OR at the Benghazi hospital. We are hoping this is not true. Do not know if Hamzamu is credible source.[61]

"Hamzamu" was a reference to Hamza Mousa, an Egyptian doctor volunteering in Benghazi's main hospital. I'd been following him on Twitter for a while and he had been reliable when it came to medical matters.

I checked @Hamzamu's Twitter stream then wrote back to the volunteer:

> I saw that. It's worrisome because he's been relatively reliable before. What have they been saying in the chatroom?[62]

She replied:

> Discouraging convo about it. Hamzamu just tweeted that he is on His way to the hospital. Said last time he was there he saw Mo's Brother crying outside the OR. My friend has been on skype with Mo's wife for the past 6 hours helping her get through this. Hamzamu will let [us] and others know when he gets to the hospital. We are all hoping it was a mistake of course.[63]

She continued her thoughts in follow-up emails.

> We are all hoping for the best. No one knows for sure. Dont' want to talk about it in chat since Mo's wife is there – perditta in chat. . . .[64]
>
> Am watching and will let you know when something definitive happens – hopefully he will walk in the door.[65]

It was one thing to hear a rumor like this from a single source. This is Libya, after all – rumors are a contact sport there. But now I'd received multiple accounts of something terrible happening to Mo, including from one of his volunteers.

As I waited to hear more, I worked my way through the remaining videos in his archive. One appeared to be the most recent session of Mo sitting in front of his laptop.[66] He looked exasperated.

> I don't know what to say anymore. Let's hope it's not true. Because if he's actually bombing the airport and bombing houses in Benghazi city. . .
>
> I don't even know how to tell people that things are not going well. I don't even know anymore what's going on. If this house was bombed, he is bombing civilians in their houses. When are the U.N. gonna take a stand? When are they gonna do something about this?
>
> So I'm gonna go with them, I'm gonna take the camera, I gonna try to take some evidence and some videos of what's happening exactly. I hope it's not that serious – you know?[67]

The video ended.

I'm gonna go with them. With whom exactly? Militia? Friends helping him with the livestream? Where exactly had he gone, and what happened while he was there?

My colleague who contacted me earlier messaged me again.

> Not for posting yet, but Mo is dead.[68]

No. Mo *couldn't* be dead. I mean, I saw him online a few hours ago. What could've gone so wrong that he'd been killed?

The volunteer who had emailed me earlier emailed me again.

> sadly it is true. announcement just made in [the chatroom] by his wife.[69]

I received another message from one of the chatroom moderators, a Libyan expat living in North America. I pictured the tears raining down her cheeks.

> plz come andy to Mohammed Nabbous room 2 report He has left us He died this morning as a martyr please help us spread the news[70]

I went to the chatroom with a terrible sense of dread. The people there – many had worked with Mo every day for the last month – were in absolute shock.

> WeekiWacheeWoman: He was MURDERED.
> CalyxxNC: How is Perditta?
> Anonymoosh: All we know is he was shot, and died of his unjuries
> freedom0001: we will all carry on his great work
> CalyxxNC: My heart is with her[71]

Dear God. What the hell had happened to him?

I went back to the stream archive to watch the two remaining videos.

The first one begins with static.[72] There isn't any new footage – just a freeze-frame of that china cabinet from the previous video. The audio quality is abysmal, with an enormous amount of noise overloading Mo's mobile phone mic. I hear a voice yell in Arabic, then English. It's Mo, reporting live from somewhere in Benghazi, and he's shouting at the top of his lungs.

> Hello everybody, check check check, if you can hear me. Right now we are attacked in Benghazi from everywhere. A plane has crashed right now, near the area of the university in Garyounis, near the area of Garyounis, and right now I'm behind on, on, on, on a pickup, I'm talking to a guy about what I know. He has a 12 and a half [mm anti-aircraft gun] on the back of his car. We are trying to go here from Benghazi to go do something.[73]

Then the machine-gun fire starts.

> *Imshee, imshee, yalla ya shabab!*[74]

Go, go, let's go, guys! He then switches back to English.

> We have bombs right here in front of us right now, in front of us right now.[75]

For a few moments it becomes almost impossible to understand what is being said. More machine-gun fire, yelling – sheer chaos – and what sounds like "Hey, Abdallah, let's go!" in Arabic.

> Right now, I'm in the back of the truck. . .Right now I'm going to be –[76]

More machine-gun fire, so loud it once again overloads his phone's small microphone.

> *Yalla, yalla! Ya Abdallah!*[77]

Let's go! Let's go, Abdallah!

Mo continues narrating the frightful scene around him.

> Everybody, I can't see everything from here, we are on *top of this bridge. I can't see everything from this side. You can hear the shooting.*[78]

I listened to it, stunned, terrified. I could only imagine how Mo must've felt at that moment. How was he keeping his composure under fire? He had learned the hard way, of course – under fire at Benghazi's courthouse during the initial days of the revolution.

> We are actually inside – they're shooting right now. . .We're in the back of a. . .We're in the back of a. . .[79]

More machine gun fire, shouting, mayhem – and then a sharp electronic *zing* – the kind of sound you sometimes hear when a cellphone call drops unexpectedly.

The audio goes silent.

Nothing. No sound for what seems like an eternity, though in reality covers probably only half a minute. Then suddenly, *beep* – as if the call had been terminated.

The silence resumes for at least two unbearably awful minutes. Then the stream switches to a music video – Khaled M and Low Key's Libyan independence anthem, "Can't Take Our Freedom." Whoever was managing the stream back at Mo's house probably started playing the music to put an end to that agonizing silence.[80]

And that was it. Mo had live-streamed the moment of his death, and God only knows how many friends, family members and supporters were listening live when it happened.

La illaha illahallah. Allahu Akbar.

I returned to the live chat and scrolled back as far as possible, to see what people had been writing. Eventually someone sent me a copy of the chat log from the moments when Mo was streaming that awful video. What I read was just as chilling as what I'd just heard.

At first, the members of the chatroom struggled to translate what Mo was saying.

FreeBenghazi: Mo is sayng keep going
FreeBenghazi: God with you
FreeBenghazi: (inaudible)
FreeBenghazi: (oh, abudlla)
FreeBenghazi: there he is
FreeBenghazi: where is the fire coming from?
FreeBenghazi: sorry wrong
4evrlonghorn: WE ARE THE FIRING FROM
FreeBenghazi: Where is the fire (ie. Why are you not shooting)
Skillethead: PLEASE TWEET TO THE WORLD THAT BENGHAZI IS UNDER ATTACK BY GADDAFI'S FORCES[81]

Then Mo's connection dropped. Mo's wife was the first to notice, responding instinctively with a mic check.

Perditta: check check
Moam84: we lost him
FreeBenghazi: Perdita?[82]

We lost him. When Moam84 wrote those words, it was just a few seconds after the phone call was terminated; she was likely referring to the loss of the connection. Yet fear quickly spread amongst the other participants. Some prayed it was only a technical problem. Others prayed as you would when a friend or family member is martyred.

hamidlibya: allah akbar
jbntly: NO!!!!!!!!!!!!!
Denythenice: no sound !!!!
Persecuted_Mind2011: lets pray for mo
hamidlibya: allah akbar
Habbabi: ALLAH AKBAR
CalyxxNC: Perditta – Mo ok?
hamidlibya: allah akbar
benghazi2011: is Mohammed OK
4evrlonghorn: WE JUST LOST THE SOUND
Glibyan: Alllllllllllllllllah akbaaaaaaaaaar
hamidlibya: allah akbar
free_libyan1: prayers from Canada

hamidlibya: allah akbar
leeby: Allahu akbar, may God grant them victory
Habbabi: ALLAH AKBAR
hamidlibya: allah akbar
Atayy7: god be with all of you
pennyvane: I pray Mo is okay
hamidlibya: allah akbar
Persecuted_Mind2011: may god have mercy upon us and deliver our brother Mo from the hand of our enemies
BobGreeley: IS MO OK?
hababbi: ALLAH AKBAR
fairuz: perditta no sound
malik_libya: ya Allah
hamidlibya: allah akbar allah akbar
FreeBenghazi: everyone tweet[83]

Everyone tweet. That was my job, yet I wasn't there during Mo's final moments; I had been fast asleep. Irrational as it might sound, I felt I wasn't there when he needed me most.

There was one video I hadn't watched yet. I played the clip, which contained only audio and that same freeze-frame of that damned china cabinet. I immediately recognized the voice as the Libyan woman I assumed was Mo's wife, Perditta.

It was one of the most heartbreaking, shattering recordings I've ever heard.[84]

> Hello? Check, check, check. Can everyone hear me?
>
> *[She takes a deep breath and sniffs her tears away.]*
>
> I'm Mo's wife, and – *[tears]* – I want to let all of you know that Mohammed. . . has passed away. . . for this cause.
>
> *Lā ʾilāha ʾillà l-Lāh, Muh□ammadun rasūlu l-Lāh.*
>
> *[The shahada – "There is no God but God, and Muhammed is his prophet."]*
>
> *[Silence, then quiet chatter off-camera, and a long sigh.]*
>
> He died for this cause and – *[deep breath]* – let's hope that Libya will become free.
>
> *[The sound of sobbing.]*
>
> Thank you everyone, please pray for him.
>
> *[She sobs again for a moment.]*
>
> And let's not stop doing what we're doing until this is over. What he started *has got to go on,* no matter what happens.

> I might not be able to come online much because of the funeral and all, but I need everyone to just. . .I need everyone to do as much as they can for this cause. Please keep the channel going. Please keep videos, post videos, and move just. . .every authority you have to do something against this. There is still bombing, still shooting, and more people are gonna die.

After sniffing away more tears, she lets out the most plaintive sigh I've ever heard. I could easily imagine her looking up toward the heavens, begging God for strength.

> Don't let what Mo started go for nothing, people. Make it worth it. He has. . .*[A deep breath, then a pause]* I envy all the *shuhada* [martyrs], so I think God gave him his wish, and *inshallah, ya rab* [God willing, oh God].
>
> I have to go now. Please keep the channel moving, and keep the videos posting, and just – I will try, if I have any news, I will try and come to give you the news we have, even though that Mo. . .
>
> There isn't much to do. But I will try my best to keep this going.
>
> *[Another long, grief-stricken sigh]*
>
> Goodbye everyone.[85]

It was just before noon in Washington, D.C. After several hours of hoping that the initial reports were wrong, there was no doubt now that Mo had died. I went offline for a while to start processing my shock and anger, and spend some quiet time with my family.

Eventually, I sent out a tweet letting my followers know what was going on.

> Hi folks. . .I'm sorry I've been offline a couple of hours but I've been soaking up the news that Mo was killed today. Absolutely devastating[86]

I was just about to write more – I so desperately needed to talk about this – but I then noticed an alert from Reuters, which I immediately re-tweeted.

> Reuters: [President] Sarkozy announces French planes are in the air to protect civilians in Benghazi.[87]

Incredible – the NATO fighter planes that Mo had demanded in his final days were likely taking off when he was killed. He didn't live long enough to find out that he had succeeded in helping save Benghazi.

I paused for a moment to collect my thoughts.

> Mohammad Nabbous was my primary contact in Libya, and the face of Libyan citizen journalism. And now he's dead, killed in a firefight.[88]
>
> "I'm not meant to die easily. Don't worry about that. I'm being saved for a bigger. . ." Mo said today on his stream, then changed the topic.[89]
>
> A few hours ago he went out to record some more audio and was caught in a firefight. Audio stops 6:30 into it. http://bit.ly/h4tphZ[90]
>
> For several hours we heard rumors that he had been shot but we didn't want to say anything until we knew for sure.[91]
>
> And then an hour or so ago, his wife released this audio. http://bit.ly/ed4lx0 Absolutely heartbreaking, but she is so, so brave to do it.[92]
>
> The saddest part is that French planes are over Benghazi now. Mo didn't live long enough to see his cries for help being answered. RIP, Mo.[93]
>
> And now I can't stop thinking, what if those French planes began to arrive 12 hours ago. Would Mo be alive now? I just don't know.[94]
>
> I live-tweeted Mo's stream last night until 1:30 a.m. Then I went to bed. I feel so fucking selfish. I should have stayed up. If I'd known. . . .[95]

If I'd known *what* exactly? That he would soon die? That through some miracle I might've been able to save him? I felt this all-consuming guilt for not being online when he died, as if somehow my presence in front of a keyboard in Washington, D.C. could have kept him alive. I wasn't making sense.

One of the first replies I received lifted my spirits. It was from Xeni Jardin, one of the co-founders of the blog Boing Boing, and a longtime online role model for me. She's one of the best out there – smart, funny, compassionate.

> RT @xeni: Andy, it's awful but don't go there. You're doing important work. You staying up a few hours later would not have saved Mo's life.[96]

I replied:

> I know, I know. It was just a moment of anger. It's just that he was doing what I would've done if I'd been in his shoes.[97]
>
> . . .I can't go down that dark, dark hole. There's nothing I could've done. I just I could've been there to bear witness. RIP Mo.[98]

Xeni wrote back:

> RT @xeni: The nature of your connection to Mo is something we don't have language for yet. But it was important. I am sorry for your loss.[99]

I responded:

> Thank, you, Xeni, I truly appreciate it. It's just more proof that there's no separation btwn online and offline relationships.[100]

It was the hug I needed, even though she was 3,000 miles away in California.

All across Twitter, journalists, activists and everyday people expressed their grief. Few of us had met Mo in person, but we all felt like we had lost someone important: a colleague, a trusted source, a comrade, a friend. One of the few journalists on Twitter who had met him was CNN's Ben Wedeman, who was the first reporter to make it into Libya after the start of the revolution.

> RT @BenCNN: A true hero, Mohammed Nabbous of Sawt Libia al-Hurra, the Voice of Free Libya, was killed in fighting in Benghazi today. #Libya[101]

> RT @BenCNN: Mohammed Nabbous was one of the courageous voices from Benghazi broadcasting to the world from the beginning. Smart, selfless, brave.[102]

@LibyanInMe, a Libyan expat who had been active on Twitter since the earliest days of the revolution, expressed a fear felt by many activists – that Mo was irreplaceable in terms of his impact in getting the world's attention.

> RT @LibyaInMe: @Tripolitanian I am EXTREMELY depressed. This revolution is nothing without him :'(:'(..I wish I can just get over it.[103]

In Dubai, Palestinian businessman and online activist Iyad El-Baghdadi noted how Mo's death would easily overshadow the joy that otherwise would've been expressed now that NATO had finally intervened in the conflict.

> RT @iyad_elbaghdadi: Mo's death is going to paint everything today in a dismal shade. Can't help it guys, sorry.[104]

As tributes to Mo spread over the Internet, more of my Twitter followers began to reach out to me. While condolences via Twitter might seem inappropriately superficial, like learning of someone's death via text message, the intimacy of my Twitter community made everyone's sincerity shine through.

One of them, a Unitarian minister who goes by @UUJames, hit upon this very point.

> @UUJames: it is one of the gifts of this new journalism that you and we feel that we have lost one of our own.[105]

> @UUJames: I am a chaplain not a journalist. Own your grief and live through it. This connection we share is a major value-add of your work.[106]

Sometimes, the messages came from unexpected sources, such as philanthropist and former supermodel Bianca Jagger.

> RT @BiancaJagger: Mo was a hero, please accept my condolences RT @acarvin[107]

Someone named @thepinebox, a complete stranger to me, wrote:

> RT @thepinebox: This is the real twitter revolution. I want to tell @acarvin how sorry I am for the loss of his friend Mo.[108]

"You just did," I replied. "Thank you."[109]

Over the afternoon, tributes to Mo appeared on newscasts and websites around the world.[110] Many of them described Mo as a "citizen journalist," a term that I often use but have never felt totally comfortable with. All too often, people in the news business use that term to separate them from professional journalists. Some even use the phrase to denigrate such work. I felt the need to put that to rest.

> Let's drop the word citizen from citizen journalist. Mohammad Nabbous was a journalist who died in the line of duty. He was Libya's Cronkite[111]

> One thing to take away from Mo's death this morning. His final reporting made it clear to the world that Gaddafi's ceasefire was bullshit.[112]

> Is it safe to say that Mohammed Nabbous was the first independent journalist in Libya? Certainly the first independent broadcaster, right?[113]

A country's first independent journalist. Not some hack peddling pro-government propaganda through state-controlled media. An actual journalist – among the first in his country in well over a generation. Can you imagine it? This was a guy who just five weeks earlier was a young entrepreneur who knew how to install satellite dishes. No matter the ultimate fate of this revolution, his role in it was now a part of history.

I couldn't help but think of Perditta, who had so bravely gone online to announce his death and ask his supporters to continue their work for Libya. Perditta and Mo were expecting their first child later that spring – a baby who would never meet its father.

> Mo's wife is pregnant. I hope many people get to tell that child what a brave, brave man his father was, and he died for his country.[114]

> I was really looking forward to visiting Mo in Libya some day to ask him how he did all he did. Hope I get to meet his family instead.[115]

My mind drifted as I thought about Mo's unborn child. U.S. Secretary of State Hillary Clinton was on TV discussing the beginning of NATO's intervention, but I barely heard anything she said. Then my four-year-old daughter Kayleigh came into the room. She walked over to the TV and promptly turned off the secretary of state.

"Don't watch her," she said. "Let's eat some chocolate."[116]

Kayleigh reached out and handed me something. A Hershey's Kiss never tasted better.

I needed to unplug from the revolution, even for a brief time: play with my kids, talk more with my wife about what had happened that day. The support I'd received online was incredibly touching and generous, but sometimes you need to look someone in the eye while confronting your grief.

As always, Kayleigh lifted my spirits with her antics. At one point, though, she asked me what had happened that day. I wasn't sure how to explain it. My wife and I did our best, saying there was a man in a faraway country who was very bad to his people, so one good person decided to go online every day to tell all of us what was the bad guy was doing. And today, the good guy died.

"Was he a hero?" she asked.

I paused. "Yes, he was."

"Are there any other heroes left?"

"I hope so, Kayleigh. I really do."

It was just past 9:30 p.m. I'd been online for yet another entire day. As cathartic as it would have been to continue discussing Mo's loss online with those who cared about him, I needed to disengage.

> Calling it an early night. Have lots of sleep to catch up on. Stay safe, folks. We don't need to lose another journalist out there. RIP, Mo.[117]

Mohamed Nabbous was among the first journalists to die during the Arab Spring. Unfortunately, he wouldn't be the last.

Tilting at Rumor Mills

With the proliferation of online sources in Libya, it was only a matter of time before we began to see an echo chamber of rumors popping up on a daily basis. Sometimes these stories would be about whether opposition forces had captured or lost a particular town. On other occasions, it'd be a blame game as to who killed civilians depicted in a particular YouTube video.

And then there were the Gaddafi-Is-Dead rumors.

These shouldn't have come across as a surprise, of course. Gaddafi – not to mention his family – had subjugated Libya for more than four decades, and there were probably few people on the side of the opposition who didn't wish at least some of the family dead.

In mid-March 2011, just a few days prior to NATO's first bombing raids, Libyans were buzzing about reports that some kind of explosion had occurred at Gaddafi's main Tripoli compound, known as Bab al Aziziya. It was an enormous complex, a mix of military barracks, parade grounds and Gaddafi's private residence. Depending on whom you followed on Twitter, word had it that there was a mutiny in progress; or perhaps it was a car bombing. Others embraced a bolder narrative: a kamikaze airplane attack.

While some Twitter users passed along the rumors as fact – or perhaps more accurately, wishful thinking – others were wise enough to couch their tweets with caution. Two of my Twitter sources were among the latter crowd. @Tripolitanian, a Libyan who kept his identity close to the vest, was among the first to note the rumors, as was UAE resident Iyad El-Baghdadi, who volunteered his time mapping clashes across the country.

> RT @Tripolitanian: Rumours of gun fights, executions and mutiny in #Gaddafi compound of #BabAzizya – all are still unconfirmed[1]

> RT @iyad_elbaghdadi: Reports of protests in Tripoli, and a fire in Bab al Azizia, #Gaddafi's residence compound. #Libya[2]

I forwarded their tweets, asking if anyone knew more about what was going on. I also reached out directly to other sources. One of them, @feb17libya, appeared to be one of the originators of the kamikaze theory, along with a questionable Libyan expat news site called Al Manara.

> @feb17libya can u give any more details about how you confirmed the kamikaze attack? Only u and Al Manara reporting it so far.[3]

I was more hopeful about getting solid information from my friend Brian Conley, aka @BaghdadBrian, who had previously developed the citizen journalism blog Alive in Baghdad.[4] He was volunteering in Benghazi, training locals to tell their own stories through video.

> @BaghdadBrian what are you guys hearing about a kamikaze attack on Gaddafi's compound? Hearing rumors, no independent confirmation.[5]

Brian soon replied; apparently people in Benghazi were celebrating the rumor, which now spread to local TV.

> RT @BaghdadBrian @acarvin just heard it hear, allahu akbar coming loudly from where people are watching television[6]

In Qatar, *Foreign Policy* managing editor Blake Hounshell was thinking precisely what I was thinking.

> RT @blakehounshell: I will believe this story about a Libyan kamikaze jet crashing into Qaddafi's compound when I see a picture[7]

While we continued to express skepticism, Libyan state TV aired another Gaddafi speech. It supposedly was live but lacked an outdoor backdrop, so there was no way of verifying where or when it was recorded. Arabic speakers translated it in real time. Their tweets overlapped, providing a handy cross-reference to compare translations.

> RT @LeShaque: #Gaddafi's speech being broadcast inside tent with fancy-ass chandeliers. #Libya[8]
>
> RT @Abdulla_AlAthba: #Gaddafi: We will win, regardless it is internal war or foreign invasion, they wont ruin our peace, and love.[9]
>
> RT @LeShaque: #Gaddafi: Whether it is a foreign or local conspiracy we are determined to crush it. #Libya[10]
>
> RT @Egyptocracy: #Gaddafi: Internal, external, or military conspiracy, we will crush it. Crush it. Crush it. (He is hitting the table hard) #Libya #Feb17[11]
>
> RT @Abdulla_AlAthba: #Gaddafi screaming: This isn't first war to win, we will defeat USA![12]
>
> RT @Hisham_G: Gaddafi: "devils, sick ppl, children of imperialists, we R going 2 destroy them" – send sum intelligent missile get that idiot psychopath[13]

Rumors regarding Gaddafi's death continued to spread on Twitter, Facebook and other social networks. Some even stated that two of his sons, Saif al-Islam Gaddafi and Khamis Gaddafi, were among the casualties. I reminded people there was no evidence.

> Lotsa rumors of a kamikaze mission into Gaddafi HQ, injuring and/or killing 2 sons. Seen *no confirmation* from independent sources. Anyone?[14]

My concerns were echoed by Libyans @Tripolitanian and @IbnOmar2005, who saw the rumor-mongering as counterproductive.

> RT @Tripolitanian: Guys, please wait for confirmation.. remember the rumours about #Gaddafi fleeing to Venezuela?[15]

> RT @IbnOmar2005: everyone. . . noone knows if saif or khamis r in the hospital!!! these are UNCONFIRMED! #libya #gaddafi[16]

At least one reporter on the ground in Tripoli, the AP's Hadeel al-Shalchi, had heard the rumor, but saw no evidence to back it up.

> RT @hadeelalsh: Rumors in #tripoli about explosion in bab al aziziya; checked out the town nothing going on. Gadhafi later spoke from the compound #libya[17]

By now it was early morning in Libya and approaching midnight in D.C. It felt like we were going in circles.

> Still hearing Libyans saying Gaddafi's HQ was attacked either by bombs or a kamikaze plane. Seen nothing from western media. Rumor run amok?[18]

One of the Libyan Twitter accounts spreading the story, @libyanewstoday, wouldn't back down.

> RT @libyanewstoday: Khamis Gadaffi is in hospital in the burn unit and in critical condition.[19]

"Still don't believe it," I replied. "Suspicious."[20]

It wasn't only Libyans buying into the rumor. A Twitter user named @DougPologe asked me, "What is suspicious about it?"[21] I responded:

> @DougPologe Only anti-Gaddafi media sources have reported it. Not a single other media source has said _anything_. Doesn't make sense.[22]

For the next few days, the rumor seemed to die down. By March 20, it resurfaced, with a new focus on Gaddafi's son Khamis, who commanded one of the regime's most ruthless military brigades. I first heard it from a Twitter user named @Lawilc01.

> RT @Lawilc01 @acarvin In al hurra chatroom, mod just reported hearing from reliable source that Khamis is clinically brain dead.

In other words, she was pointing out that a moderator in the chatroom created by Mohammed Nabbous was making this claim from one of their own sources. Mo had passed away the previous day, but the chatroom had continued its work, collecting and discussing information gathered from Libya.

I wrote back to @Lawilc01.

> @Lawilc01 Heard that last week and the week before that. If Khamis is hurt or dead, I want to see it. Too popular an ongoing rumor.[23]

> @Lawilc01 It's entirely possible Khamis is hurt. But people have cried wolf regarding him so many times it's hard not to be skeptical.[24]

Egyptian-American writer Mona Eltahawy also attempted to nip the rumor in the bud.

> RT @monaeltahawy: UNCONFIRMED RT @operationlibyia: Khamis Gaddafi is confirmed Dead :)[25]

This was getting terribly frustrating. Libyans and non-Libyans alike continued to propagate the rumor of Khamis' death. It didn't help that many of them used what they perceived as the jargon of journalism, with words like "confirmed" or "breaking news," often in all-caps for emphasis.

Lebanese blogger Imad Bazzi (@TrellaB) reported he had spoken with an Associated Press photographer.

> RT @TrellaLB: got a call from AP photographer in #Libya saying Khamis #Gaddafi has died![26]

Back in the U.S., political blogger Liza Sabater, who was actively tweeting about the Arab Spring, wasn't sure how to interpret this claim:

> RT @blogdiva: so this is semi-confirmed or confirmed-confirmed?[27]

I replied:

> Keep hearing that rumor every other day. Not one word in the wire services, almanara untrustworthy. Very skeptical.[28]

> Feel like I'm the only person on twitter who doesn't believe the khamis-is-dead story. Would rather be right than first.[29]

Like Khamis Gaddafi himself, this was the rumor that wouldn't die. As the days and weeks passed, mainstream news outlets propagated it further. Al Arabiya TV, for example, began making the same claim, as noted by reporter Abeer Allam of the *Financial Times*.

> RT @abeerallamFT: khamis might have been killed in a raid, Alarabiya tv says, citing unnamed sources[30]

Perhaps Khamis Gaddafi had discovered the perfect method to save himself in the long run – spread one rumor after another about his death until it got to the point that no one would ever fully believe it one way or another. I pictured the man sitting on a faraway beach, sipping a daiquiri as news outlets reported his death. Minus the appearance of a body or other tangible evidence, I'd never believe he was dead.

> Maybe I'm just stubborn and cantankerous, but the more people insist to me that Khamis Gaddafi is dead, the more I think he's alive. #libya[31]
>
> I think he's like Keyser Soze. He doesn't need to be seen; just feared.[32]

Despite our inability to fully debunk the Khamis Gaddafi rumor, my Twitter followers and I had more success on a larger story about illicit arms sales. Libya was awash with weapons, many smuggled in from abroad. You'd often hear claims that one particular country or another had engaged in smuggling arms. But how might the Libyan revolution change if that country happened to be Israel?

On March 12, 2011, I received a tweet from someone going by the name @jan15egy. I didn't know much about him – or her – except that he or she tweeted a lot about Egypt. On this particular day, the topic was Libya.

> RT @jan15egy @acarvin pic of mortar in libya http://goo.gl/iaF9C could u get any info on manufacturer?[33]

The link brought me to a photo with a URL suggesting it was stored on a Facebook server. It was just the photo, with no other context. The picture showed a man dressed in camouflage, a black-and-white plaid scarf around his neck. He was with three other men, wearing a mix of civilian and military clothing. The photo appeared to be from Libya, probably a group of opposition fighters, or *thuwwar* ("revolutionaries") as they preferred to call themselves.

The man at the front of the photo was holding a large artillery shell that had seen better days. It didn't appear to have been fired, but was covered in specks of rust, with a large rusty streak on the left side. The stabilizing fin at the bottom didn't look screwed in properly, jutting off at an angle, like a hastily sealed pickle jar.

The information on the front of the shell was the point of contention in the photo:

81 mm M

ILLUM

PARA L 20A

L 2 Y

Between the third and fourth lines of text, there was a pair of symbols. The first one looked liked a crescent facing downward. The second was a six-pointed star.

"Do you know where and when it was found?" I asked @jan15egy.[34] I received a link to the Facebook page of Al Manara, the Libyan expat news service that had been unreliable on several occasions, including the reported death(s) of Khamis Gaddafi.[35] The site had published the photo with the headline, "Israeli industry against the Libyan people." The six-pointed star on the shell, they implied, was evidence that Israel was supplying weapons to support Gaddafi.

It was one hell of an allegation – and it made almost no sense. Gaddafi was an avowed enemy of Israel; why would Israel want to support him? Sure, the Israelis were worried about the instability the Arab Spring was causing in the region, but this seemed ridiculous. I tweeted to my followers:

> For argument's sake, let's say Israel sold mortars to Libya. Would they be so dumb as to put a star of david on them? http://on.fb.me/dTpmVs[36]

Yes, there was a six-pointed star on the shell. But to take that symbol and jump to the conclusion it was Israeli-manufactured and supplied by Israel to Gaddafi – it didn't make sense. But sometimes the most viral of rumors are the most preposterous.

I began poking around for more information, asking if anyone on Twitter could help identify the shell.

> They ID it as Israeli. Maybe, maybe not. Need help to ID it. Anyone? RT @jan15egy: it's posted on Al Manara Press FB http://goo.gl/LMfeU[37]

One of the first to reply was a Twitter user named @HarisAlisic.

> RT @HarisAlisic @acarvin 81mm calibre – it's not eastern. Probably British[38]

I replied:

> @HarisAlisic Do wonder what the Star of David and crescent signify? Seems like an odd combo.[39]

> RT @HarisAlisic: Actually it's not a crescent if u look again. More like a wave or umbrella http://bit.ly/gNw7Dp[40]

I clicked the link and it brought me to a Google image search for "81mm illumination." The page was filled with photos and drawings of mortar shells, many sporting variants of the symbols in the Libya photograph. The word "illumination" suggested it was an illumination round, a shell filled with flare material that burns so hot it lights up the sky at night, allowing troops to see what's happening on the ground. Others agreed.

> RT @sonomadiver @acarvin Looks like an 81 mm illuminating mortar. The "crescent" is a parachute icon and the star could be "flare" icon.[41]

> RT @jasonhansman @acarvin it's a parachute. . . illum uses parachute to keep airborne longer. . . Likely not a company logo but a graphic to describe what it is[42]

> RT @shorepatrol @acarvin If re:illumination shell, I'm guessing star is symbol for flare. Still odd. But shell could come from anywhere.[43]

We'd reached an initial consensus: we were dealing with an illumination round rather than an explosive shell, with serious doubts about the meaning of the six-pointed star. Given the nature of online conspiracies, especially regarding Libya, it was important to keep investigating the shell and identify the country of origin if possible. Even if Al Manara's reporting was incorrect, as appeared to be the case, animosity toward Israel could cause the story to spread and distract us from covering what was actually happening on the ground in Libya.

I put out another request to my followers.

> Anyone want to hunt throught Google pics of 81mm illumination rounds – http://bit.ly/gNw7Dp -to match this logo? http://goo.gl/LMfeU[44]

One of the most intriguing discoveries came from @brhone in Vancouver:

> RT @brhone @acarvin an illumination round contains flare suspended from parachute, which is what that graphic looks like http://bit.ly/dZ6q0w[45]

@brhone had found a schematic of a star shell, another name for an illumination round. The hand-drawn rendering described it as a "Mark II" star shell designed for a British 10-pounder mountain gun. The beige canister was marked with a red six-pointed star inside a white circle.[46]

Below the schematic, I found a citation:

> Plate XXXI, Page 194, 197 in "Treatise on Ammunition" 10th Edition, 1915.

1915? The schematic dated from World War I, more than 30 years before the creation of Israel. The six-pointed star had apparently been used on shells for a very long time.

As I marveled at the nearly 100-year-old drawing found by @brhone, Shakeeb Al-Jabri, a Syrian living in Beirut who had helped translate numerous Gaddafi speeches, uncovered leads from weapons manufacturers in India.

> RT @LeShaque @acarvin This one looks similar http://qvie.ws/hg0mwo[47]

He linked to mortar shell on a website called weaponsindia.com. It was a long, off-white 81mm shell with a black tip and fins, decorated with a pair of red stripes around the cylinder. It had a line drawing of a parachute and a six-pointed star: not an exact match to the shell found in Libya, but very similar.[48] The text on the page said that it "belongs to the family of illuminating ammunition extensively used to support night warfare. . . It provides intense illumination for identification and engagement of all types of moving and stationary objects."[49]

Shakeeb found two other similar shells.

> RT @LeShaque: @acarvin This one too: http://qvie.ws/fZYywo Again, India, not Israel. . .[50]

> RT @LeShaque @acarvin Here's a third http://qvie.ws/eyTx9w (middle of page, high quality image)[51]

The first appeared identical to the shell manufactured in India. The second, also Indian-made, was photographed at an arms fair. It was 115mm rather than 81mm, but it featured the same pairing of parachute-and-star symbols.[52 53]

By this point, the issue seemed settled. We had found the same symbols on Indian and British illumination rounds. Though we couldn't prove that "our" shell wasn't manufactured in Israel, we were positive that the so-called "Star of David" couldn't be used as evidence that it was Israeli.

I thought that was the end of the story, until I heard from Shakeeb Al-Jabri two weeks later.

> RT @LeShaque @acarvin Remember the logo we looked up? The one that turned out to be Indian? Rebels on AJA now claiming it to be Israeli[54]

He sent me a link to an Al Jazeera Arabic video on YouTube.[55] The video included an interview with a Libyan opposition fighter who not only claimed the shell was Israeli in origin, but that it was an illegal cluster bomb.

> These weapons are being used against unarmed civilians who don't have any weapons. They are using cluster bombs which are prohibited.

> And they are also using Israeli-made weapons: 84mm, and as you see, there's this six-pointed star. The corrupt regime has asked for help from Israel against the people to destroy us. He's using prohibited weapons to massacre us.

The rumor, initially reported by a relatively obscure Libyan news service, was now being perpetuated by the most influential Arabic-language news channel. It was only a matter of time before others news organizations would likely pass it along as fact, just like the Khamis Gaddafi rumors. So once again I brought it up on Twitter, to see if anyone wanted to dig up additional evidence to debunk the story.

> How many times to we have to debunk this? They're illumination rounds: parachute + 6-pointed star. Doesn't mean Israeli. http://j.mp/ib34BV[56]

Unfortunately, the first time we attempted to debunk the rumor, we didn't document our findings beyond Twitter. This time I assembled sources on Storify to archive the evidence as we collected it.[57]

> OK, folks: to those of you who helped me with the "israeli" mortars in Libya story, do you still have the links you dug up?[58]

Along with the information we'd found previously, people continued to dig up new sources.

> RT @ingefl @acarvin looks like the French illumination round on p. 57 http://64.78.11.86/uxofiles/enclosures/Iraq_NAVEOD_Guide_Projectile.pdf[59, 60]

The page in question showed several photos of an illumination round with this description:

> FRENCH CARTRIDGE, 81-MM, ILLUMINATION, MORTAR, MK68
> Ordnance used with:
> FH-81B, PROJECTILE, MT
> M68, 81MM, ILLUM
> MK 68, 81MM, ILLUM
> FH-55, PROJECTILE, MT[61]

Another Twitter user, @MadcapMagician, found a similar British schematic to the one from World War I, though dated to the Second World War.[62] The text described it as a "British 4 inch 35 lb star shell, circa 1943." It also had a six-pointed star.

To top it off, a man named Amin El Shelhi sent me this tweet:

> RT @AminES @acarvin Hope this helps, go to page I-1-7b http://www.scribd.com/doc/34065603/NATO-AOP-2-C-The-Identification-of-Ammunition-2008[63]

It was an official NATO manual regarding the proper labeling of munitions, titled *(NATO) AOP-2(C), The Identification of Ammunition – 2008.*[64]

I skimmed through the document until I reached the 28th slide, which featured the title "SYMBOL DENOTING COLORED & NUMBER OF STARS EJECTED." It showed five different examples of what symbols should be used on NATO illumination rounds, depending on the number of stars it ejected and their color. All five featured a six-pointed star as its primary symbol. Below this was the crescent-like parachute on the original photograph from Libya. According to the text, this was the "SYMBOL DENOTING THE PRESENCE OF A PARACHUTE."

We now had nearly a century's worth of examples demonstrating that a six-pointed star *did not mean it was an Israeli weapon.* I tweeted a link to the NATO manual and annotated it with one word: "DEBUNKED."[65]

I was glad we had managed to put the issue to rest. My Arab Twitter followers seemed relieved, too; the Israeli weapons conspiracy theory had become an unwanted distraction.

> RT @NajiAnaizi: I'm Libyan and no fan of Israel but im tired of people draging Israel into this. They're no fan of qadaffi.[66]
>
> RT @_saadlatif_: agreed man, us arabs are just too paranoid of israeal.. 'gadaffi: israel took my lollypop and unicorn.'

Soon enough, though, Iran's Press TV kept running a story titled "Gaddafi forces use Israeli weapons."[67] Admittedly irritated, I CCed them on a tweet about our efforts.

> More proof that @PressTVchannel doesn't read my twitter feed. Debunked, people. http://dlvr.it/M5kwl[68]

Let's face it: Twitter can serve as an easy vector for spreading rumors – especially when those rumors are spread by mainstream media outlets. But Twitter can also be a place where rumors go to die. In this particular case, a rumor perpetuated by several news organizations was easily debunked by a group of people on Twitter who don't know each other and likely will never meet in person. After a few more days of making the rounds on Twitter, the rumor faded altogether.

A similar online collaboration took place on May 6, 2011, when photographer Ali Alramli and other members of a Libyan citizen journalism group called the 17 of February Media Center documented a number of munitions that had fallen on the city of Misurata. The city had been under siege by Gaddafi forces for nearly three months. At least one of these munitions exploded, damaging a white van. Alramli's footage captured how the left side of the van was blown apart, leaving a dozen or so holes on the driver's side windshield.[69]

The device itself wasn't very large, about the size of a man's foot. A piece of green cloth, apparently a tiny parachute, covered a squat plastic cylinder, also green. Below the cylinder protruded a closed tripod comprised of metal shafts, each with a sharpened tip. It looked like something you would hammer into your backyard to scare away pesky gophers.[70]

Each photo included a brief description from the 17 Of February Media Center, claiming that the dispersal of the devices was a violation of the no-fly zone (NFZ) established by NATO over Libya:

> THAT GADDAFI FORCES VIOLATED NFZ YESTERDAY WITH HELICOPTER ATTACK ON PORT OF MISRATA.
>
> Details and evidence are emerging. Our source has interviews with witnesses and video of the damage, which will be furnished ASAP (this is a reliable source we have used repeatedly). Yesterday, helicopters were flying over the port of Misrata, guards became alerted so they investigated what was happening and furthermore they contacted NATO to confirm they were OK. NATO told them they were Red Cross helicopters and were told to hold any fire. Helicopters entered harbor without permission but guards were told they could not be fired upon. Shortly thereafter, the helicopters released explosives which are currently being described as "land mines" being dropped from the helicopter into the harbor in an apparent effort to damage the port.

The team that photographed it also uploaded a brief video.[71] One of my Twitter followers, @tasnimq, volunteered to translate. The person behind the camera interviews a Libyan man on the scene, who claims landmines are being dropped on the city by either helicopter or airplane.

> *Do you know anything about these mines?*
>
> This is an anti-personnel aerial mine. The way it is delivered. . .you can see the parachute. It explodes at the slightest movement.
>
> You can see the tripod, it fell this way on the asphalt on its side. It should root itself in the ground endangering any passing cars or people.
>
> *How was it delivered?*

By air.

A plane? Helicopter?

We heard a plane at 9 p.m. yesterday. We saw it and left it alone because we couldn't deal with it at night, it wasn't something we were familiar with. Then at 6 a.m. we came back and everything was dealt with. At around 9 p.m. on Thursday Gaddafi forces used two helicopters marked with the red cross/red crescent to drop several mines, around 50 of them, in the port. This is one of them.

Our fighters met the planes, which then flew off, and then they dealt with the mines.

What about the damage caused yesterday?

A vehicle which some of the fighters were using was hit and several were wounded. But thank God no one was killed. And as for other damage, some trucks and cars. Thank God and God is with us: God is great!

Meanwhile, on the ground in Misurata, Pulitzer prize-winning foreign correspondent C.J. Chivers was investigating the situation for the *New York Times*, working with his own sources to identify exactly what type of munitions they were.

> RT @cjchivers: Story is not up yet. Still working. ID almost solid. Need a little more time. . . . it's an exotic.[72]

While C.J. went about his work, I issued a challenge to my Twitter followers to see if we could figure out what they were by pooling our collective knowledge and research, using the hashtag #IDthis.

> OK, military geeks, new assignment: we need to ID what this is. Some claims it's a mine. Is it? flic.kr/p/9F8yAA #IDthis[73]

One of my followers, @der_bluthund, sent me an extended response:

> It's an aerial dispersal mine, fired out of a pod slung under a jet aircraft or helicopter. Some have vicinity fuses, some timer fuses, some vibrational fuses, and some impact fuses. The idea is the enemy on the ground don't know which one is which until its too late. It is to deny territory to an enemy force by making the area too dangerous to traverse.[74]

He added:

> It is a NATO standard mine, but western arms manufacturers do not give a shit who they sell arms to.[75]

Other people weren't so sure we were dealing with a land mine.

> RT @shava23 @acarvin very like a fragmentation grenade bit.ly/jjf9oj more generally bit.ly/mhFDS3 note handle, form factor[76]
>
> RT @ProfdelaPaz @acarvin That's a pic of a gas mask.[77]

While it was the same color and had a similar form factor as the fragmentation grenade @shava23 suggested, the grenade lacked both a parachute and the metal tripod. And as for gas mask, that seemed like a dead end to me, though I could see how the cylinder could be confused with a gas mask's air filter.

I then heard from @cultauthor, who was convinced he had seen them in a previous war.

> RT @cultauthor @BristleKRS @acarvin I've not seen one that looks like that since Yugoslav Wars of Dissolution, but looks like a 'smart' mine[78]

"Smart how?" I asked.[79]

> RT @cultauthor @acarvin 'Smart' as in meant to be self-destructing and self-deactivating after a set time.[80]
>
> RT @cultauthor @acarvin So you drop them, have them maim, kill and wreak havoc, but deactivated by time you send your troops in. That's theory anyway.[81]

I reached out to @der_bluthund to see if he had a particular mine in mind.[82] While I waited for his reply, @tetreaultaj wrote:

> RT @tetreaultaj @der_bluthund @acarvin is it confirmed to be of NATO design? I'm not sure about that. Link?[83]

I found some of the original photos and passed them along as reference.

> These pics definitely appear to show off its supposed parachute better: flic.kr/p/9F8yZ9 flic.kr/p/9F5Dzn #IDthis #libya[84]

A few moments later, a Twitter user named @nolesfan2011 chimed in. I didn't know him personally, but I'd seen him tweeting a lot about Libyan weapons and opposition military tactics.

RT @nolesfan2011 @net_anon @libyaalhurratv GOT IT! they are the syrian variant of Chinese type 84 land mines[85]

RT @nolesfan2011 @net_anon @libyaalahurratv they are techincally "anti tank" mines but that doesnt matter. they can be timed or contact explosives[86]

RT @nolesfan2011 @LibyaAlHurraTV have these been defused/deposed of properly? they could be LIVE on a time fuse please BE CAREFUL very DANGEROUS[87]

As I reviewed @nolesfan2011's tweets, @der_bluthund also replied with the same conclusion.

RT @der_bluthund @tetreaultaj @acarvin Could be a chinese type 84 or more recent variant: http://ordatamines.maic.jmu.edu/displaydata.aspx?OrDataId=6837[88]

By this point, we had been working on IDing the mine for around half an hour, as I noted:

So @cjchivers will have a NYT story on the munition shortly. Will be interesting to see how close we got after 30 mins of research. #IDthis[89]

We then heard from @urbanmilkmaid, who had a source suggesting the mines were delivered via helicopter.

RT @urbanmilkmaid @acarvin @cjchivers A friend on FB says the same thing Chinese 84 (Syrian supplied?) dropped from helicopters. Citizen journalism! Woot![90]

C.J. Chivers, still working on the piece for the *New York Times*, chimed in, though he sounded skeptical of the helicopter angle.

RT @cjchivers @UrbanMilkmaid @acarvin very close. helo dropped?[91]

Several others, including @der_bluthund, also disagreed with the helicopter theory.

RT @der_bluthund No, small artillery piece fired: j.mp/jTHyvl j.mp/mrKP0c[92]

RT @papakila @cjchivers @UrbanMilkmaid @acarvin I'm thinking they said helo because it floats down, but normal delivery is 122mm cannon, no?[93]

Soon enough, C.J.'s article appears on the *New York Times* website:

> . . .The land mines were delivered by a Chinese-made variant of a Grad rocket that opens in flight and drops mines to the ground below, each slowed slightly and oriented for arming by a small green parachute, according to an identification of the sub-munitions by specialists who were provided photographs and dimensions of the weapons. . . .
>
> . . .The use of such mines also introduces a new menace to the city. The Type 84 Model A is fired by a mobile multiple-rocket launcher system that can carry up to 24 rockets containing 8 mines each. The system's range is slightly more than four miles, according to a publication of Jane's Information Group.[94]

Though our team of volunteers hadn't settled on a delivery mechanism for the mine, at least they had IDed it correctly. Was this an academic exercise? In some ways you could argue yes. C.J. Chivers was on the ground in Libya; his investigative skills and military background made it not at all surprising he managed to identify the mine quickly.

So did we even really need to go through this exercise? I certainly thought so, and Twitter user @BCubbison managed to capture what I had in mind.

> RT @BCubbison Follow @acarvin and you'll watch citizens become journalists #ff[95]

Honestly, I didn't know if my Twitter followers would figure it out – just as I wasn't sure if they would be of any help investigating claims that Israel had supplied weapons to Libya. If we had done nothing, someone would've figured it out eventually.

But a group of people scattered around the world took a break from whatever they were doing to become detectives. They put on their thinking caps and collected various bits of information, working together to come up with an answer. Did they do it better than a professional journalist would have? Not necessarily. But the simple act of working together made them more discerning online citizens. They gave back to the Internet – and in turn, made us all better informed.

The Road to Liberation

In May 2011, the Libyan revolution could fairly be described as a civil war. Fighting raged along the central and eastern coasts of the country and in the western mountains. The streets of Misurata, about 90 minutes east of Tripoli, had been transformed into an urban battlefield reminiscent of Beirut in the 1970s. Despite all odds, opposition forces held the city, pushing Gaddafi forces westward.

Tripoli, however, remained securely under Gaddafi's yoke. The protests in the capital at the start of the revolution had been quashed, forcing remaining opposition underground. NATO forces routinely pounded military targets across the city as part of the U.N. mandate to protect Libyan civilians.

Communication with people in Tripoli remained extremely haphazard. Mobile phone networks and Internet service providers were disrupted, and landlines were assumed to be tapped by Libya's intelligence services. Many of my Tripoli sources, including @Abukhit, @alitweel and @flyingbirdies, hadn't been heard from in more than two months. I was extremely concerned for them, but because no one knew much about their true identities, it was difficult to get reliable information about them.

A few opposition supporters remained online, using satellite phones and clandestine Internet connections. Among them was a mysterious Libyan man calling himself Niz Ben-Essa. Over the spring, Niz demonstrated his bona fides by tweeting about protests and bombings from Tripoli, often before Libya-based Western reporters could report them:

> RT @Niz_FGM: 31/5/11- #Tripoli public protest.Thousands on street. http://http://bit.ly/mb1Rb5[1]
>
> RT @Niz_FGM: 31/5/11 – Another explosion. Louder, heavier, closer. #Tripoli. Jets continue to circle above. . .[2]
>
> RT @Niz_FGM: 5/6/11 – Another 2 loud explosions. Windows shaking. Jets circling low. #NATO bombing in #Tripoli continues. . .[3]
>
> RT @Niz_FGM: 35/6/11 – 2 more #NATO hits in #Tripoli. Looks like its going to be a long night for Gaddafi. Cannot yet verify location.[4]
>
> RT @Niz_FGM: 7/6/11 – From eye witness just now – "I saw huge chunks of a building flying into the air. My car as i drove past almost became airborne"[5]

Niz was also co-founder of a shadowy opposition group called the Free Generation Movement (FGM). Unlike other partisans, they weren't armed resistance fighters. They attacked the regime in their own unique way: conducting acts of civil disobedience and uploading the footage to YouTube.

Video from Tripoli was rare. Yet FGM somehow got around Gaddafi's Internet firewall. By uploading footage of their acts of civil disobedience, FGM activists inspired Libyans beyond the dictator's grasp. They became a constant embarrassment for Gaddafi and his government, which routinely claimed unanimous popular support in Tripoli.

An early FGM video in May 2011 begins with a closeup on a wooden box containing three paint rollers doused in red, black and green, the colors of the Libyan independence flag. The scene switches to a major road, presumably in Tripoli, late at night. A person runs back and forth across the road, rolling bright red paint onto the asphalt. The video ends before the other colors are applied.[6]

Another video starts with a large canvas banner. A pair of hands painstakingly traces Arabic letters with flairs of red, black and bluish-green paint. The camera cuts to another scene: the banner is drying, with silver dumbbells holding it in place. Soon, we're in a car, on a busy highway at night. The car makes two trips under an overpass. During the first pass, the lettered part of the banner hangs from the overpass. The second time, the entire banner is unfurled, displaying an enormous Libyan independence flag.[7]

A week later, FGM activists uploaded more footage. It starts with a closeup of a portable audio system. Someone with a glue gun pastes Libyan independence flags on top of it. There's a jump cut, and the PA system, wrapped in paper, is placed in a white shopping bag. The scene then shifts to a busy square. A man walks through the square with the white shopping bag. He places it at the top of some marble steps and walks away, disappearing into the crowd. Almost immediately, the PA system blares a Libyan independence anthem. For about 30 seconds, the music echoes across the square, a choir singing a rousing chorus of "Libya, Libya, Libya!" Suddenly it stops; someone has knocked over the speaker.[8]

With each new video, Niz Ben-Essa and FGM jab another finger into Gaddafi's eye. The footage was circulated widely among online Libyans and routinely received international news coverage. Pro-Gaddafi Libyan state TV asked for the public's help capturing Niz. For every secret policeman hunting him, though, that was one less officer targeting other opposition members.

FGM's videos appeared on YouTube well into the summer; someone even designed a professional-looking, animated Free Generation Movement logo to introduce each clip. The videos capture various forms of dissent. People cheer NATO bombs falling on Tripoli;[9] volunteers create incendiary devices and burn down giant billboards of Gaddafi.[10]

A particularly powerful FGM video takes place on a rooftop. The camera zooms onto a pair of distant minarets to confirm that it's Tripoli. Several men begin assembling hot-air balloon lanterns. Some hold the lanterns as others light candles to fill them with hot air. Slowly, the lanterns float away. As they rise, they reveal a large Libyan independence flag dangling below them. The flag soars into the distance, visible for miles.[11]

In another video, a man whose face can't be seen sits at an outside table. It's a beautiful day; birds are singing. He's got a small cellophane packet, and he's inserted a handmade paper button in it – a round cardboard button sporting the Libyan independence flag. He seals the packet, places it in an envelope and stacks it with two dozen other envelopes, each destined for an opposition supporter.

The man picks up a pillowcase and shakes it open. Scores of handmade Libyan independence flag buttons dump onto the table. The camera zooms in on a single button: red, black and green, a star and crescent moon at its center. These buttons were distributed across Tripoli. While dissidents might feign support for Gaddafi, they could wear the buttons inside their clothing. If you were caught with one, it was entirely possible that it could get you jailed, tortured or even killed.[12]

Along with his work on Twitter and YouTube, Niz Ben-Essa routinely communicated with reporters through a variety of backchannels. On journalists' email lists and Facebook groups, it wasn't unusual to see messages begin with "According to Niz" or "Niz just reported."

In mid-July, Niz suddenly went quiet. Rumors circulated that he had been arrested and FGM disbanded. If true, it would be a major blow to opposition forces. Niz soon reappeared on Twitter, assuring people everything was fine, though he later admitted FGM was dealing with a hacker attack.[13] It seemed that Niz had dodged a bullet. He gave his contacts a larger scare in late July, when he disappeared again. No tweets, no Facebook posts, nothing. A mutual contact sent me a direct message: there were reports that Niz had been betrayed, and was now on the run. Others speculated he had been detained – truly a terrifying prospect.

Thankfully, Niz reappeared online on August 7, insisting he had merely been traveling.

> RT @Niz_FGM: Hi all.Apologies for the absence.FGM is now in tunis undertaking some humanitarian work for Ramadan.All is well. . . .[14]

It was a plausible explanation; the border with Tunisia wasn't completely sealed. Yet Niz's tweet didn't ring true. Something more serious must have happened.

By mid-August 2011, Libyan rebels had made significant progress toward Tripoli, but there were no signs of a decisive victory any time soon. Six weeks, six months, six years – anything was possible. It wasn't unusual to see the word "quagmire" in the mainstream media. [15, 16, 17, 18, 19]

Online, volunteers from around the world continued to assist the opposition however they could. The video channel that formed around Mohamed Nabbous continued to post video from across Libya. UAE resident Iyad El-Baghdadi routinely updated maps of the Libyan battlefield. The Twitter user @nolesfan2011, an expert at identifying Libyan munitions, continued to help whenever mysterious weapons appeared.

Other non-Libyan volunteers, both offline and online, raised money and shipped equipment across the Tunisian and Egyptian borders into Libya. Online volunteers reportedly passed bombing coordinates from local sources on the ground to NATO, and then helped NATO verify strikes.[20] It was like the groundswell of American volunteers in the 1930s who joined republican forces in the Spanish Civil War – except this time you didn't have to leave home for Libya. Collaborating with partisans had become a virtual affair.

Despite the many challenges, the Libyan Twitter community remained adamant that Gaddafi would soon fall. On August 13, one of my contacts wrote:

> RT @Liberty4Libya: By the 17-18th of August #Libya is planned to be liberated including #Tripoli.[21]

In less than a week? *Yeah, right.* We'll see about that.

August 17 and 18 came and went. Nothing major happened in Tripoli, apart from the usual NATO bombing raids. Opposition forces were still well outside city limits, beyond the furthest exurbs. False alarm, apparently.

On the 19th, though, anticipation was in the air – at least among the Libyans I followed on Twitter. Opposition forces were advancing on Tripoli from three different directions. Even so, it wasn't obvious that a final showdown was imminent. Yet their tweets increasingly radiated hope and optimism.

One Libyan I followed closely, @Tripolitanian, captured the mood the night of the 19th – and offered a warning to Gaddafi supporters.

> RT @Tripolitanian: Called some friends in #Tripoli, they're ecstatic. Haven't heard them this confident since Feb 20th. #Libya #Feb17[22]

> RT @Tripolitanian: Defect now before your head defects off your neck! #Libya #GaddafiCriminals[23]

I wasn't the only Twitter user in the U.S. picking up vibes from Tripoli. Justin Long, a resident of Plano, Texas, who conducts research for missionary groups around the world, was among my Twitter followers detecting intriguing Twitter chatter. He also wondered about the reliability of a particular Twitter source, @tripoli_latest, dropping hints about something brewing in the capital.

> RT @justindlong: Hey @acarvin seeing a lot of activity on twitter on Libya tripoli, but I don't know if it's really happening. . .[24]

> @justindlong I am too. Stuff is going on. What exactly, and at what scale/intensity, is still tbd. #Tripoli #Libya[25]
>
> RT @justindlong: @acarvin is tripoli_latest a quality person to follow?[26]
>
> @justindlong I know a lot of Libyans who seem to rely on it, but I can't vouch for who runs the account.[27]

Approaching dawn on August 20, @Tripoli_Latest seemed to be preparing Twitter followers for action.

> RT @Tripoli_Latest: We urge everyone to please show patience with the phase we are beginning. please retweet & spread.We'll do it properly, not quickly #Tripoli[28]

Soon afterward, I saw another Libyan contact using a hashtag I'd never seen before.

> RT @IbnOmar2005: #Tripoli has been fighting from day one. She is no longer stranded. #DawnofTheBride #Libya[29]

Dawn Of The Bride? I had no idea what that meant; it sounded like the title of a 1950s horror movie.

A few moments later, this came from @feb17voices, the team of U.S.-based volunteers who recorded phone calls with reliable sources in Libya.

> RT @feb17voices: OppContact: Action in #Tripoli being referred to as Operation Dawn of the Mermaid #Libya[30]

First *Dawn of the Bride*, now *Dawn of the Mermaid.* Something was lost in translation, but the implication was clear: opposition forces were launching an operation on Tripoli.

I asked my Twitter followers for insight.

> So where has the operation and its name been confirmed? Just seeing a lot of chatter but not pointing to verifiable source.[31]

@Tripoli_Latest, that mysterious account that seemed so plugged in, tweeted:

> RT @Tripoli_Latest: correct English name for zero hour is Operation #MermaidDawn – Spread and rejoice my friends. Coming soon – videos inshallah in next days.[32]

Operation Mermaid Dawn? I wrote back:

> @Tripoli_Latest can you point to any source that's confirmed the name of the operation – or is it just word-of-mouth?[33]

The reply:

> RT @Tripoli_Latest: @acarvin The name in english is subject to translation but the arabic name is fixed – *3aruset al ba7r*. I cant reveal sources im afraid.[34]

Another Twitter contact, @libyaoutreach, added:

> RT @libyaoutreach: @acarvin I think *3arusat al ba7r* was translated wrong in english b/c those 2 words combined means mermaid just like *kalb al bahar* means seal[35]

Kalb al bahar, I figured out, literally meant "dog of the sea," but as @libyaoutreach said, the phrase was used for the word "seal." So "bride of the sea" – *3arusat al ba7r* – was the phrase Libyans used for "mermaid."

But why "Mermaid Dawn," of all things? I did a quick Google search for *Mermaid Dawn Tripoli*. After a few clicks, everything began to make sense: one of the local nicknames for the city was "Mermaid of the Mediterranean."

Operation Mermaid Dawn meant a new day was about to rise in Tripoli.

"It's gonna be a long night," I tweeted.[36]

> RT @N_Benghazi: The sun is rising but I'm not going to sleep until the *thuwwar* [revolutionaries] do. I don't want to miss a thing. #Libya[37]

I stayed online well past midnight in D.C., trying to get a handle on what was happening as the sun came up in Tripoli on August 20. Unfortunately, enthusiasm outnumbered hard facts by a significant margin.

> RT @ceoDanya: i am soooooo excited about what is happening in tripoli i can barely sit in my seat!!! omg pleaaase plesseee grant us freeedom allah! #LIBYA[38]

DJ Meddi in Atlanta, one of the first Libyans I had connected with, asked people to pray for opposition freedom fighters, also known as *FFs* on Twitter.

> RT @DJMeddi: Amazing News coming out of #Libya. . . Lets keep our Prayers with The #FF's *inshAllah* [God willing] it will all be over soon![39]

Also in the U.S., munitions expert @nolesfan2011 was ecstatic.

> RT @nolesfan2011: this is it boys (and girls) this is what we worked months for and poured our hearts into. lock n load yall! #libya #feb17 #tripoli[40]

The team behind @ShababLibya, which began tweeting about the revolution before it even started, kept its ears to the ground.

> RT @ShababLibya: Lots of news coming out of Tripoli tonight, we will try to confirm what we have and tweet as soon as possible #prayforTripoli #Libya[41]

Rumors ran rampant for hours. Reports via Facebook claimed opposition forces had taken Tripoli's international airport, and opposition marine forces had stormed the shores of Tripoli. There was no way of confirming these rumors.

One credible story, however, kept coming up again and again, thanks to expatriate Libyans who remained in audio contact with family in Tripoli: residents were shouting "God is Great" from their rooftops.

> RT @HafedAlGhwell: #libya #Allahuakbir — *Takbeer* (*allah akbar*) being heard from roof tops around Tripoli[42]

Whether this was the final push into Tripoli remained to be seen. But the citizens of Tripoli seemed prepared to stand up and do their part.

While reports of the opposition's advance on Tripoli continued to circulate all over Twitter, details remained thin. Government officials took reporters on a tour of the airport to deflate rumors that it was in rebel hands.[43] Later that evening, though, Western journalists in Tripoli, including Missy Ryan of Reuters, the BBC's Matthew Price and Jomana Karadsheh of CNN, noted increased gunfire.

> RT @missy_ryan: Sounds of heavy gunfire in distance. #Tripoli #Libya[44]
>
> RT @matthewwprice: I'm no expert but the explosions are not #Nato as far as I can tell. No sound of jets. Gunfire still heard. Lots of it. Distant. #Libya[45]
>
> RT @JomanaCNN: sounds of explosions & gunfire in #Tripoli tonight- more than usual.. eyewitnesses say its clashes. #Libya

NBC's Richard Engel received word that fighting had broken out in multiple areas around Tripoli.

> RT @richardengelnbc: reports of fightng in souq al jumaa, feshloum, tajoura and zawit al-dahmani in #tripoli[46]

The person behind @Tripoli_Latest, who was among the first to declare Operation Mermaid Dawn, posted:

> RT @Tripoli_Latest: Mosques calling God is Great, ALLAHU AKBAR, from Ben ashour mosque. #Tripoli #MermaidDawn[47]

Was this the official signal for the population to rise up against Gaddafi? A tweet by Libyan student and UAE resident Danya Bashir seemed to reflect this possibility.

> RT @ceoDanya: on the phone with my aunt in #TRIPOLI – says she can hear people in TRIPOLI saying ALLAHUAKBR EVERYONE IS OUT![48]

It seemed that Tripoli residents were taking it upon themselves to fight, but would the opposition government in Benghazi, known as the National Transitional Council (NTC), back them up? Danya became increasingly anxious.

> RT @ceoDanya: You know what screw the NTC . . . Tripoli is liberating itself I JUST can't STAND the lies they made to our families in #TRIPOLI[49]

> RT @ceoDanya: Now if you have any friends or family in #TRIPOLI you would like to speak to, because they will probably die ..now is the time to call them[50]

> RT @ceoDanya: THIS IS PISSING ME OFF !!!!!!!!!!!!! MY COUSIN WAS JUST SHOT AND THEY HAVE NOTHING NOTHING TO PROTECT THEMSELVES !!![51]

On the morning of Sunday, August 21, Western journalists in Tripoli continued to report clashes around the city. Nearly 36 hours had passed since the phrase "Mermaid Dawn" first appeared on Twitter, but it was unclear how the operation was progressing.

Al Jazeera's Zeina Khodr observed the fighting along a main road into Tripoli.

> RT @ZeinakhodrAljaz: #Libya, Battles taking place along a highway as opposition pushes towards #Tripoli, #Gaddafi, #Libya[52]

NPR's Lourdes Garcia-Navarro was also on the ground, following rebel movements.

> RT @lourdesgnavarro: rebels in #zawiyah say anti gaddafi fighters in #tripoli outgunned in certain neighborhoods. #gaddafi forces using heavy weapons.[53]

> RT @lourdesgnavarro: Fierce fighting begins just after dawn outside #zawiyah. Heavy weapons, grads [rockets], mortars again #libya.[54]

> RT @lourdesgnavarro: Families fleeing #tripoli to the west, saying rebel cells inside city are in control of some areas but outgunned in others #libya[55]

The Associated Press reported that opposition forces had seized the Maia military barracks, run by Gaddafi's son Khamis, just west of Tripoli:[56]

> RT @ShababLibya: AP reporter w/FFs saw them take over the base of the Khamis Brigade, 16 miles west of the capital, #Tripoli on Sunday.

> AP: Libya rebels reach western outskirts of capital Tripoli, meeting no resistance as they advance.[57]

> Maia base, 10 miles from Tripoli, in opposition hands. Dumpster trucks full of GRAD missiles captured. #libya[58]

Lourdes Garcia-Navarro corroborated the report.

> RT @lourdesgnavarro: Hundreds of rebels cars stream into Khames's base in Maia, taking weapons and celebrating. Spoke to prisoners who escaped. #libya #tripoli[59]

> RT @lourdesgnavarro: #libya rebel in maia tells me "these are the rockets gadhafi used against us, now they are ours". Huge dump truck overflowing with grads.[60]

Danya Bashir, who had been fearful that the operation was premature, regained her confidence as she spoke with family in Tripoli.

> RT @ceoDanya: on skpye with my cousin in TRIPOLI everyone is screaaaming allahuakabr! [God is Great!] i can hearrr them all saying allahuakabr[61]

> RT @ceoDanya: My aunt is crying she says inshallah [God willing] we will all be free allahuakbr god protect TRIPOLI . . . .wow amazing hearing people in #TRIPOLI[62]

Then a pair of tweets made me do a double-take.

> Libya Libya Libya Ibialibia Libya Libya Libya Ibialibia Libya Libya Libya Ibialibia Libya Libya #Libya[63]

> There is no turning back . . .[64]

It was @Abukhit, one of my contacts in Tripoli who had vanished from the Internet after Gaddafi pulled the plug in March. I immediately recalled the day in February when he risked his life and his family's by secretly uploading video of a firefight outside his home. He had been so scared, yet maintained his composure to show the world the fighting in his neighborhood. Despite my fears, @Abukhit had made it through the summer.

A few minutes later, his friend Ali Tweel reappeared, using another Twitter alias, @TrablesVoice.

> RT @TrablesVoice: Did you miss me? I'm glad that i managed to survive this! I missed you all.[65]
>
> RT @TrablesVoice: I'm fine and my family are fine, we still have some clashes in my area, I'm 2km away Bab Azezya [Gaddafi's Tripoli compound], the area has many of his supporters[66]
>
> RT @TrablesVoice: It's almost impossible to reply on every tweet, especially with slow connection, but i'm trying[67]

Then we heard from the third friend, @flyingbirdies, for the first time in more than six months.

> RT @flyingbirdies: Thanks again for all who kept asking about us in #Tripoli #Libya[68]

I had feared we would never hear from the trio again. Tripoli had become such a dangerous place, anything was possible. Yet all three had survived. I was so relieved for them and their families.

> I remember that day in early March when so many of my Tripoli contacts vanished when the Internet was shut down. Welcome back. #libya[69]

Through Sunday night local time, opposition forces continued to maintain the initiative. Tripoli's eastern and western neighborhoods were reportedly seeing little resistance. Alex Crawford of Sky News, broadcasting live atop one of the convoys entering the capital, marveled at traffic jams created by caravans of rebel trucks entering Tripoli.[70]

One Twitter source after another reported opposition forces streaming into town.

> RT @ShababLibya: The citizens of Tripoli welcome Freedom Fighters to their city, The suburbs of Tripoli are out to greet them with Independence flags #Libya[71]

> RT @Gheblawi: Called family in (Seyahia) west #Tripoli all happy as freedom fighters arrive to our neighbourhood, mosque is calling Allahu Akbar #Libya[72]

> RT @Gheblawi: Our house is being liberated :)) :)) V V #Tripoli #Libya #feb17[73]

> RT @MyFreeLibya: Okay sooo my friends from Zintan have just passed my house in Tripoli,,,#TRIPOLI #FajrAl3aroos [Mermaid Dawn][74]

Amidst the excitement among Libyans on Twitter, Danya Bashir offered a harsh reminder about the danger.

> RT @ceoDanya: My father's two friends just passed away in #TRIPOLI . . . may god rest their souls in peace . . . .[75]

Despite enormous risks, the opposition remained confident – so much that one noteworthy Twitter account made an unexpected revelation.

> RT @Tripoli_Latest: Safe to announce that @Tripoli_Latest is in fact @Niz_FGM from The Free Generation Movement.Niz & team remained in #Tripoli the entire time.[76]

> RT @Tripoli_Latest: @Niz_FGM is now out on the streets getting first hand information, I will be communication what he tells me on here #Tripoli #MermaidDawn[77]

So @Tripoli_Latest was actually Niz Ben-Essa and his team. I had to tip my hat to them; after six months of working clandestinely in Tripoli, they would have one hell of a story to tell.

Muammar Gaddafi's world was collapsing. The advance on Tripoli had become a rout. Sky News' Alex Crawford, who two hours earlier was outside Tripoli's city limits, entered the heart of the capital with rebels as jubilant residents cheered them.[78] "They feel liberated," she reported live on air. "Fireworks going off, guns going off, truly an amazing sight."[79]

Twitter user @ChangeInLibya, living in Malta, couldn't believe what he was seeing on Sky News.

> RT @ChangeInLibya: Tears pouring down my face listening to Alex Crawford in Tripoli #libya #feb17[80]

> RT @ChangeInLibya: Better start packing my bag and charging my digital camera. I can finally go back to my city. #tripoli #libya[81]

Libyan American @Libyan4life tweeted what so many of us were thinking:

> RT @Libyan4life: CONFIRMED: Alex Crawford is BAD ASS[82]

As Crawford and other Western reporters broadcast from what was fast becoming a liberated Tripoli, online rumors about Muammar Gaddafi began circulating.

> RT @MonaShark: @acarvin Some tweeps are saying #Gaddafi has been shot dead. Is this true?[83]

I responded:

> RUMOR RUMOR RUMOR. Take with grain of salt.[84]

Similar inquiries came in from other Twitter followers. "He's alive, he's dead, he's in Tripoli, Sirte, Algeria, Disney World," I told them. "Take your pick."[85]

Gaddafi could be dealt with later. For most Libyans, this was a moment to celebrate.

> RT @EEE_Libya: 41 years, 355 days give or take a few leap years. Loser you'll never reach 42 #libya[86]

> RT @IbnOmar2005: Congratulations to all who have sacrificed for this day! thank you all non libyans for your support![87]

> RT @Libyan4life: IS THIS A DREAM IS THIS A DREAM!?!?!!?!! ![88]

> RT @Libyan4life: I cant even cry.. I am so emotional I cant even display any. . . *Alhamdulilah AllahWhoAkbar* [Praise God, God is Great][89]

> RT @ShababLibya: 21st August 2011 Remember the date, your kids will probably be asking you for help with their history homework #Libya[90]

I had to marvel at everything I'd witnessed remotely over 48 hours.

> One week ago, Libyan contacts told me to expect an uprising and attack in 5-10 days. I honestly didn't believe it'd happen. Still stunned.[91]

> When we have some free time we should search google news for "libya" and "quagmire" so we can point fingers and giggle a bit. #libya[92]

> I just realized I've been doing this for 8 months straight. Wow. #tunisia #egypt #yemen #syria #bahrain #libya #whoknowswhatsnext[93]

I received a reply from @nolesfan2011, who had helped debunk rumors and ID munitions throughout the revolution.

> RT @nolesfan2011: @ACARVIN SPECIAL THANKS TO YOU FOR ALL YOU DID THANK YOU THANK YOU THANK YOU. WE DID IT!!!!! WE DID IT!!![94]

It was very kind of him to say that, but I thought his sentiment was misplaced. I didn't play any active role in the revolution; I simply covered the story through the lens of social media.

> @nolesfan2011 Thank you, but all I did was report Libya as best I could. Hopefully some people have gotten something out of it.[95]

I wondered, though, what he meant by "WE DID IT!!!!" Did he think his tweeting somehow impacted the revolution? Or had @nolesfan2011 contributed support more directly? Given his vast military knowledge, it was certainly possible. I made a note to try to find out someday.

Watching Libyans celebrate what I had been considered impossible/what some had considered impossible/what many/what had been considered impossible, I thought back to the beginning six months earlier, and about the Libyans who risked their lives to tell the world what was happening. An image of a young man with a shaved head and giant headphones appeared in my mind. It was Mohammed Nabbous, who died while documenting Gaddafi's assault on Benghazi just hours before the NATO intervention began.

I wasn't the only one thinking of Mo.

Jill Collins (@Bashert54) was watching the liberation of Tripoli from her home in California.

> RT @bashert54: @acarvin all I I can think about is Mo, this was his dream.[96]

"He's watching, from somewhere," I told her.[97]

Mosa'ab Elshamy, the Egyptian pharmacy student who documented almost every major protest at Tahrir Square, invoked Mo's name from Cairo.

> RT @mosaaberizing: Mohammed Nabous.[98]

A Twitter user named @Zlatxlat recalled the phrase Mo uttered on CNN the first week of the revolution:

> RT @Zlatxlat: "I'm not afraid to die. I'm afraid to lose the battle" -Mohammed Nabous[99]

Kurdish human rights activist @RuwaydaMustafah responded to @Zlatxlat:

> RT @RuwaydaMustafah: He won! He won! He won![100]

Mo's wife Perditta had been pregnant when he was killed. She gave birth that June – a little girl. She would grow up in a Libya free of Gaddafi. A Libya where people would tell her stories about her brave father – a father she would never meet.

I invoked Mo's favorite quote, which he had used repeatedly during the revolution: *A candle loses nothing when lighting another candle.*

> Mo Nabbous, wherever you are: it looks like you're winning the battle. And your candle never went out, because it's everywhere.[101]

The L-Team

Following the liberation of Tripoli, the hunt was on for Muammar Gaddafi. At some point during the assault on the capital he had escaped. Gaddafi sightings streamed in from all over Libya, from the remote oasis town of Ghadames to his coastal hometown of Sirte. Others thought he had fled the country, hiding in the deserts of Algeria, Chad or perhaps Niger. Venezuela was a dark-horse candidate. Libyans teemed with confidence that Gaddafi would eventually be captured, but when exactly was anyone's guess.

One figure in the revolution would not play a role in the search for Gaddafi. It was Niz Ben-Essa, who had revealed his true identity: Nizar Bhani, a 30-year-old oral surgeon who lives in Cardiff, Wales, but returned to Libya at the start of the revolution to join the protests.

"I wanted to really annoy the regime by doing something they most hate, and that is telling people what is really going on," he told the *Washington Post*. "The fact it annoyed them so much means we must have done something right."[1]

In late September, Niz announced his departure.

> RT @Niz_FGM: After coming to Tripoli on 21stFeb,to take part in the uprising,Im finally leaving,closing this chapter of my life&my role in the revolution[2]
>
> RT @Niz_FGM: Thank you everyone for your well wishes and kind words following my decision to leave Libya. Your support is incredible.[3]

Niz had been pretty incredible, too, in the fight for his native country. Now he could go home.

While the search for Gaddafi continued, I received a message from @NolesFan2011. Despite our many exchanges on Twitter, I didn't know much about him, except his Twitter handle suggested he was a Florida State Seminoles football fan. The man knew his munitions, no doubt about it, from small arms to landmines to artillery shells. I suspected he was active military or retired – maybe a civilian defense analyst. It really didn't matter to me as long as his contributions were constructive.

His message was tantalizingly cryptic.

> RT @NolesFan2011: @acarvin you up this morning? I got a story you might be interested in please DM your email to me[4]

Of course I was interested, I replied, and told him I'd get back to him shortly.

"Shortly" turned out to be wishful thinking. Wrapped up in the drama of Gaddafi on the run, plus catching up on more than eight months' of work for my usual day job at NPR, I almost forgot about his offer. A couple weeks later, @NolesFan2011 asked me again if I was interested. We scheduled a Skype call. I had no idea what to expect.

I started by asking him what I should call him; there are few things more awkward than talking to someone in real life and knowing only their Twitter name. He introduced himself as Steen – Steen Kirby.

With a Twitter name like @NolesFan2011, I figured he'd have a Southern accent. Steen spoke in a slow North Florida drawl that I'd rarely heard since moving away from my hometown in Central Florida to attend college in Chicago.

"Basically, from the period of early March 'til when Tripoli fell," he began, "me and a group of others formed a group to provide military assistance, advice, training and that type of thing to the freedom fighters in different areas."

Military assistance? As far as I knew, this guy had been based in the U.S. throughout the Libyan revolution. What was he doing – training rebels via Skype?

Steen then rattled off the names of Libyan towns that experienced significant fighting at one point or another. "We've personally been able to assist the freedom fighters in Tripoli, in Misurata and the Nefusa Mountains area: Kikla, Yefren, etc."

In other words, almost every strategic point along the western Libyan front.

"We started by identifying stuff like weapons and things like that," Steen continued. "I realized it would be great if we could identify [what] these mines or small arms or artillery pieces or whatever are, but can we help them to use them to defend themselves against the Gaddafi forces?"

He and a small team of volunteers recruited over Twitter, I learned, had put together manuals on a wide variety of military and medical topics, then had them translated into Arabic and shipped off to Libya. They also answered questions for opposition forces over the Internet.

Essentially, @nolesfan2011 had set up a virtual help desk for the militias.

Seriously?

At first, he explained, they focused on producing medical guides. Over time, he recruited volunteers to tackle military topics, from small arms to artillery. Medical professionals, weapons experts and former military types got involved, putting together more than four dozen different manuals – "handmade and personal," as he put it.

"Do you have a military background?" I asked.

"No, I'm what you might call a military junkie," Steen said. "I've always studied it and have a real interest in it."

Mine detection, targeting tanks, cleaning guns, dressing wounds, you name it – they had a manual for it. This was beginning to sound like a covert op – I envisioned a group of scruffy CIA guys parachuting in and dressed as locals to teach everyone Kalashnikov 101. But @NolesFan2011 and his volunteers were doing all this remotely. I tried picturing Ernest Hemingway operating an ambulance in Europe via a game console as he sipped daiquiris in Havana. Sure, that was a bit of an exaggeration, but what Steen and his team did wasn't that far off.

I paused to soak in what @NolesFan2011 – I mean Steen – was telling me. Right under the noses of pretty much everyone on Twitter, he pulled together a team of experts from around the world to teach freedom fighters how to actually be, well, freedom fighters. It was such as simple idea. As long as a handful of Libyan rebels maintained Internet access, they could receive training manuals and distribute them across the front.

If this had been a novel I would have dismissed it as absurd. I needed to learn more about this guy.

"So what can you tell me about yourself? Based on your Twitter name, can I assume you were at FSU?"

"No," he replied. "Actually, I'm in high school, but I'm from Tallahassee."

He's from Tallahass –

Wait, what?!?! He's in frickin' high school?

"So when you say '@nolesfan2011,'" I continued, dumbstruck, "are you in the class of 2011 at your school?"

"Yeah, ummm. . ." he replied, then paused.

"I'm 15 years old."

"Really???"

"Yes."

"Wow."

Honestly, I didn't know what else to say. *Fifteen years old?*

"Most of us are young people," Steen continued. "There's like a college student – he's a sophomore in college. The rest are in their 30s and 40s. There are some ex-Special Forces who are older. But my co-founder is in his 20s, so we're all young activists, pretty much."

"Does your family know about this?" I had to ask.

"Yes, they do. My parents, I don't know if they even believed me half the time. They weren't really interested in Libya – just, you know, working, American people. So Libya was kinda like my thing."

Kinda like my thing?

"So did this group of yours have a name or anything like that?" I asked.

"The L-Team," he replied. "L as in Libya." A fitting name since they were basically a virtual "A-Team," though that old TV show had been off the air for years by the time Steen was born.

I asked him if he could send me copies of some of his manuals. He paused for a moment; I could hear him typing. An email with a bunch of attachments popped up in my in-box.

One by one, I opened them.

> *Freedom Fighter's Field Manual for Booby Traps (IED), Working Version 2.0.*
>
> *How to Use an AK-47 & AK-74.* "It is rugged, incredibly durable, and very easy to use."
>
> *A Brief Guide to Defeating Qaddafi Armor*
>
> *Medical Booklet Lite.*
>
> *Protecting Against Artillery: Holding The Line.* "Digging holes all the time might get a bit tiring, but do you want to be tired or dead?"
>
> *(Suggested) Handling Procedures for Captured daffy® Forces Radios.* "Do NOT talk to daffy® forces via radio – do NOT taunt them!"

One of the manuals was dedicated to defeating Gaddafi's Russian T-72 tanks: page after page of schematics, detailing every inch of the tank from various angles, identifying its weakest points. If you could remember these points on a tank and aim well, you might actually take one out – just as Libyan opposition forces had been doing all summer.

"So who else was involved writing these manuals?" I asked.

He started rattling off Twitter users. "You know Niz in Tripoli? We worked with him a lot."

I smiled. Niz Ben-Essa seemed to be involved in just about everything during this revolution.

Steen continued to name his other partners. He described one of them as "Our main special ops guy. Tactics, weapons, he did a lot."

"Is he former Special Forces?" I asked.

"Nah, he's just a college student."

Just a college student. Unbelievable.

On top of it all, most of these people weren't strangers to me. Some of them I'd been interacting with on Twitter since the beginning of the Libyan revolution – just as I'd been doing with @NolesFan2011.

"It's funny how I know all these people. . ."

"I know," Steen replied, laughing. "See, we were doin' it right under your nose. You never know what people are up to."

I guess not.

After my conversation with Steen, I talked to his father – he was awfully proud of his son – then contacted half a dozen of his team members. They came from all walks of life: activists, nurses, a Special Forces vet.

I also reached out to Niz Ben-Essa, now back home in Wales. My question for him was simple: what exactly did Steen's L-Team do for Libya?

"I can absolutely confirm and verify that Steen and his team were involved heavily in the distribution of information material to freedom fighters and activists in and around Tripoli," Niz told me. "The physical distribution involved people on the ground, but Steen's team provided us with the raw material to then go ahead and distribute. . .They were a huge asset."

A huge asset. They were like the proverbial Internet geek, sitting in a basement in pajamas, hunched over a laptop to connect with friends – the only difference being that these Internet users could teach rebels how to clear a minefield and blow up a tank.

Talk about one hell of a way for a student to spend his summer vacation.

Steen's connection to Niz...
"The L-Team"

Multi-Camera Shoot

For two months, the Libyan opposition – now effectively the Libyan government in the form of the NTC, the National Transitional Council – hunted Muammar Gaddafi. Over those weeks, there were countless rumors that he had been cornered or even killed.

Early in the morning on October 20, I received word that the Libyan opposition had captured the central coastal town of Sirte, Gaddafi's hometown and one of the last pro-regime holdouts. Many speculated that Gaddafi or his sons could be hiding there.

Evan Hill of Al Jazeera tweeted that a convoy had just been spotted fleeing the city.

> RT @evanchill: Convoy leaving Sirte that may contain high-level regime figures reportedly heading west to Misrata. Maybe the only way they could get out?[1]
>
> RT @evanchill: AJE: NATO reportedly firing at a convoy of cars leaving Sirte. #Libya[2]
>
> RT @evanchill: NTC fighters in Sirte believe Gaddafi himself is in the convoy fleeing Sirte, but that needs to be taken with more than a grain of salt.[3]

More than a grain of salt was right. The convoy leaving Sirte certainly could contain high-value targets, but nothing was confirmed. An NTC representative went on Libyan TV, though, hinting that a "big fish" had been captured. He offered no details.

Al Jazeera's Sherine Tadros tweeted that an NTC source had information on Gaddafi.

> RT @SherineT: #NTC official tells #AJE that #Gaddafi has been captured and is injured in both legs UNCONFIRMED STILL[4]

"Very unconfirmed," I tweeted for good measure.[5] The NTC had a long history of officials contradicting each other; I reminded my Twitter followers to remain cautious.

> With Sirte taken, anything is possible. Let's just wait and see what happens. Maybe they have Gaddafi, maybe they don't. *No* confirmation.[6]

Soon, reports came flooding in that people in Tripoli were celebrating the Gaddafi rumors.

> RT @libyansrevolt: Everyone shooting wildly in the air in #tripoli – don't want to get my hopes up! #Libya #feb17 #Gaddafi[7]

In the United Arab Emirates, Libyan student Danya Bashir pointed out a simple way of confirming the rumors.

> RT @ceoDanya: COME ON show us a god damn picture!!!! who did you CAPTURE!![8]

I added:

> Does no one in the NTC have a cameraphone? Got Twitpic? #gaddafi #libya[9]

Everyone online seemed to have an opinion about Gaddafi's status. After a while it felt like a game.

> Awaiting confirmation from NTC on Gaddafi's capture, Khamis' death, [Yemen] President Saleh's resignation, and J-Lo's dating status.[10]

Then the BBC reported Gaddafi was in custody.

> MT @BBCBreaking: NTC has captured Gaddafi, one of their commanders says[11]

"So one source is good enough for a breaking news alert?" I tweeted, incredulous.[12] Yes, there was a reasonable chance that Gaddafi had been nabbed. But I didn't want to get ahead of ourselves. We needed details; a single source wasn't good enough.

Al Jazeera reported that Gaddafi had been captured and injured, which seemed to me an opportunity for confirmation.

> AJE sources saying Gaddafi was critically injured. That should suggest he's not moving around much and could indeed by photographed. Please.[13]

I added:

> One group of sources: Gaddafi shot in legs. Another group: he's in critical condition. Libyan TV: he's dead. Me: I have no frickin' clue.[14]

Many Libyans, such as @N_Benghazi, felt these reports were more just than the usual rumors.

> RT @N_Benghazi: Ok but seriously guys……..this seems legit.[15]

Certainly the residents of Tripoli believed it, based on the vast amount of celebratory gunfire I could see on television.

> Too bad that the noise level in Tripoli isn't a reliable truth detector; if it were, it'd now be reporting that Gaddafi is very, very dead.[16]

Al Jazeera English had become more nuanced in its Gaddafi coverage. I kept pushing for details.

> AJE now says Gaddafi "appears to have been captured." "Appears" is somewhere on the spectrum btwn "reports" and "confirmed." I want more.[17]

Less than one minute later, AJE reported that sources were claiming Gaddafi was indeed dead. "Which sources, unclear," I noted.[18]

Reuters, meanwhile, had an intriguing lead: an opposition fighter who claimed to have witnessed Gaddafi's capture.

> NTC fighter tells Reuters that Gaddafi was hiding in a hole and yelling "don't shoot! don't shoot!"[19]

The varying reports left me as confused as everyone else on Twitter. One of my followers, Josh Shahryar, offered an elegant, yet indelicate explanation.

> RT @JShahryar: Gaddafi was captured, injured and then killed – problem solved! #libya[20]

Maybe Josh was correct: Gaddafi had been captured, injured, then killed. Depending on your source, it was entirely conceivable to get only one piece of the story. Each part true, but not the whole truth. It felt like a repeat of prior rumors about the Gaddafi family, including his son Khamis, who "died" and rematerialized many times, as Sultan Al Qassemi reminded us.

> RT @SultanAlQassemi: I remember the 3rd time Khamis Gaddafi was 'killed' #NTC[21]

"I remember the 9th," I bragged, jokingly.[22]

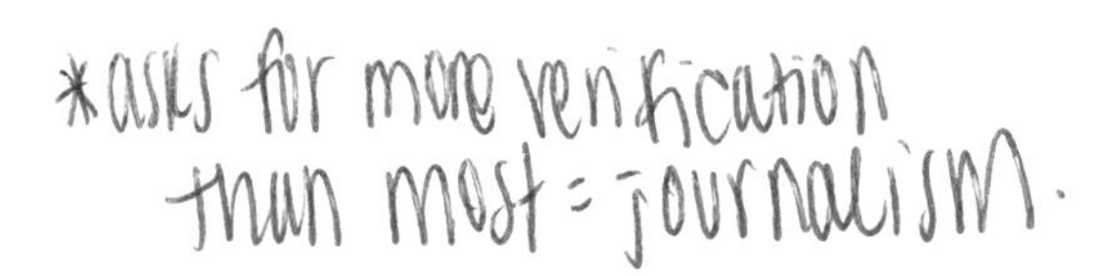
*asks for more verification
than most = journalism.

Soon, a provocative photo began circulating by way of French news agency AFP. The photo showed a video camera's viewfinder, with superimposed text indicating the length of the video, battery level and various camera settings. The scene was disorienting: a bit of someone's jacket to the left, someone's arm on the right, plus the leg, torso and left arm of someone wearing bloodied khakis. In the middle of this human pretzel was another man, slumped over, blood on his face and clothes, his eyes blank and skin ashen. If he wasn't dead, he certainly looked close to being dead.

He also looked a lot like Muammar Gaddafi.

I asked my followers to scrutinize the picture. Was it photoshopped? My instincts told me the photo was authentic. But we had to be sure.

Back in Tripoli, Ali Tweel – one of the Libyans who reappeared online after the Internet was restored in western Libya – felt the image wasn't good enough:

> RT @AliTweel: The shot taken of that cam corder doesn't show the edges of the camcorder screen, it's too good to be true. show us a video.[23]

Danya Bashir wasn't fully satisfied, either:

> RT @ceoDanya: allahauakbar . . .this is so weird i still cant believe what is happening i want a picture just one fucking good picture so i can be SURE![24]

Suddenly many news organizations were more confident that Gaddafi truly was dead. Reuters suggested Gaddafi's body had been taken to a secret location in Misurata, citing NTC information minister Mahmoud Shammam as the source.[25] Sherine Tadros of Al Jazeera English noted reports that Gaddafi had been found "hiding in a hole and then shot in the head."[26] That certainly could explain the "Don't shoot! Don't shoot!" rumor circulating earlier in the morning.

Just before noon in Washington, D.C., Reuters released a breaking news bulletin.

> RT @Reuters: Gaddafi killed as Libya's revolt claims hometown http://t.co/zYWNrAPT[27]

Reporters then began sharing a range of details regarding Gaddafi's capture and death. Abdurahman Warsame of Al Jazeera English cited new information from a military officer.

> RT @abdu: Libyan field commander says Gaddafi was alive with few wounds when captured, the Libyan revolution forces then executed him #Libya[28]

Neal Mann of Sky News reported that his network had interviewed an eyewitness.

> RT @fieldproducer: Man who says he saw the capture of Muammar Gaddafi on Sky News says he hit him with his shoe #Libya[29]

A report from Al Jazeera's Tony Birtley finally convinced me that Gaddafi was indeed apprehended. Birtley was among the first to interview opposition soldiers who had captured Gaddafi; they also showed him the raw video from which that AFP photo had been taken. I tweeted the highlights of his interview.

> AJE's Tony Birtley: Gaddafi firefight, then tried to flee in convoy, then captured. Says someone showed him Gaddafi's shoe and watch.[30]

> "He was captured, I saw him. . . I recognized him. . . . He was lying on the floor. He was alive." -AJE's Tony Birtley on a video of Gaddafi.[31]

> So far, AJE reporter Tony Birtley's account of watching a video of Gaddafi's capture has been the most credible, in my mind at least.[32]

But was Gaddafi dead or alive? The initial photo suggested he was dead, or at least near death, though Birtley stated he was still alive in that video. So what exactly had happened to him? I thought again about Josh Shahryar's tweet earlier that morning.

Captured, injured and then killed.

A video obtained by Al Jazeera erased any doubts. Apparently recorded on a camera phone, the footage is very choppy. The camera points toward the ground, showing a number of boots and camouflaged pants surrounding a body on the ground. It zooms in on the body. It is indeed Muammar Gaddafi. The men drag him by the shirt, nearly pulling it off. They kick the corpse, again and again.[33]

Shortly after the release of the video, the Associated Press issued a bulletin.

> AP: Libyan Prime Minister Mahmoud Jibril says Moammar Gadhafi has been killed. #libya[34]

The major news networks cut to a live press conference with Prime Minister Jibril. "We have been waiting for this moment for a long time," he announced. "Muammar Gaddafi has been killed."[35]

After nearly eight months of civil war in Libya, I could finally utter the word that so many people were waiting to hear from me.

> I guess it's time to say it: *Confirmed.* Muammar Gaddafi is dead. #libya[36]

Many Libyans like @ChangeInLibya, who had just returned to Tripoli from Malta, celebrated the death of their former dictator.

> RT @ChangeInLibya: Gaddafi is dead. Libya is free. Long live Libya. Allahu Akbar[37]

> RT @ChangeInLibya: Gaddafi met his appropriate end. Good for him, straight to hell inshallah. #Libya[38]

> RT @ChangeInLibya: Someone told me Libyans can't resist Gaddafi's army and should try to work out a political deal. We persevered and destroyed his regime.[39]

Libyan-American Assia Amry (@Libyan4life) compared the sense of elation to the holiday marking the end of Ramadan.

> RT @Libyan4life: Today feels like Eid. It feels like a new day. Its amazing.[40]

Some activists, including Iyad El-Baghdadi in the UAE and Nasser Weddady in Boston, were blunt in their assessment of Gaddafi's death.

> RT @iyad_elbaghdadi: What a fitting fate that the big rat should be found in a sewer. #Gaddafi #Libya[41]

> RT @weddady: My only regret is that Gaddafi wasn't given a field court martial, red his charges and sentence, then shot on camera. #Libya[42]

> RT @weddady: Did Mohamed Nabbous get a trial and the trappings of justice? no he didn't. He got a bullet..[43]

Ali Tweel in Tripoli was overcome with emotion.

> RT @AliTweel: words can't express what I feel. few moments ago.. I cried.[44]

His friend @Abukhit responded:

> RT @Abukhit: @AliTweel that means u r a human[45]

In the midst of these celebrations, new videos emerged. They documented Muammar Gaddafi's final hours, and they were brutal.

The first video that surfaced is chaotic and brief. Someone with a camera phone is scurrying around the back of a pickup truck. Several men sit in the truck bed. Muammar Gaddafi is slumped among the men. He is most certainly alive, though injured. Several of the men grab Gaddafi. He stumbles out of the truck bed. His face and hair are matted with blood. Hatless, he has a bald spot. The men force him to stand and then escort him away from the truck.[46]

A second video takes place later. A crowd of men greet an ambulance, chanting "Bye bye, *Shafsufa*!" *Shafsufa* means "frizz head." The camera reaches the back of the ambulance, where Gaddafi's corpse is splayed inside. There is a bullet hole in his left temple – it appears to be a *coup de grace* shot.[47] The crowd dances, celebrating their kill.[48]

The next video to appear online shows Libyan opposition forces shouting *Allahu Akbar*! and firing AK-47s into the air. The camera zigs and zags all over the place, unable to maintain focus. The celebratory gunfire increases. Then, in the back of the truck, there's Gaddafi, slumped over and dead. It's the same pose seen in the very first photo distributed by AFP.[49]

Later that day, the online news site Global Post released an extraordinary video that starts just a few seconds after Gaddafi has been pulled from a drain pipe. The cameraman is actually standing on the pipe; he jumps down and runs toward the soldiers holding Gaddafi. For a fraction of a second, it appears someone is sodomizing Gaddafi through his pants with a stick or a knife.[50]

The camera jumps to Gaddafi's face. The soldiers force him to the ground and begin kicking him. At least one pistol-whips him on the head. Gaddafi tries to stand, but stumbles; soldiers hold him down by the arms. Chaos ensues as they compete over beating him. For a moment, you see his eyes, gazing into the distance. He doesn't seem to comprehend what is happening.

The soldiers continue to tussle over Gaddafi. Someone helps him get back on his feet. He is forced to walk, hands behind his back. More soldiers strike him on the head. Then the camera is right in his face, but the commotion makes it difficult to get a proper view. For a split section, there's a close-up of his right eye; Gaddafi looks stunned, maybe even afraid. Soldiers taunt him, telling him he's going to Misurata, the city he nearly destroyed in a three-month siege. "Misurata! Misurata, dog – to Misurata!"

The crowd thins momentarily; copious amount of blood stain Gaddafi's head, face and clothing. A soldier spits at him. They continue to taunt him: "Misurata, you dog! To Misurata!"

They force Gaddafi onto the bed of the truck.

"Misurata! Misurata! TO MISURATA!!!"[51]

Other videos of Gaddafi prior to his death emerge over the next 24 hours. One shows soldiers surrounding him; he's kneeling on the ground, the left side of his face covered in blood. A soldier sarcastically calls him *habibi* – "darling" – as others address him by his first name, Muammar, an intentional show of disrespect. Gaddafi is lifted onto the bed of a truck, his shirt hiked up and belly exposed. Gaddafi looks around, dazed, trying to understand what is happening to him. He realizes there's blood on his hand, then touches the wound on his head, confused, trying to wipe away the dampness.

The cameraman walks away from Gaddafi for a moment, and then a boot appears on screen. It's Gaddafi's own boot, and someone begins hitting him with it. A young revolutionary jumps in front of the camera, shouting *Allahu Akbar*! at the top of his lungs. He then howls in the air, a howl for his comrades and his country, a howl more than 40 years in the making, and claims his prize: a dictator, conquered.[52]

These videos stirred up an impassioned debate over both how Gaddafi was abused and the subsequent media coverage of the clips. One angry Twitter follower chastised me for retweeting them.

> RT @solbutterfly: Y share this? This is sick sensationalism. RT @acarvin: Gaddafi vid: still alive, dazed, face covered in blood,Soldiers take his boots.[53]

"Not sensationalism," I insisted. "Documenting it just as I have the hundreds of other videos of Libya's dead."[54]

Lorenzo Bondi of the newspaper *Europa* noted that it's the duty of reporters to present what happened to Gaddafi, no matter how distasteful.

> RT @lorbiondi: @acarvin As a journalist, one has to watch this. But it's hard to watch a man dying, whoever the man is[55]

I also commented on the challenges of doing this type of reporting when working from home.

> One laptop has Gaddafi videos on it and the other has previews of the kids' school photos. Note to self: do NOT show kids the wrong one.[56]

Iyad El-Baghdadi exhibited mixed feelings.

> RT @iyad_elbaghdadi: As happy as we are today, there's no honor in beating a critically injured 69 year old man who's already captured & unarmed. #Libya #Gaddafi[57]

> RT @iyad_elbaghdadi: Morally I can't justify or condone summary justice, but I also can't sympathize with a tyrant like #Gaddafi. #Libya[58]

In contrast, @ChangeInLibya had no qualms.

> RT @ChangeInLibya: FLASH: No one here in Libya cares about how Gaddafi died, we're just glad he did. Plus he doesn't deserve to dirty Libya's sacred soil.[59]

While the debate raged online, perhaps the most intriguing development was how mainstream media embraced the footage. For months on end, I was one of the few people in the news industry routinely posting uncensored videos; people could make an informed choice to view them or not. Broadcasters and online news outlets had generally steered away from those videos.

But here was this assemblage of graphic footage, plastered wherever the media had room for it. CNN played the clip of Gaddafi being beaten by his captors. Al Jazeera put a still image of Gaddafi's body on the screen for nearly two minutes – plenty of time for a screen-grab if you were so inclined.[60] Newspapers ran graphic, bloody front-page photos of his corpse. And some news websites, including Global Post and the Huffington Post, conducted frame-by-frame analyses of footage so readers could determine for themselves if someone had sodomized Gaddafi.[61] [62]

Had something in our culture changed? We were now so desensitized that no one cared how graphic the Gaddafi footage was? Or was this just the latest example of people seeking closure by seeing a deceased enemy with their own eyes? It reminded me of the footage of Saddam Hussein's dead sons – or Saddam's hanging, for that matter – and the images of Mussolini after his execution during WWII. As a society, we shy away from graphic depictions of the dead – except for the really bad guys. We need visual evidence that they are indeed gone, however we choose to rationalize it: for closure, curiosity, vengeance or satisfaction. *Ding dong, the witch is dead.*

The Libyan revolution began eight months earlier with videos of impassioned protesters marching in the streets of eastern Libya. Citizen journalists like Mo Nabbous died covering the bloodshed; mysterious partisans like Niz Ben-Essa mocked the regime by documenting acts of civil disobedience. And Muammar Gaddafi – ruthless, indomitable, untouchable – suffered a most ignominious demise, vanquished in a hail of camera phones.

YEMEN

Conflicting Reports

> RT @acarvin: So to summarize, Yemeni pres Saleh is/isn't/could be/perhaps is/supposedly/according to twitter/according to Reuters/sort of/who knows dead.[1]

The basket case of the Arab world. That's how I've heard various pundits dismiss Yemen.

The poorest country in the region, Yemen is also among the most tribal. Every Yemeni identifies with a particular clan with roots going back to when southern Arabia was an assortment of Bedouin alliances. The tribalism runs deep – it's still not unusual for fighting to break out between clans, community versus community.

For several decades, the country was divided into two separate nations, north and south. Despite reunification, distrust remained rampant. The tensions and factionalism allowed Al Qaeda to gain a foothold in parts of the country. And complicating matters further, Yemen is the second most armed country per capita in the world, behind only the United States.[2]

Overseeing this political tinderbox in early 2011 was President Ali Abdul Saleh. In power for more than three decades, he stayed atop the pyramid by playing different factions off of each other: tribe against tribe, political party against political party. Yemen constantly seemed to be stumbling into yet another civil war, and Saleh reaped the benefits, positioning himself as the only person who could hold the country together.

Over the previous five years, a number of forces had pushed hard to loosen Saleh's grip. On one end of the spectrum were established political parties that form the loyal opposition, working the system to solidify their own power gains. On the other end were NGOs and youth groups, eager to oust Saleh and put him on trial for crimes against the nation. Looming in the background were several well-armed tribes with long-standing beefs against Saleh and his own tribe – not to mention the Al Qaeda presence in remote parts of the country.

As the Arab Spring took hold in Tunisia, Yemeni opposition groups seized the opportunity to press for political reform. Young activists in Sana'a, the capital, set up tents in the main square, known in English as Change Square, while established political parties organized rallies across the country.

It didn't take long for things to get violent. Rooftop snipers targeted demonstrators on the streets of Sana'a. Saleh's government brushed off the snipers as rogue elements, but everyone presumed the snipers were actually government-sanctioned thugs. Week after week, more people would die – and in turn, more people would march on the capital. As other countries attracted global news coverage for rallies drawing tens of thousands of people, Yemen experienced weekly marches of hundreds of thousands of protesters, yet rarely got its fair share of headlines.

For all of 2011, Yemen was trapped in a dangerous stalemate. Neighboring countries repeatedly presented peace proposals to allow President Saleh to retire quietly, receive immunity and be replaced by a unity government. Saleh offered to sign the document on many occasions, but never followed through. It was easy to lose count of his promises. Activists, meanwhile, continued to march, demanding that Saleh be put on trial for corruption and the murder of protesters.

As the Egyptian revolution reached a fever pitch in early February, word spread that Yemeni activists planned protests against President Saleh on February 18. I was utterly unprepared to cover Yemen; almost all I knew about the country was that it had a reputation prior to 9/11 as a place where foreign tourists were kidnapped, treated hospitably by their kidnappers – as if honored guests – and then released. But that world was long gone.

Fortunately, people I followed on Twitter were preparing for the protests by creating Twitter lists of tweeps in Yemen. Two lists in particular – one created by @ArabRevolution,[3] another by @habibahamid[4] – laid the groundwork for my initial identification of sources. Compared to other countries in the region, my potential pool of contacts seemed limited. As the poorest country in the Arab world, Yemen was also among the least wired, so getting real-time reports would likely prove difficult.

One of the first sources I relied on was an American woman named Jane Novak. I'd heard about her blog, Armies of Liberation,[5] from a number of people, and she seemed to be a well-regarded Yemen analyst, especially when it came to national politics and security issues. The thing I found most interesting about Jane is that she's a stay-at-home mom in New Jersey who doesn't speak Arabic.[6] She developed an interest in Yemen after the 9/11 attacks in 2001, and started her blog a few years later. I immediately felt like I had a bond with her – a non-expert who initially jumped in headfirst because of sheer curiosity. But she had nearly a decade's head start on me.

Over the first week of protests that February, Jane routinely tweeted updates that helped me understand what was happening in Yemen.

> RT @JNovak_Yemen: Injuries, Arrests as Hundreds in #Taiz protest #Yemen Post English Newspaper http://bit.ly/fqyd5M[7]

> RT @JNovak_Yemen: #Aden #Yemen video snipers open fire in al Mansoura http://youtu.be/l4BxToiHGnE #feb17[8]

> RT @JNovak_Yemen: Game changer in #Yemen as protests swell http://exm.nr/hmssgo my article at Examiner re todays events and shifting alliances[9]

RT @JNovak_Yemen: In the six years I have been studying #Yemen, I have never seen any evidence of learning. #AliSaleh uses fail tactics over and over #YF[10]

By February 26, I was actively encouraging my fellow tweeps to follow her.

To keep up on the violence in Yemen, please follow @JNovak_Yemen. A treasure trove of updates that no one else seems to have.[11]

It was also through Jane that I discovered the #YF hashtag, for "Yemeni Freedom." Monitoring the #YF hashtag became more important for me than following the more generic #Yemen hashtag, which was often overrun with off-topic tweets or spam.

For the next month, I did my best to keep up with Yemen. The relatively limited number of online English-speakers there made it difficult to get minute-by-minute information. If I was going to crack Yemen, I needed to do a better job of tracking down potential sources.

The morning of March 18, I heard from Al Jazeera English colleagues that something bad was happening in Sana'a. A tweet from AJE reporter Rawya Rageh was particularly troubling.

RT @RawyaRageh: AJE Presenter: Even tho images we're showing now (from #Yemen) may be horrid, they're nothing like the stuff we've edited out[12]

While I continued to follow my Yemen Twitter lists and the #YF hashtag, I began to scour YouTube. The video-sharing site had become one of the best ways to find citizen journalism from countries across the Arab world. I dedicated a browser window to a YouTube search results page displaying the most recent uploads referencing different spellings of the capital – Sana'a, Sana and Sanaa – as well as the Arabic spelling of the city.

One of the first sets of images from Sana'a came from Gilles Frydman (@gfry), a master at keeping tabs on the Arab revolutions.

RT @gfry: *GRAPHIC* RT @South_Arabia #fb http://plixi.com/p/84901931 http://plixi.com/p/84901905[13]

Thankfully, Gilles labeled the photos graphic, which prepared me for them. The first photo was a portrait of a young man, lying face-up on a blanket. He's covered with bloody rags. His left eyelid is half-open, his pupil fixed on the empty void, while his right eye is closed. Coagulated blood surrounds his nose; there appears to be brain matter just to the left of the top of his head. The second photo was just as bad: a stocky young man, dead on the floor with his bloodied shirt pulled open, an enormous pool of blood next to his left temple.

Evan Hill, one of the Al Jazeera reporters I followed closely in Cairo, reported on the violence.

> RT @evanchill: Reports of 30+ deaths in Yemen as security forces put down protests. . . .[14]

On a Yemen Twitter list, a user named @25FebFreedom said:

> RT @25FebFreedom: Help #Yemen a young boy killed very graphic don't know if u saw this http://is.gd/laxEuT[15]

I took a deep breath and clicked the link. The boy, perhaps 12, is splayed on a gurney, his red soccer shirt covered in blood. A white cloth placed on his neck is blood-soaked. A gaping hole in his right temple oozes more blood across his sealed, swollen eyelids.[16]

Most of the information I found regarding the violence in Sana'a was via Al Jazeera, which had solid contacts in Yemen. I was still struggling to reach sources on the ground. I checked in with my followers.

> The last I heard from AlJaz re: #Yemen massacre was 30 dead, 200+ injured. Any reliable updated numbers?[17]

Correspondent Sherine Tadros had the latest information.

> RT @SherineT: 41 dead, over 200 injured in #Yemen today according to medical sources there[18]

Other news networks soon reported the story. This update from BBC Arabic came via columnist Sultan Al Qassemi in Dubai.

> RT @SultanAlQassemi: BBC Arabic: Yemen president declares state of emergency & a ban on carrying weapons.[19]

Whatever was happening in Sana'a, the government was on high alert. The scale of this attack was more than anything we'd seen so far. More and more people on Twitter began calling it a massacre.

Back on YouTube, I trawled for whatever footage I could find. One video, just over two minutes long, begins with the scene in Change Square.[20, 21] The camera pans counter-clockwise, revealing a man flat on the ground, bright red blood pooling around his head. The cameraman moves out of the way as the dead and injured are brought away from the scene. The gunfire is nearly constant. The cameraman then approaches a crowd of men trying to lift another protester, his chest covered in blood. They chant "There is no God but God" as they whisk him away. Others point across the street; someone else has been shot. As a handful of people tend to him, others pass by, carrying more casualties. Several people flinch at the sound of gunfire; a handful stand their ground, aiming their cameras in the direction of the shooting. There is a high-pitched *zing* – a bullet has just missed the camera.

This was no fight between protesters and government supporters, with two sides attacking each other. The protesters were being picked off by snipers.

I found another video of a Sana'a rooftop, where several snipers direct rifle fire toward the crowd.[22] They're accompanied by spotters, pointing out protesters to target. In another video, one group of men after another recover an endless flow of dead and wounded protesters. They carry out someone every 10 or 15 seconds. I tweeted that video to my followers with a brief description with the only word I could think of: *horrifying*.[23]

One person who popped up on my Twitter lists proved to be an amazing source of information for the rest of the year: Maria al-Masani (@al_masani). She lived in Canada and competed in beauty pageants in her free time. She had even stirred up a bit of controversy when she competed for a slot in the Miss Universe Canada competition in a sari rather than a bikini, because of her Sufi Muslim beliefs. She ended up advancing one more round.[24]

More relevant to my work, Maria was originally from Yemen and had an academic background in international security and intelligence. As she explained in a tweet, "I grew up with Saleh's family. My father advised him. I know those guys & their games."[25] She also published a blog called Yemen Rights Monitor,[26] which became a go-to source for breaking news.

Two days after the massacre, the situation became even more volatile, as I learned from Al Jazeera's Rawya Rageh and Reuters:

> RT @RawyaRageh: BREAKING Yemeni President sacks Cabinet #Yemen[27]
>
> RT @REUTERSFLASH: Yemen president fires government – state news agency[28]

To deflect the public's rage, Saleh had blamed his cabinet and sacked all of them. Heads were rolling, but not his.

The next day, March 21, brought even more surprising news.

> RT @AJELive: Tanks, armored vehicles deploy in Yemen's capital as top commander defects to opposition – AFP[29]

Ali Mohsen, one of the most powerful generals in the country, had defected with his entire division and sworn an oath to protect the protesters. For some, it was a sign that the end was near for President Saleh; for others, it was just another authoritarian figure positioning himself to be the last man standing.

Abdulkader Alguneid, a physician and public health specialist in Yemen's cultural capital, Taiz, was among those who thought Saleh was now in deep trouble.

> RT @alguneid: Amazing,What a signal was it!! Ali Mohsen quitting. All jumped from the ship. #Yemen #yf[30]

Others, such as Jane Novak and a Yemeni man I only knew as @al3ini, were more skeptical.

> RT @JNovak_Yemen: CNN: Ali Mohsen negotiating with #Saleh to leave #Yemen by the end of the year. ??!! No thats not going to work.[31]
>
> RT @al3ini: Ali Mohsen negotiating with Saleh to leave by the end of the year. This man has bad intentions.[32]

For the next week, determining the truth was next to impossible. Local news organizations would claim one thing and then retract it, while President Saleh used his mastery of rhetoric to talk his way through each step of the crisis. But Dr. Alguneid was convinced that Saleh would blink first, rather than the Yemeni people, as he put it in his halting English:

> RT @alguneid: ANALYSIS: In the crowd game between SALEH and PEOPLE.#Saleh can do it as a stunt. PPL , can do it indefinitely.[33]

Jeb Boone, one of a handful of Western journalists based in Sana'a, became a key source for sorting out what might or might not be true, as noted by Princeton-based Yemen scholar Gregory Johnsen, an important analyst in his own right.

> RT @gregorydjohnsen: Very Wise words on #Yemen RT @JebBoone No march; Media rumor[34]

Reuters reported that President Saleh was prepared to hand over power, but only to "safe hands," which likely meant one of his cronies or sons. The will-he-or-won't-he rumors went on for days.

Ibrahim Mothana, co-founder of a Yemeni youth political party, was incredulous.

> RT @imothanaYemen: #Saleh will not step in 2 HOURS. He is just dancing his so called dance with Snakes #Yemen #yf[35]

And Iona Craig, freelancer for the *Times* of London, jokingly linked the political crisis to the city's notoriously bad power grid.

RT @ionacraig: Electricity outage again. Is that Sana'a equivalent to white smoke in the Vatican? #yemen[36]

Beauty pageant contestant and intelligence specialist Maria Al-Masani reached out to her own sources.

RT @al_masani: From the tribes, I hear Saleh to step down within days, but wrangling his personality something else #yemen[37]

And Jeb Boone again warned against rumor-mongering.

RT @JebBoone: Saleh is still president. More reason for you not stop believing all these rumors in #Yemen.[38]

RT @JebBoone: Being a journalist in #Yemen is like asking for directions from NASCAR drivers during the Indy 500[39]

While trying to sort out fact from fiction, a number of Twitter users introduced me to the YouTube channel of Yemeni surgeon Hamza Shargabi.[40] Unlike much of the other video I found from people on the scene in these uprisings, he didn't merely upload raw footage; he narrated it as a reporter might, providing context and analysis. He also used a high-definition camera rather than a phone.

One video begins with Hamza walking down the main road occupied by the protesters. It's filled with tents, stretching as far as the eye can see. "It's 7 a.m.," he says. "It's very strange weather; it's foggy in Sana'a. . .People have been awake all night, cussing the president. . .I'm on my way to record my log for the day."

The footage then dissolves to another nearby location, essentially a pile of sooty rubble. "As you can see, the leftovers of the tires that were burned to create a smoke curtain for the snipers to shoot at us."

Hamza then turns the camera on himself as he strolls down the street. He's a young man wearing stylish wire-rimmed glasses and a black cap, sporting a well-groomed beard.

"Yemeni people are snipers and they know about military tactics," he acknowledged. "The other thing is this. This is the house where they shot us from. They were basically stationed on the rooftop. . .It's the [home of a] governor of a nearby governate. How could normal folks go up on the house of a governor of the country?"

He shakes his head cynically and laughs. "I don't know what to say. . .I don't know what to say. All I can say is, from this spot, 50 lives or more were lost."[41]

Hamza's video conveyed two important points. First, it didn't make sense that snipers were themselves rogue elements, as claimed by President Saleh; given the location of the snipers, nest, they must have been given permission from someone in the government to kill protesters. His second point was more ominous: all Yemenis know how to shoot and defend themselves. Yemen has a long tradition with guns; almost everyone in the country owns at least one and knows how to shoot it. In other words, it's not the type of place where you'd want violence to escalate.

As the crisis in Yemen entered early April, I received an email from one of my Yemeni sources on Twitter. It was in response to my practice of asking people to cite their sources and clarify what's been confirmed. I had done it hundreds, perhaps even thousands of times, since the start of the Arab Spring, and no one had ever raised a concern about it – until I received this email from him.

> I hope you don't mind questioning my sources in private, and not so publically. I was quite embarassed, as I use the intelligence metric of accuracy x validity for sources on the ground. Its more intelligence to me than evidence. I am not a journalism school graduate.
>
> Please don't be too hard on us in public, you've been at your job for years. . . .We started reporting as of January with no training. Losing face and reptuation is a part of Arabic culture. So messaging me in private would be greatly appreciated, and same for most Yemenis actually. I know you mean welll. . . . It's just a cultural thing, I hope you understand

It's just a cultural thing. My sincere requests for more details had been interpreted by at least this Yemeni as questioning his integrity, even his honor. When it came to online collaboration, Yemen would be a whole other ballgame.

The same day I received that letter, I also received an invitation to a private event at the U.S. Institute for Peace in Washington. It was a video conference call with several opposition leaders in Yemen, organized for journalists and Middle East policy wonks. I read through the list of names of those who would be joining us remotely from Yemen and didn't recognize them – I had so much catching up to do when it came to Yemeni politics – so I decided to contact Maria al-Masani to see if she knew any of them.

I had expected her to reply with a brief yes or no, and perhaps a sentence or so on the ones she knew. Instead, she wrote me detailed biographies. One by one, she went through the names, describing their political affiliation, any alliances they had, their role in the protests, even their status among established politicians versus the youth protesters.

One person on the list stood out. She was the founder of an association of women journalists fighting for press freedom, and she was affiliated with one of the main Islamist opposition parties. She was married and had several children, but spent almost every night in her tent in Change Square in solidarity with the other protesters. She was also the person who called for the protests in the first place. Her name was Tawakkol Karman.

I hung on every word she spoke during the video conference. She spoke bluntly, confidently. The video connection was terrible – she was basically a headscarfed blur seated at a large, pixelated table – but the audio was good enough that I could tweet the highlights of her remarks.

> Karman: It's a historical moment #Yemen, where the country can regain itself and its role in the region.[42]
>
> Karman: The solution is the ouster of the regime. #Yemen[43]
>
> Karman: The people in Sanaa are taking the banner of peace and aren't waging war against anybody. #Yemen[44]
>
> Karman: If you come to Change Square, you'll see people from warring tribes sitting under one tent, sharing food, demanding the same. #Yemen[45]
>
> Karman: First we must mediate the departure of the regime. #Yemen will be well governed and better off without Saleh.[46]
>
> Karman: We'll need your help, your assistance in building this civic state. #yemen[47]
>
> Karman: We demand now that the US call upon Saleh for an immediate departure of Yemen and freeze his assets and his family's. #yemen[48]

Like the majority of protesters in Yemen, Tawakkol Karman spent little or no time online. Eventually she got a Twitter account, but almost never used it. This revolution lacked much of the Internet presence of other uprisings in the region. For Karman, it was much more important to be in her tent, night after night, supporting the protests. In all uprisings, ultimately it's the people on the ground making the sacrifices, whether they succeed or fail. No revolution has ever been won through the Internet alone.

Over the next six weeks, Yemen seemed mired in an endless cycle of violence. Huge crowds of protesters, often hundreds of thousands, marched each week, demanding the ouster of the president. Snipers took pot shots at activists, often killing a number of them, wounding more. The protesters would then respond with equally large marches the following week.

In the aftermath of one sniper attack on May 11, I learned from reporter Jeb Boone that he had barely made it out alive.

> RT @JebBoone: When they opened fire on protesters, there was so much shooting it just sounded like a steady hum. Never heard anything like it. #Yemen #YF[49]

> RT @JebBoone: @YemenPeaceNews I just made it out of change square. I think they're going to storm the place, so I left.[50]

> RT @JebBoone: Most news outlets reporting 1 dead in Sanaa. BS, scores were killed. #Yemen #YF #Sanaa[51]

I asked Jeb if he had any sense of how many people had been hit.

> @JebBoone How many casualties did you see, approximately? #yemen #sanaa[52]

He wrote back:

> RT @JebBoone: @acarvin Saw two dead bodies in the field hospital but saw scores gunned down while I was running.[53]

"Jesus," I uttered, in shock.[54]

Elsewhere on Twitter, I saw a note from Laura Kasinof, who freelances on Yemen for the *New York Times*.

> RT @kasinof: 120 shot today in Sanaa #Yemen according to a doctor at the field hospital on the phone. He's shouting. very upset.[55]

The scale of the massacre was devastating. Yet this scene would repeat itself in Yemen's cities and towns throughout April and May. And things were about to get much worse.

On a Sunday morning in late May, I saw an urgent tweet from Dr. Abdulkader Alguneid in the Yemeni city of Taiz.

> RT @alguneid: #TAIZ 1 martyr, 11 wounded in Alssafwah Hosp.[56]

As a doctor, @alguneid was well placed within the local medical community to learn about casualty figures. If something bad were going down, he'd be among the first to know.

He continued:

> RT @alguneid: #Taiz #Youth went to Qahera District police station. Demand release kins.Shot at by plainclothes men. 1Martyr, many wounded[57]

A Yemeni woman who went by the name @YusraA1A frantically sent out a river of tweets about the violence in Taiz.

RT @YusraAlA: Snipers are spreading widely on the roofs of building near Freedome Square of #Taiz #Yemen #yf[58]

RT @YusraAlA: Heavy explosion shakes the city of #Taiz and sounds of gunfire- unknown location. #Yemen #yf[59]

RT @YusraAlA: Appeal from #Taiz: Everyone has to go the Freedom Square to support the protesters who are getting attacked. #Yemen #yf[60]

Maria al-Masani, who was archiving Taiz-related footage on her blog, shared a particularly disturbing video.

RT @al_masani: upclose video from bushes two meters away from thugs shooting protesters in #taiz #yemen http://on.fb.me/lOoqwR WOW[61]

The video shows two men in plain clothes, standing in front of a door, firing rifles directly toward the cameraman, who almost seems within reaching distance of them. The video then cuts to another sniper operating from a rooftop. He approaches the edge of the roof, aims downward, and fires. It was like a human turkey shoot.

@ArabsUnite then reported that the protesters' tents were being set on fire.

RT @ArabsUnite: Security forces burning the remainder of the tents & contents in Freedom Square – #Taiz #Yemen #YF[62]

God, I hoped people were able to get out first. Unfortunately, that turned out to be wishful thinking, as I learned from Dr. Alguneid.

RT @alguneid: #TAIZ horrid stories, still coming about #Saleh men mass killings in sit-in Al-Huriyah sq. Some are looking for mass graves #HRW #AI #UNHRC[63]

RT @alguneid: #TAIZ Handicapped tent in sit-in sq,set on fire.Couldn't escape.Found charred at morning.Buried,in mass grave[64]

"Any other info?" I asked.[65]

He responded:

RT @alguneid: @acarvin Just received this info,from an MP [member of parliament] who is very active n the sq and demos.(It was 2nd tent,hit by a rolling tier set on fire)No more[66]

Digging for footage of the burning tents, I went back to YouTube, setting up searches for Taiz using a variety of possible spellings in English and Arabic.

One of the first clips I found takes place in the middle of the night. It shows protesters' tents in Taiz's Freedom Square. They're chanting *Allahu Akbar* – God is Great.[67, 68] In a second video, all is black, except for intense flames in the distance. What appear to be collapsed tents are burning, as several calls to prayer can be heard in the background.[69, 70] A third video captures the torching of the tents up close, from just across the street. Several tents are completely ablaze, and the flames are spreading from one tent to another. People cry out *Allahu Akbar*! as snipers continue to rain bullets in their direction.[71, 72]

Journalist Tom Finn, editor of the *Yemen Times*, offered a grim assessment of the ruthlessness used against the protesters.

> RT @tomfinn2: After setting tents alight, the army bulldozed the entire square, death toll expected to rise, protesters too afraid to return #yemen #taiz[73]
>
> RT @tomfinn2: After Mar 18 this is by far the most brutal crackdown on protesters we've witnessed in Yemen's 4-month uprising #yemen #taiz[74]

Within hours of the crackdown in Taiz, reports came in from Sana'a: another major attack was under way. Yemeni-American Raja Althaibani was among the first to report on fighting in Sana'a's Al Hasaba neighborhood. It wasn't just gunfire; this time it was artillery.

> RT @RajaAlthaibani: Wow.. I can here the explosions in Alhasaba all the way over here by 50th street! #yemen[75]
>
> RT @RajaAlthaibani: Are they trying to wipe al-hasaba out of #sanaa? #yemen[76]
>
> RT @RajaAlthaibani: Alhasaba: This is absolutely devastating and horrific! #yemen #sanaa[77]

Amr Al-Zain, in another part of town, noted the intensity of the gunfire and shelling.

> RT @AmrAlzain: . . .i normally can't hear them from where I live in #Sanaa, but tonight I have been hearing them clearly[78]

I asked him:

> @AmrAlzain what general area are you in? How far are you from the fighting? #yemen[79]
>
> RT @AmrAlzain: @acarvin Algiers st. (southeastern) part, abt 5 miles from Hasbah, where most fighting has been so far. Unclear where fighting is tonight.[80]

@YusraA1A also noted the scale of the explosions.

> RT @YusraA1A: Yet another VERY powerful explosion shaking hasaba now in #Sanaa #Yemen #yf[81]

Another Sana'a resident, French reporter Benjamin Wiacek, described the fighting taking place in an area ironically known as Tahrir.

> RT @Nefermaat: very strong explosions, heavy gunfire, from #Tahrir I feel like a war is going on "next" to my house #Sanaa #Yemen[82]

The violence in Sana'a continued for the next several nights. Raja Althaibani urged caution, as fears of an all-out civil war spread throughout the city. She was also prepared to defend herself if necessary.

> RT @RajaAlthaibani: Rumors of #saleh security forces heading to the square. I dont think thats true. Lets not allow what happened in #taiz assume the same for #sanaa. Unlike Taiz, Sanaa is heavily armed and Saleh knows this. #yemen[83, 84]

> RT @RajaAlthaibani: Everyone reporting from #Yemen. This is a scary time, lets remain calm. Remember: SILMIYA! "Peace"!Ignore what ur hearing right now and focus on the task at hand. We are peaceful and the is a family dispute and IT WILL REMAIN ONE! #YEMEN[85]

> RT @RajaAlthaibani: I OWN THREE RIFLES AND LOTS OF AMMO. THEY ARE IN MY CLOSET&WILL REMAIN THERE UNTIL SALEH STEPS DOWN!! #FUCKVIOLENCE! #YEMEN #SANAA #YF[86]

> RT @RajaAlthaibani: PEOPLE HAVE A RIGHT TO DEFEND THEMSELVES! ONLY WHEN NECESSARY. RIGHT NOW WE ARE FREAKING PPLE OUT AND NOTHING HAS BEEN CONFIRMED. #YEMEN[87]

> RT @RajaAlthaibani: People lets stay CALM!Reports of gunfire around change square's perimeter. NOT INSIDE. This is not new. There have been many incidents where clashes happened at the squares perimeter. Lets not jump to conclusions unless we are SURE! #Yemen #sanaa[88]

Reporter Iona Craig, who lives in Sana'a, offered a play-by-play from her vantage point.

> RT @ionacraig: Northern Sana'a emploded in last 20mins. Shelling heavy gunfire from northwest, north (arhab) & northeast (Hasaba)[89]

> RT @ionacraig: If they keep aiport open now & you're planning on leaving or arriving in Sana'a this a.m. I'd stay at home if I were you. #yemen[90]

> RT @ionacraig: Huge explosins echoing across the north. You wouldn't want to be living in northern Sana'a right now. #yemen[91]

I became increasingly worried for all of them.

> Getting very concerned for my contacts in Yemen. How many close calls can they get through unscathed? Please keep your heads low, folks.[92]

Maria al-Masani responded.

> RT @al_masani: @acarvin contacts are still protesting in the change square and bullets have reach the podium #yemen – very determined people[93]

> RT @al_masani: @acarvin I worry too but what can you do. :-)[94]

Another Twitter user going by @Priapus_D countered:

> RT @Priapus_D: @acarvin I think they should keep their heads high![95]

No doubt, the escalation in violence was taking its toll on the people of Sana'a, whether they were directly in the line of fire or not. As Raja Althaibani remarked that awful night:

> RT @RajaAlthaibani: never did I think I'd be sitting on a bldg roof in Sanaa listening for signs of warfare. :(they've hijacked my #Yemen[96]

The fighting continued for several more days, without decisive gains by one side or the other. By late afternoon on June 3, reports suggested there had been an attack on President Saleh's residence.

> RT @JebBoone: Seems as though the Presidential Palace has been shelled in #Yemen #YF[97]

> RT @gregorydjohnsen: Lots of rumors out of Sanaa right now, as everyone tries to make sense of the chaos following a strike on presidential compound #Yemen[98]

Soon, the names of potential casualties began to circulate.

RT @gregorydjohnsen: Mareb Press reporting the identities of a number of prominent govt. figures injured in strike on mosque within presidential palace #Yemen[99]

RT @gregorydjohnsen: They include speaker of parliament, gov. of Sanaa, prime minister, deputy prime minister even Salih reportedly sustained light injureis[100]

RT @YusraAlA: Arabia: Yemeni president was in the mosque during the attack and was slightly injured. #Yemen #yf[101]

RT @Yemen411: AJA: Presidential complex in #Yemen was shelled and officals were injured including speaker of parliement~No official confirmation yet #yf[102]

RT @alguneid: #BREAKING Great loss of life and charred bodies inside presidential residence #Sanaa[103]

RT @alguneid: #Sanaa Ahmar's mortar missile hit the mosque inside presidential residence and injured top officials while Saleh rushed away. (by phone)[104]

I asked Dr. Alguneid how he was getting his information. I knew he was in Taiz and was on the phone with his Sana'a contacts, but who were they?

RT @alguneid: always the same. A source close enough. This is a very Yemeni thing to know someone who knows someone[105]

RT @alguneid: @acarvin insider enough and wounded, as well[106]

Many of my contacts monitored local independent TV channels, including one called Suhail TV.

RT @YusraAlA: Suhail: Reports that Ali Saleh's forces targeted the mosque by shelling to expand the scope of battles in Sana'a #yemen #yf[107]

Gregory Johnson, the Yemen scholar at Princeton, wisely cautioned:

RT @gregorydjohnsen: Suhail TV leading the charge in rumor mongering #Yemen[108]

I seconded his tweet.

Lots of rumors around, waiting for more indie confirmation.[109]

The number one question on everyone's mind was whether President Saleh had been hit. Unsurprisingly, confusion reigned into the evening.

> RT @YusraAlA: Suhail said #Saleh escaped to #Aden at night, now they're saying he died in the bombardement on the mosque #Yemen #yf Uhmm *_*![110]
>
> RT @JebBoone: Suhail opposition channel reported that President Saleh was killed in the shelling #Yemen #YF[111]
>
> RT @JebBoone: Yes, do not consider reports of Saleh's death to be credible #Yemen #YF[112]
>
> RT @gregorydjohnsen: 1 piece of advice to #Yemen watchers, be wary of any piece of information coming from Suhail TV[113]
>
> RT @alguneid: #Yemen State tv: "president Saleh, god bless him, is fine and well" No trurh to what is promoted by gossip channels channels @suhail_tv and #AJA[114]
>
> RT @Yemen411: Presidential Palace in #Yemen was attacked earlier senior government officials were injured no causalities & President was not killed #YF[115]
>
> RT @imothanaYemen: Brief: Suhail TV: #Saleh is dead. Yemeni TV: Saleh is fine. Alarabiya: Saleh was slightly injured in his head. I am LOST.#Yemen #Sanaa[116]

As the night went on, I reminded my Twitter followers to beware initial casualty reports, particularly regarding President Saleh.

> Lots of rumors that pres Saleh was killed, but one opposition station reporting it doesn't make it confirmed. Need more than that. #Yemen[117]
>
> It looks like a mosque in the pres palace was shelled, some casualties, but actual details remain unclear. #Yemen[118]

The scale of these rumors reached epic proportions when some of them got picked up by international news outlets such as Reuters, only causing more confusion.

> RT @mpoppel: REU: YEMENI RULING PARTY OFFICAL TELLS ARABIYA PRESIDENT SALEH IS "FINE"[119]
>
> RT @Reuters: FLASH: Yemen President Saleh killed – Opposition TV says"[120]
>
> RT @Reuters: FLASH: Yemeni president Saleh alive – al Arabiya[121]
>
> RT @Reuters: FLASH: Yemeni president Saleh alive, will hold news conference – Sanaa deputy mayor"[122]

By this point, I had no idea what to believe.

> So to summarize, Yemeni pres Saleh is/isn't/could be/perhaps is/supposedly/according to twitter/according to Reuters/sort of/who knows dead.[123]

Government-connected sources, meanwhile, were eager to prove President Saleh was alive. They announced he'd give a press conference, but that only led to more confusion.

> RT @Yemen411: President #ALISALEH will host a press conference momentarily #YEMEN #YF . . .[124]

"Define momentarily," I asked – to which Shakeeb Al-Jabri in Beirut dryly responded:

> RT @LeShaque: In the Arab dictator lexicon that could be up to 12 hours.[125]

Maria al-Masani chimed in as well.

> RT @al_masani: @acarvin If there is no press conference it means they want to hide something – i.e. injured govt officials or damaged palace #Yemen[126]

Just as she had predicted, the press conference was called off.

> RT @BBClysedoucet: #Yemen TV now says no press conference by Pres Saleh but a statement will be issued. @BBCWorld[127]

As we waited for clarification – or the lack thereof – surgeon and video blogger Hamza Shargabi reported that his house had been hit in the fighting.

> RT @ichamza: bombing around my house in Hadda for the past 3 hours.. my house was hit with many bullets .. #Yemen[128]

> RT @ichamza: my house is now directly hit in Sanaa- hadda #Yemen[129]

Yemenis gave him a variety of advice on what to do next.

> RT @WomanfromYemen: @ichamza LEAVE LEAVE LEAVE LEAVE.[130]

> RT @al_masani: @ichamza the best thing you can do now is take the large mattress from the bed, put it on top of you and lie on the ground :-([131]

> RT @AlaaAjJarban: @ichamza Hamza, please stay safe! And please if you want to move to my place on the other side of Sana'a, let me know! PLEASE, Okay?[132]

But Hamza was adamant. He wasn't going to budge.

> RT @ichamza: 1 thing I have to make clear! We are not afraid! #alisaleh and his thugs r bringing fight towards residential areas caus they r dumb #Yemen[133]

Hamza wasn't the only one affected by the fighting, as shelling continued across the city.

> RT @imothanaYemen: Another HUGE explosion in Bait Baws in #Sanaa !! My house is literally SHAKING. #Yemen #Saleh #GCC[134]

> RT @ionacraig: And more shelling now. Can't confirm if palace or residence of Hamid al-Ahmar. I'm about half a mile away.[135]

> RT @imothanaYemen: Today is the most dramatic day I have ever lived in #Yemen. #Sanaa #Saleh #GCC[136]

With the cancellation of the press conference, attention turned to the possible extent of President Saleh's injuries, as few people now believed he got through the attack unscathed.

> RT @iyad_elbaghdadi: There are reports that Saleh has been moved to a hospital in Saudi Arabia for treatment. Can anyone confirm? #Yemen[137]

> RT @iyad_elbaghdadi: #Yemen's deputy minister of information describes Saleh's injuries as "scratches".[138]

> RT @kasinof: official: saleh is suffering from burns on his face but going to be fine #Yemen[139]

> RT @JNovak_Yemen: If the #Saleh regime says he is slightly injured, likely its more serious because their first instinct always is to lie #yemen[140]

Out of the blue, Saleh went on air to announce he was okay. There was no video – just audio – which raised more questions about his condition. And he didn't sound like himself, which caused people to speculate that he was seriously wounded, or perhaps even dead, with an impersonator making the audio statement.

> RT @AlaaAjJarban: I can swear it's not Saleh's voice on his audio tape now! This is crazy, could he really be dead? WTH is going on?? #Yemen #Sanaa[141]

> RT @gregorydjohnsen: Woah, he does not sound like himself – Salih #Yemen[142]

> RT @Hisham_G: #Yemen president #Saleh just gave very short audio address on state TV. His voice sounded terribly frail.[143]

> RT @AlaaAjJarban: #Saleh's audio speech is the weirdest thing I have ever heard my whole life! Could he really be dead? I'm pretty sure it wasn't him. #Yemen[144]

> RT @blakehounshell: Just hearing Saleh's statement now. . . heavy breathing and it sounds like his mouth has been damaged or something. Marbles.[145]

> RT @gregorydjohnsen: Well so much for Salih's speech putting an end to the rumors – twitter can sometimes function like a virtual qat chew. #Yemen[146]

> RT @YemenPeaceNews #Saleh doesn't sound good in that recorded message. But he doesn't sound dead, either. #Yemen[147]

Eventually the facts began to emerge, by way of the Saudi Arabian government: President Saleh had been injured and transported out of Yemen to Riyadh for treatment.[148] The exact nature of his injuries remained unclear, but there were numerous online reports of him being wounded in the back of the head.

As we awaited more details, I received this tweet from a political science student who goes by the name @menablog:

> RT @menablog: @acarvin Could it be real? tinyurl.com/6xgff4m[149]

The link brought me to an Arabic news story on the Yemeni website Alhasela.[150] It was about Saleh's injuries, and it showed a picture of him, intubated and apparently gravely ill, being treated by doctors.

I didn't buy it. The article said the photo was from an anonymous source, which rarely bodes well in circumstances such as this. And the photo just didn't look right. So I threw it over to my tweeps to see if they wanted to dissect it.

> Ok, photoshop geeks, scrutinize this pic. Could be really Saleh; fake; or dated. RT @menablog: Could it be real? tinyurl.com/6xgff4m[151]

No one else believed it was authentic, but everyone had different reasons.

> RT @Nasser_elMasri @acarvin The Doctor is wearing a name-tag holder with the word Palestine all over it. Impossible to be in Saudi[152]

> RT @warpafx: @acarvin He also seems to have grown another ear behind his left ear[153]

> RT @MaxDReinhardt: @acarvin It looks doctored. No pun intended.[154]

I noted some inconsistencies in the picture.

> Look at his forehead by the pillow and his neck along the gown he's wearing. I think I see crop marks. #SalehPic tinyurl.com/6xgff4m[155]

My Twitter followers continued their assessments.

> RT @toea: @acarvin Well for one, look at the skintones and color balance of the faces. The doc's is reddish, but Saleh's is yellowish[156]
>
> RT @menablog: @acarvin Some things that i noticed; timestamp says 2:26:26, does that correspond with his arrival in KSA[157]
>
> RT @GypsyDesert: @acarvin pillow is too fluffy fir the weight..[158]
>
> RT @franniefabian: @acarvin Looks false. Looks like different camera iso's (you can see the graininess) on the doctor than on saleh's face.[159]
>
> RT @danjukic: @acarvin PS for sure. Tip offs: Neck line. Can see color through mask that doesn't fit. Skin tone off. Size of head too large.[160]
>
> RT @volks: @acarvin Photoshopped for sure: Using error level analysis, you can see the points where it was shopped: tinyurl.com/3hfvygr[161]
>
> RT @GypsyDesert: @acarvin his hair was silverish, but in hospital pic is jet black![162]
>
> RT @SubMedina: @acarvin tyrant hair club for men syndrome.[163]

Some of the most damning evidence came from trauma nurse @sandymaxey in Asheville, North Carolina.

> RT @sandymaxey: @acarvin The length of the endotracheal tube/junction of where ventilator tubing connects is too long. I am skeptical of legitimacy[164]
>
> RT @sandymaxey: @shiftingbalance @acarvin The pic suggests a naso-tracheal intubation, yet the proportions and attachments are not accurate.[165]
>
> RT @sandymaxey: acarvin If he was truly *critical* can't fathom anyone in their right mind would slap tape on a bandage/attach to a gown.[166]
>
> RT @sandymaxey: @acarvin If he were a head trauma, I would expect him to be in this postion, except his head wld be in alignment w/body. Blood flow issue[167]

> RT @sandymaxey: @acarvin Look at the diameter of the tube as it comes out of his nose. Not congruent w/diameter of tubing connecting to vent tubing.[168]

As we concluded our debate about the photo, Bahraini doctor @MoMustafaMD pointed out that the news site that originally circulated the photo had now retracted it for unknown reasons.

> RT @MoMustafaMD: @acarvin bit.ly/j66tMQ they just updated the page, the title says the photo is fabricated now.[169]

A picture may speak a thousand words, but in this case it could have sparked a thousand rumors if we hadn't nipped it in the bud.

In the days following President Saleh's evacuation to a Saudi hospital, more details emerged about his condition. CNN reported that 40 percent of his body had been burned, including his hands and face, and he had a collapsed lung.[170] Over the course of several weeks, Saleh would occasionally appear in front of a camera, which documented – and sometimes raised more questions about – his recovery. Two months after the assassination attempt, he left Saudi Arabia, but did not return home to Yemen.

The two sides maintained a fragile ceasefire, but it didn't last long. On several occasions, the bloodshed resumed, leaving more dead protesters in its wake.

In late September 2011, President Saleh returned to Yemen, appearing weaker than usual, but undeterred. While he and politicians across the region debated the terms of his resignation, protester Tawakkol Karman – the woman I first encountered in a video conference call six months earlier – was awarded the Nobel Peace Prize. Most people expected an Arab Spring-related Peace Prize would go to someone from Tunisia or Egypt, particularly someone who had been active both online and offline, but for some of us she was a dark horse candidate.[171] Her win gave many Yemenis an immense sense of pride, but it was bittersweet; President Saleh was still around, dithering about resigning as protesters continued to die on the streets of Yemen.

In late November 2011, Saleh finally put pen to paper and confirmed he would resign. As many protesters feared, it took an immunity deal brokered by regional diplomats to get him to step down. There would be no trial, no prison term. Though he was no longer in office, the activists felt that Saleh had gotten away with murder. His vice president, Abd Rabbuh Mansur al-Hadi, became interim president, and free elections were scheduled for February 2012.

The election could have been a transformative moment for Yemeni politics, but that wasn't in the cards. Interim President al-Hadi was the only name on the ballot.

Al-Hadi received nearly 100 percent of the vote. Just as President Ben Ali of Tunisia, President Mubarak of Egypt and yes, President Saleh of Yemen, did before him.

SYRIA

Outing A Gay Girl in Damascus

> We do not know who took her, so we do not know who to ask to get her back. . .If they wanted to kill her, they would have done so. That is what we are all praying for.[1]

Gay Girl In Damascus. If you put together the world's savviest bloggers and challenged them to come up with an attention-grabbing name for a blog, I'm not sure they could think of something more provocative than that. A Syrian-American woman named Amina Abdallah Arraf came up with the title when she launched her blog in February 2011, just prior to the start of the Syrian uprising.

Her timing couldn't have been better. Amina lived in the U.S. before moving to Syria in 2010, well before the Arab Spring was on the minds of anyone. Once the uprising started, she was positioned to be one of its most unique chroniclers.

Amina's blog posts were blunt, passionate, in-your-face. She made no bones about being a lesbian living in a conservative Muslim society, and was openly contemptuous of President Bashar al-Assad and his government. Of all of her prolific writings, it was her post "My Father The Hero" that captured the imagination of Internet users in the West. The post tells the story of her father confronting two policemen trying to arrest her.

> "Did she tell you that she likes to sleep with women?" [the policeman] grins, pure poison, feeling like he has made a hit. "That she is one of those faggots who fucks little girls?" (the arabic he used is far cruder . . . you get the idea)
>
> My dad glances at me. I nod; we understand each other.
>
> "She is my daughter," he says and I can see the anger growing in his eyes, "and she is who she is and if you want her, you must take me as well. . . ."
>
> "Your father," he says to the [other policeman] who threatened to rape me, "does he know this is how you act? He was an officer, yes? And he served in . . ." (he mentions exactly and then turns to the other) "and your mother? Wasn't she the daughter of . . .?"
>
> They are both wide-eyed, yes, that is right,
>
> "What would they think if they heard how you act? And my daughter? Let me tell you this about her; she has done many things that, if I had been her, I would not have done. But she has never once stopped being

> my daughter and I will never once let you do any harm to her. You will not take her from here. And, if you try, know that generations of her ancestors are looking down on you. Do you know what is our family name? You do? Then you know where we stood when Muhammad, peace be upon him, went to Medina, you know who it was who liberated al Quds, you know too, maybe, that my father fought to save this country from the foreigners and who he was, know who my uncles and my brothers were . . . and if that doesn't shame you enough, you know my cousins and you will leave here. . . ."
>
> "And right now, you two will both apologize for waking her and putting her through all this. Do you understand me?"
>
> The first one nodded, then the second one.
>
> "Go back to sleep," he said, "we are sorry for troubling you."[2]

Amina became the poster child of the Arab Spring blogosphere. Media outlets profiled her, including the *Guardian* newspaper – which somehow managed to conduct an in-person interview in Damascus, despite travel restrictions on journalists.[3] With each feature story, Amina's notoriety spread to a broader mainstream audience; it also encouraged other news outlets to play catch-up and chase down interviews with her. Her stock was rising faster than any other blogger in the Middle East.

And then she was kidnapped.

In early June 2011, I noticed a tweet from Rami Nakhla, a Syrian activist tweeting as @MalathAumran.

> RT @MalathAumran: Amina Abdallah: Please read the latest post on her blog http://j.mp/j5L2dZ #Syria[4]

When I read the post, written by a cousin named Rania Ismail, I was stunned.

> Amina was seized by three men in their early 20s. According to the witness (who does not want her identity known), the men were armed. . . .
>
> . . .We do not know who took her, so we do not know who to ask to get her back. It is possible that they are forcibly deporting her. From other family members who have been imprisoned there, we believe that she is likely to be released fairly soon. If they wanted to kill her, they would have done so. That is what we are all praying for.[5]

I couldn't believe what I was reading. The most prominent English-speaking blogger in Syria had been nabbed. I retweeted Rami Nakhla, exclaiming, "Dear

God – she's been kidnapped?"[6] then dashed out another tweet emphasizing the gravity of the situation:

> According to a post on her blog, Gay Girl in Damascus has been kidnapped. Absolutely horrible if true. http://bit.ly/j5L2dZ #syria[7]

It didn't take long for word of Amina's kidnapping to spread across the region. You could almost sense the horror in the tweets of Leil-Zahra Mortada, herself a lesbian activist based out of Egypt.

> RT @LeilZahra: People at home, plz start making noise about the abduction of blogger Amina Abdallah. Fax #Syria embassy in ur country. #FreeAmina[8]

Another activist, @Razaniyat, issued a call-to-action to organize a campaign on Facebook for Amina's release.

> RT @Razaniyat: Join our call to free Amina Arraf author of Gay Girl in Damascus here on Facebook http://on.fb.me/kBDwep #Syria[9]

And in Canada, far from the chaos of the Middle East, Amina's girlfriend Sandra Bagaria quietly joined in, her words plaintive and direct.

> RT @sade_la_bag: Please #FreeAmina http://damascusgaygirl.blogspot.com/2011/06/amina.html[10]

The race was on to find Amina Arraf.

I had no illusions; it would be next to impossible to determine her location. She could be imprisoned in a police station, an army barracks, or in – I didn't even want to consider worse places she might be detained. Syrian civilians had been brutalized in ways scarcely imaginable: children castrated, women skinned and dismembered. The depravity of their torturers knew no bounds. And now, at that very moment, Amina could be staring into the eyes of one of those monsters.

I privately messaged my Syrian contacts to learn more about Amina. According to one of them, she had attended at least one meeting of the Damascus Local Coordination Committee, the core group of activists organizing protests in the capital. He wasn't at the meeting, but was told by a fellow activist that she participated.

In public conversations on Twitter, Amina's friends and supporters mobilized. The hashtag #FreeAmina gained steam. Competing Facebook pages sprung up supporting her cause. One featured an ink-like rendering of Amina. "Borders mean NOTHING when you have WINGS," it said, quoting a poem from her blog. "FREE AMINA ARRAF."[11]

The picture made me realize I didn't know what she looked like. I went back to my Twitter stream to see if any of my contacts tracked down any photos. One of them, @Bsyria, wrote:

> RT @Bsyria: These are two pictures of Amina Arraf (A Gay Girl in Damascus). I found them online http://j.mp/jmSQpm http://j.mp/lfjyPI #FreeAmina #Syria[12]

The photos looked like the inspiration for the Facebook artwork. Amina was pretty, probably in her late twenties or early thirties. She had dark brown hair, distinctive cheekbones, an elegant neck and a conspicuous mole above her left eyebrow.

Wanting more details, I tweeted:

> Can anyone confirm that these 2 pics are of #Amina, eg Gay Girl In Damascus? http://j.mp/jmSQpm http://j.mp/lfjyPI #syria[13]

Soon I got a terse reply from @Bsyria.

> RT @Bsyria: @acarvin, I got them confirmed first.[14]

I intended no offense on my part; I just wanted to be sure that these photos were authentic.

> @BSyria Yeah, I saw – thanks. . . Just trying to find people who know her in person.[15]

I messaged more Syrian contacts; they hadn't met her either, but shared mutual friends. Getting those friends to talk, though, was a non-starter. Even when you're on good terms with Syrian activists, it's often difficult to get them to connect you with other protesters. They don't want to put anyone's life at risk.

Then there was Amina's girlfriend, Sandra Bagaria. She was still doing her best to get the word out from Montreal.

> RT @sade_la_bag: Working on my social media skills to help #FreeAmina and spread the word out. . .Keep the momentum. #Syria[16]
>
> RT @sade_la_bag: #FreeAmina OK I need to think straight now. . . Since lunch I cant eat. Facebook page http://www.facebook.com/FreeAminaArraf #Syria[17]

No doubt I'd have to talk to Sandra. I could only imagine her anxiety.

After spending hours trawling through countless Twitter feeds and Facebook discussions about Amina, I almost missed the emails in my inbox.

They were direct messages from @DannySeesIt, a gay Syrian man I'd met online during the Egyptian revolution. The DMs appeared to be in reference to my earlier comment about trying to find people who knew Amina in person. He's given me permission to republish them.[18]

> I dunno if you heard about Amina, gay girl in Damas. I have it from a good source that she is a fictional character. She isn't a real person
>
> I'm asking about that today most of the day and I have some solid connection in the lesbian scene in Damascus. No one knows her.
>
> I just needed to tell someone; It upsets me as this whole madness is bringing too much attention to LGBT people in critical times like this.
>
> I believe all the negative authority attention Amina is bringing to LGBT people might eff us up all soon.

I was taken aback. Was Amina who she said she was? Syria isn't the kind of country where being openly gay is common practice. From everything I'd heard, the LGBT community in Damascus was pretty tight-knit, so you'd think many of them would know of each other.

I wrote back to him:

> I have from a good source that she is indeed real. We'll see, though.

Danny, however, was insistent.

> I can tell you from experience that the post titled my father the hero doesn't make sense whatsoever. They [the secret police] either ask you to come over. . . yourself to have a chat (usually friendly) or arrest her no matter who her father is. It's as simple as that.
>
> I asked over 40 contacts here about her. No one knows her and they all heard of her. Also, she uses [the blogging tool] blogspot to blog, which is blocked here [in Syria]
>
> The big question is if she fictionalized her arrest story too.

Was he onto something? The only way to find out was to track down someone who had met Amina in person. Her Facebook page was at least a year old, with well over 100 friends – many of whom I knew offline. At least one of them must've met her, right?

Wrong. All my queries turned up empty. I decided to ask my Twitter followers more directly this time.

> Just wanted to ask again: has anyone met #Amina (Gay Girl In Damascus) in person? If so, pls contact me.[19]

> If we can't find anyone who has met #Amina in person, is there anyone who has Skyped with her? Talked to her on the phone? #syria[20]

Among all of the journalists, protesters and fans who had sung Amina's praises for the past few months, there had to be at least a handful of people who had met her and would be willing to talk to me about it, even if it were off the record or on background.

Once again, I couldn't find anyone. This was getting really strange, because the Arab Spring's Twitter crowd is a grapevine of epic proportions: one way or another, you're never more than a few degrees of separation from everyone else. Yet here we had a woman who'd gone out of her way to make a name for herself, interacting with friends and fans on her blog, on Facebook, on email lists – you name it. How was it possible that no one had actually met her?

Later that day, a Syrian activist replied to me on Twitter and asked me to follow him, so he could direct-message me privately.[21] He sent a series of messages expressing skepticism about Amina's blog.

> You know the first post about her near brush with security?

> 1) Wayyy too dramatic

> 2) security forces sent to get you only have a list with your name on it. They don't know why they're getting you, and don't care

> 3) Security comes and gets you, then moves on. No moving father's speech will stop that.

> This is only one of many instances where I felt that her blogging were more of a catering to a special audience

> I might be wrong, and being wrong in this case is horrible. But it feels a lot like I'm right.

Just as I was about to respond, he cut off all communications with a final note to me:

> I have to unfollow you now, I'm sorry.

I tried messaging him, but all I got was an error message: *Twitter problem – not sent.*

Just as he said he would, he unfollowed me so I couldn't contact him privately.

Soon after I archived his messages for safekeeping, they vanished from my Twitter account, each one deleted in rapid succession. Wiped clean. It was as if our conversation never happened.

Not long after that exchange, I saw a tweet from a Syrian activist known as @seleukiden. I didn't know who he was or where he lived, but he always seemed to have provocative things to say. Which is why his tweet caught my attention, even though it wasn't directed to anyone in particular.

He later deleted the tweet, but I remember the gist of it:

> *This isn't going to end well for us.*

"Are you talking about #Amina?" I asked.[22]

He didn't want to talk about it.

Shit.

Even though I have no idea what @seleukiden looks like – hell, I'm not even positive about his gender – I imagined the look on his face. And that look was telling us we were being punked.

While online activists mobilized to save one of their most beloved Arab Spring bloggers, I had a sinking feeling that my Syrian sources were onto something. Sure, it was theoretically possible that Gay Girl In Damascus was simply a well-crafted hoax. But it would have to be a damn lucky one at that, since I knew a number of people who had gotten to know Amina online well before the Arab Spring.

More likely, she was a real blogger who covered her tracks to avoid arrest. This meant she could vanish without any of her real-life acquaintances knowing that she and Amina were the same person.

Maybe she'd been kidnapped. Perhaps she made up the story because she feared for her safety and wanted to disappear. Maybe she couldn't take the spotlight any more. I didn't know what to believe.

I had to tread carefully; if she truly were a kidnapped Syrian blogger, any public skepticism on my part could cause supporters to cease demanding her release. The Facebook pages might fade away; the #FreeAmina hashtag would stop trending. And all the while, Amina might be strapped down on a cold, damp gurney somewhere, with that monster breathing against her cheek, gently caressing her face with the end of a jumper cable.

For a moment I heard his voice. "Where shall we begin, *ya habibti*?"[23]

I couldn't bear something like that hanging on my conscience.

> Let me ask the question another way: does anyone know *anyone else* who's met Gay Girl In Damascus in person? #amina #syria[24]

Finally, I received several public reactions, including a tweet from a woman in Beirut going by the name of @shoofs.

> YES i do know Amina personally; I have conversed with her over chat and so have many of our common friends[25]

I responded:

> Have you met her in person or seen video of her while you chat?[26]

@shoofs continued:

> No but other friends have met her in person. why?[27]

Why?!? I guess this wasn't so obvious to everyone yet.

> It's just odd that I can't find anyone who has actually met her in person. Some people have raised questions so I'm investigating.[28]

@shoofs pushed back.

> a little propaganda theory thinking don't you agree! friends have met her personally. no need to investigate[29]

No need to investigate. I was worried I might get this reaction from her Internet friends. How could I blame them? I've known people online for over 15 years but haven't met them in person. How would I feel if some would-be investigator demanded proof of their existence?

Yeah, I'd be pissed, too.

Fortunately, not everyone was so dismissive. Paula Brooks, who ran a group blog for the lesbian community, offered her assistance:

> RT @LezGetReal: hi she blogs for me. . . . I might be able to help[30]

Good, I thought. I DMed her my email address so she could contact me privately.

And then there was the *Guardian* newspaper, the only news outlet I was aware of that had interviewed her in person. I had no idea how to go about contacting the paper's undercover reporter in Syria, but it was worth a shot. I emailed a managing editor and hoped that someone would get back to me soon.

Then I saw a blog post from the *New York Times*.

Robert Mackey is the blogger for The Lede, the *NYT's* highly regarded news blog. Mackey's a consummate pro—one of the best there is when it comes to monitoring what's happening online and distilling it into a compelling read. Earlier in the day, he had posted a story about Amina's disappearance, but now he had updated it with some observations about my recent tweets, as well as his own original reporting.

Robert described me as an "expert at debunking rumors" – I grimaced – and noted I was trawling for information on Amina. He also stated that Amina had launched another blog, four years earlier, in which she told her readers that it would contain elements of fiction.[31]

I hadn't come across Amina's older blog, so I gave it a quick look. I was stunned.

> *This blog is . . .*
> *. . . where I will be posting samples of fiction and literature I am working on.*
> *This blog will contain chapters and drafts.*
> *This blog will have what may sometimes seem likely deeply personal accounts. And sometimes they will be. But there will also be fiction.*
> *And I will not tell you which is which.*
> *This blog will sample what I'm writing.*
> *This blog is not a diary.*
> *This blog is not about politics.*
> *This blog invites your comments.*[32]

And I will not tell you which is which. She was openly admitting that her writings would be a mix of fact and fiction. How on earth would we separate which was which?

Amina's credibility as a nonfiction blogger was now in question. That raised the stakes even higher. A Syrian blogger with a penchant for artistic license *is still a Syrian blogger*. But her inner novelist now imperiled her in ways she probably never imagined.

It also sank in that the *New York Times* had outed me as an Amina skeptic. I wasn't trying to "debunk" anything; I just wanted to know the truth, especially if it could lead to determining her whereabouts. And now it was on the record: I was effectively calling bullshit on at least parts of her story.

I had no choice but to lay my cards on the table, so I posted a note online and tweeted a link to it.

> Regarding #Amina, aka Gay Girl In Damascus, here is what I know and don't know. Earlier this week I got a tip from an LGBT Syrian source who didn't believe Amina existed. They had told me they had asked around other members of the LGBT community and they couldn't find anyone who knew her. They also were very concerned that her blog posts were drawing attention to Syria's LGBT community in ways that could be dangerous for them.
>
> Independently of this, two other Syrian sources I knew mentioned similar speculation to me. They didn't say she was fictitious, per se, but they were skeptical of the circumstances described in her My Father The Hero blog post. My first source also expressed similar skepticism. Given

> their collective experiences with Syrian security services, they simply did not believe it was possible her father could protect her by shaming them into leaving the house. They said the men would have dragged her way no matter what. It didn't pass their personal sniff tests. . . .
>
> . . . So where does this leave us? I still have many more questions than answers, but I currently believe Amina is a real person, but one who is much more expressive about herself online than offline. It is possible that Amina Arraf is a pen name, to protect herself in Syria, but so far I can't prove it one way or another. If it is just a pen name, that might explain why the sources I talked to said they'd never met a person by that name. Even so, I wouldn't be surprised if I indeed found people who know her in person. It's just taking longer time than I would have liked. Much of this could be sorted out by contacting her reported American mother, but I hadn't been able to do that yet, which is why I haven't had much to say about the topic for the last few hours. I also felt that I didn't want to send people on a wild goose chase when it's quite possible she is indeed detained under very harsh conditions.
>
> Despite all the questions I have, I am deeply worried that this discussion about her identity could distract people from the possibility that [she] might be being brutalized in detention, and in dire need of support from friends and strangers alike. Having a pen name and writing occasional fiction on an otherwise real blog, if that is indeed true, is an academic discussion when compared with what she might indeed be going through.
>
> Whoever she is, wherever she is, I hope she is well and with us again online soon. -andy[33]

It was really important for people to understand that this wasn't about exposing a hoax per se. Yes, it was a possibility. But proclaiming Amina as fiction could be tantamount to a death sentence if she were indeed real.

Just in case I wasn't clear enough, I tweeted:

> I repeat: my greatest fear is that we're going on a wild goose chase re: #Amina's identity when it's very possible she's being brutalized.[34]
>
> I also worry that the fact that I was asking questions publicly made some so suspicious of her they're less likely to fight for her release.[35]

Soon I heard from people exhibiting their own skepticism. One person named @GypsyDesert hypothesized it probably was all a work of fiction:

> RT @GypsyDesert: According to your up-date :she will not reveal reality from fiction.she could be sitting w/ her hubby & sipping mint tea about now![36]

I responded:

> And that's what I'm concerned people will believe. Give her the benefit of the doubt while it's possible she's detained. . .[37]
>
> This is one of those situations where I had no choice but to ask some questions publicly. And it was easy to jump to conclusions from that.[38]

Another person, Oema Soso, worried about the impact of a potential hoax, including the dangers it might create for Arab bloggers.

> RT @oemasoso: horrible if #Amina is really kidnapped but bad if exposed as hoax cause this endangers future REAL cases not being taken serious.[39]
>
> RT @oemasoso: if #FreeAmina is indeed a virtual bubble copied by serious media after zero research this is a bad dev'ment in #ME #journalism[40]

I then received an email from a friend of Amina's. He wasn't happy with my cameo on the *New York Times* website.

> I realize that it's frustrating not being able to find anyone who had met her. But this is not a reason to question her existence, with all due respect. The Lede wrote about her in a way that makes it seems highly likely that she doesn't exist or that she's a fraud. As if someone is bored enough to travel all around the world, take photos, upload them to facebook, create a fake persona, create a whole imaginary life and write about it, and for no apparent reason.

Maybe he was right; I just didn't know.

> RT @Elizrael: If Amina's story is fake this is truly one of the cruelest jokes I've ever witnessed http://on.wsj.com/kjP4YK[41]

The next morning, I saw this tweet from another friend of Amina's, Elizabeth Tsurkov. It was clear she was devastated about something that transpired while I slept. The *Wall Street Journal*, I learned, investigated the Amina photos and discovered they were, in fact, a London-based Croatian woman named Jelena Lecic.

I compared the photos. Same neck, same hair, same jawline – same mole above the left eye.

For the first time, I was really tempted to tweet the word *hoax*. But that image of Amina in an interrogation room kept haunting me, seared into my mind just like that monster of an interrogator might. . .

Stop it. I'd drive myself crazy if I kept imagining the details. I'd seen enough videos from Syria to know what the regime was capable of.

I tweeted:

> Again, people should operate under the assumption that there is a real blogger under detention in Syria. Who they are is another matter.[42]

I then heard from Egyptian-American columnist Mona Eltahawy. She expressed frustration with the potential impact of my line of questioning.

> RT @monaeltahawy: "Gay Girl in Damascus" exists. Her girlfriend has verified so. Questioning her existence can jeopardize her life. Let's focus. #FreeAmina[43]
>
> RT @monaeltahawy: I don't care what her real name is or what her father's name us. #FreeAmina and thousands of others held by #Assad regime[44]

I understood where Mona was coming from, but I had to respond.

> I assume it was a pen name too. But her fb pictures weren't of her, says the WSJ, and no one seems to have met her.[45]

Mona shot back:

> RT @monaeltahawy: Why would she put her pics online – esp on Fcebook? That would be height of stupidity.[46]
>
> RT @monaeltahawy: I've said my bit on #FreeAmina. I'm not getting into any discussions – not while #Assad troops slaughter 100s of #Syrians and jail 1,000s.[47]

Mona had a point – it would've been downright dangerous for Amina to share pictures of herself on Facebook. But if that's the case, why post any pictures at all? Why take an entire collection of photos from a woman in London and purport them to be yours – even to your online girlfriend? Amina played a dangerous game by blogging from Syria, but her chances of being found were evaporating now that her precautions were sending everyone in circles.

Finally, I heard back from the *Guardian*. My email worked its way around the newsroom until it reached Katherine Marsh, the pseudonym of the paper's Damascus reporter. Her explanation raised more doubts.

> After getting in contact with her through by her email address – got from a Syrian contact in Damascus who said she knew Amina and

> emailed her to check it would be ok to pass on her details – she agreed to an interview.
>
> Meeting in Damascus comes with risks and she said she was not sure about meeting, coming in the wake of the entry about security agents entering her home. The Guardian said it would be very keen to meet her in person or talk on Skype. She said she was not using Skype. We agreed to carry out the interview by email in the meanwhile and agreed to a meeting up a couple of days afterwards.
>
> Amina agreed to meet on morning in a public location in Damascus. She sent a photo of herself – showing the same person as in the photos circulating [e.g., Jelena Lecic] – and described herself as fairly tall.
>
> The meeting never took place. As is usual with meetings in Damascus, it was agreed that if either party felt followed, they would not go through with the meeting. Amina did not show up and later emailed to say she saw security agents around the location and was afraid to meet.
>
> A day later she emailed to say she had gone into hiding with her father. She subsequently corresponded with the Guardian by email. She gave further information for the article, some off-record details of her hiding place as well as family information that she did not want published.
>
> From these, and her knowledge of Damascus and Syria, we believe she is a real person, Syrian (and with fluent English) and, at that time, was in the country. We cannot verify the images of her or the name being used are her real ones.

The same person as in the photos circulating. Amina used Jelena Lecic's photo to help the reporter recognize her when they were to meet in public.

That meant only one thing – she never intended to meet her in the first place. It was all a ruse.

I vented my growing doubts.

> *I truly hope #Amina is real, because the many hours I've spent on this would've otherwise been spent covering Syria, Yemen & Libya.*[48]

All of those hours. Multiply that by the hundreds of other people – thousands, even – who had redirected their energies for the last couple of days working to find Amina.

Somewhere in Syria, President Bashar al-Assad was laughing at us.

The next day I received an email from Sandra Bagaria, Amina's girlfriend. I asked her who she thought Amina actually was.

> Who is Amina? What runs in my head is that she could be a brilliant writer. She could be a Syrian woman that fights everyday this conflict and has hidden her real face. The question that I have is, why did she choose me?

I didn't know what to say to her. If Amina were truly a hoax, her cruelty to Sandra was nothing short of staggering.

Sandra said she once tried to call Amina using a phone number she'd received from her via email. No one answered. Later, Amina claimed she was out with her father.

Sandra supplied the number. My colleague Ahmed Al Omran gave it a call. It was a Syrian pharmacy; they'd never heard of an Amina Arraf.

Countless people were now investigating the Amina case. The State Department tried to track her down in their databases of U.S. citizens, without any luck. People on Twitter such as Elizabeth Tsurkov chased down their own leads. Paula Brooks of Lez Get Real, Jillian York of the Electronic Frontier Foundation, online identity expert Liz Henry and the team at the blog Electronic Intifada were all hard at work.

Everyone was passing along the latest tips and theories, either publicly or via email. This had become an open-source missing-person hunt.

Back at NPR, my colleague Eyder Peralta and I worked with our librarians to search public databases for any trace of Amina or her family's names. Property records, court records, news databases – all dead ends. We also set up a white board so we could map whatever connections Amina had to other individuals.

Then Paula Brooks of Lez Get Real found a tantalizing lead. Because Amina had written for Paula's blog, she left an online paper trail, including what's known as an *IP address*. Everything that's connected to the Internet has its own IP address, which is traceable to its general location, anywhere on earth.

According to Paula, Amina posted to the blog with two separate IP addresses. She did some digging and traced the addresses to Edinburgh, Scotland.

Edinburgh? What the hell was Amina doing in Edinburgh? Then again, she had mentioned Edinburgh on her blog; she had once considered a graduate program of some sort at the University of Edinburgh.

Of course, it's not unusual for activists trying to protect themselves online to use *proxy servers*, which allow them to connect in such a way that their location appears to be somewhere else. So maybe Edinburgh was another smokescreen. Maybe not.

Either way, Paula Brooks was unnerved by the discovery, and the implication that Amina wasn't who she said she was. Back at the office, Eyder managed to get Paula on the phone – or more accurately, Paula's father, as Paula was deaf and needed him to translate.

"I am about frantic here," Paula said. "Amina and I got close in these last six months. . .I don't know what to do or think now."

"Frantic" is relative, of course; Paula was safe at home in the U.S. Members of the LGBT community in the Middle East, however, had every right to be *truly* frantic. One woman I talked with described a very troubling rumor in which Amina was an undercover operation by the Syrian regime to infiltrate their community, since many of them were also active in protest circles.[49]

> "Amina" was on some private Arab lesbian lists & as every1 on the list had access to private info about them. There is some panic
>
> I don't think she is a spy/mole, I'm trying my best to calm ever1. My hunch comes from not finding a solid benefit to anyone
>
> I really hate the course this has taken, and I want to do all my best to get the attention back on the real issues.
>
> I'm also worried if "Amina" is partially real & is under arrest, and everyone is stopping pressure, we might be handing her over.

Another lead came via Elizabeth Tsurkov. She had been contacted by a man who claimed to have known Amina for five years. If this were true, it would be a major breakthrough; we'd been unable to find anyone who had known her for more than a year. I asked Elizabeth to put me in touch with him.

The man, whom I'll call James, said he'd gotten to know Amina on a science fiction email discussion group called the Sterling list. James said she'd been on the list since at least 2006, and over the years she provided a number of details about herself.

As we emailed back and forth, James agreed to get me information from a fellow list member, whom I'll call Steven, who had contacted Amina by postal mail.

Steven refused to talk to me directly; he was concerned for his job. I asked James to serve as intermediary and ask him what he knew about Amina. A little while later, James forwarded me Steven's reply:

> I have known Amina on line for roughly five years
>
> I have never met her in person
>
> To the best of my knowledge none of my other web friends from the linked group of lists has either
>
> I have never spoken with her on the phone
>
> I have sent holiday cards for years – none ever returned by USPS [the U.S. Postal Service]
>
> I have sent other mail – none ever returned by USPS
>
> I sent a check as a wedding present – someone cashed it

A wedding present?!? By all accounts, Amina was gay, not bisexual – and there was no mention on her blog of being married. Was it possible we were dealing with two different Amina Arrafs?

James didn't think so. "Amina's views on the blog are consistent with what she's said on our lists," he wrote me. "[She] had an extremely deep knowledge of Syria and Arab ethnic history." James also said that Amina often talked about being married.

It was quite likely that Amina – the email list version – was the same person as Amina, the Gay Girl In Damascus version. They *had* to be connected. But every new lead just spawned more questions than answers. Gay or straight, real or fake, Amina was quite the hydra.

James supplied me with Amina's postal address – *Amina Arraf & Ian Lazarus, care of Mr. and Mrs. Abdallah Arraf-Omari* – similar to her father's name on her blog.

The address itself was in Stone Mountain, Georgia. This was also consistent with her blog, as she claimed she attended school in Georgia. My colleague Eyder contacted her high school and university; neither had any record of her.

I passed along the address to one of NPR's research librarians, who went back to take another look at some of databases we had tried previously. We got some hits in a property records database, but they didn't seem very helpful. There were three names associated with the address, and none came close to a match. All we could find was a Newson, a Branch and a MacMaster.

"Do you know about Cresentland?" James asked me.

I didn't, so I googled and found TheCrescentLand, an email discussion list. It was a private group, which meant I couldn't see its messages or members, but the public description suggested it was about finding common ground in the Middle East.

I submitted a request to join the list, then received an automated email. *Request denied.*

Whoever was managing the list either didn't know who I was or didn't want me joining it. I mentioned it to James and he said I should try again and include a note saying he'd vouch for me.

So that's the kind of list it was – only people who knew the secret handshake could participate.

This time, I received a reply approving my membership. I posted a short note to the group, explaining who I was and that I was interested in talking with them about Amina's disappearance.

Shortly after I posted, someone deleted the entire list.

Nuked it. *Gone.* One of the administrators of TheCrescentLand had taken the extraordinary step of erasing everything – its archive of thousands of messages, the membership list, even the public description. It was as if it had never existed.

Seems like I had just spooked the crap out of someone.

I immediately contacted James. He said only two people had authority to delete the list. One of them was a friend of his who allowed me to join it a few minutes earlier. The other was Amina Arraf. Having said that, James continued, Amina once admitted sharing her password with Rania Ismail – the cousin who had supposedly authored the blog post about Amina's kidnapping. Theoretically, Rania might've been the one who deleted it.

I went on Facebook to try to message Rania. Her account had been deleted. I then checked Amina's account – also gone. A Facebook page promoting her blog had also been wiped clean from the social network. Even *online dating profiles* she had created on other websites had vanished.

Someone out there was panicking, erasing Amina's virtual paper trail.

Almost a week had passed since this mess began, and I had to go to New York for an event at Columbia University's journalism school. No doubt there would be interest in discussing Gay Girl. I planned to collect my thoughts during the four-hour train ride from Washington.

Somewhere en route, I started getting messages from people asking if I'd seen the latest blog post from the guys at ElectronicIntifada.net. I hadn't. The article, written by Ali Abunimah and Benjamin Doherty, was called "New Evidence About Amina, The 'Gay Girl Damascus' Hoax."

There was that word: *hoax.* And they put the blame squarely on an American living in Edinburgh.

His name was Tom MacMaster.

Abunimah and Doherty had tracked down the people who also once lived at Amina's address in Georgia. One of the prior residents, MacMaster, was a graduate student at the University of Edinburgh. He is also married to someone named Britta Froelicher – a Syria expert at the University of St. Andrews, Scotland.

They confronted MacMaster via email, but he denied any involvement:

> I am not the blogger in question. Whomever that person 'really' is, I have doubtless interacted with her at some point. I do not know further than that about hert. . . .
>
> Unfortunately, we're on vacatio. . . . We have already been 'confronted' by the Washington post with these and have denied them and will continue to do so."[50]

So the *Washington Post* was hot on their trail, too? Not surprising.

Abunimah and Doherty had taken the disparate information that had been assembled about Amina and connected the dots before the rest of us: Tom MacMaster, former resident of Stone Mountain, Georgia, now living in Edinburgh. The IP addresses from Paula Brooks pointed to Edinburgh. A photo on Amina's Facebook page was almost identical to a photo Tom's wife had posted at Picasa.com.

All the evidence pointed at Tom MacMaster and Britta Froelicher. But they categorically denied it.

My NPR colleague Eyder Peralta tracked down Britta and emailed her for comment. She replied tersely:

> "I'm in Turkey at the moment on vacation. I don't have the time or inclination to talk about it."

Meanwhile, blogger Liz Henry posted her own thoughts on the research collectively done by her, me, Paula Brooks, the Electronic Intifada guys and others. She made a staggering accusation: that Paula Brooks herself might be in on it.

> A couple of days ago I realized LezGetReal.com editor Paula Brooks, who had worked with Amina, was being interviewed by mainstream media. Brooks had not communicated by voice to the reporters — only over email or chat. Brooks' online presence looked a bit thin. Ben and Ali [of Electronic Intifada] tried to verify any of the facts of her education and employment, and could not find evidence of Paula Brooks' existence. I spoke with people who were close to Brooks and should have met her — but who had never seen her.
>
> I have no direct evidence that Brooks is Tom MacMaster, but circumstantial evidence shows it is a good avenue for research. If Brooks is *another distinct hoaxer*, that will be very odd, and will need more investigation.[51]

Was Paula a red herring? It was certainly possible, but truly strange if true, since Paula was the person who helped us connect the dots to Edinburgh. So if Paula were indeed MacMaster, that would only make sense if she – or do I mean *he?* – wanted to get caught and confess to being Amina.

Then there was the other possibility Liz Henry raised – that Paula was a fake persona created by someone other than MacMaster or his wife. Two fake lesbians who accidentally collided in a vortex of deception and geopolitical intrigue? I wasn't ready to go there.

I still had one more lead to investigate – the Picasa photo gallery mentioned by Electronic Intifada. Battling the gremlins of crappy Internet access as my train crossed the Chesapeake, I looked at the pictures, including an album of photos from a Syria trip in 2008.

Amina's girlfriend Sandra, meanwhile, began texting me via Skype. She'd read the Electronic Intifada post and was now digging for information about MacMaster and Froelicher.

Then she emailed me.

> I GOT HER!!
>
> 
>
> The Syrian pictures that she put of Syria corresponds to the one I have received!!!!

Sandra told me that Amina had sent her several photos identical to the ones in Britta Froelicher's album. She sent me the photos and Amina's comments about them.

"here're a couple around the neighborhood," Amina wrote of one of the photos, which she claimed to have just taken for Sandra. When Sandra had asked her why she wasn't in any of them, Amina replied, "no; i took all the pictures and never posed for any."

I asked Sandra if she could look at the metadata of the photos she had received. Metadata are the bits of information that a digital camera includes with each photograph – the time and date it was taken, the shutter speed, and so on. Meanwhile, Eyder and I looked at the metadata of the photos on Britta's photo album; there wasn't much there. Most likely she had cropped the photos or edited them in such a way that the original data was lost.

Sandra's copies of the photos, however, gave up their secrets immediately. One of them, an image of a mosque, looked just like one of Britta's photos. It was photographed from exactly the same angle and featured the same blue sky – even the same three birds circling around the minaret. The metadata dated it February 7, 2008.

Other photos appeared to be exact matches. But the metadata was even more damning. Whoever sent Sandra the pictures possessed the original, unaltered photos from 2008. Britta had uploaded cropped versions of them to the Web three years later. There was no way that Amina could've taken these pictures for Sandra in 2011; they were old pictures. This was probably as close to a smoking gun as we'd get.

Eyder and I emailed Britta one more time, including our metadata analysis. And then we waited.

I was now somewhere just north of Philly; the Internet connection from my wireless card was crashing every few minutes.

Why the fuck can't wireless companies get their signals to work on the most traveled train route in North America?!?

Less than an hour later, Britta replied; we had reached end game.

> The blog is being updated. We urge you to read that statement. We are on vacation in Turkey and just really want to have a nice time and not deal with all this craziness at the moment.

The blog is being updated. That could only mean Tom MacMaster and Britta Froelicher were ready to confess to the world.

I don't think I've ever reloaded a website so many times in my life. There was nothing new on the Gay Girl In Damascus homepage, but assuming Tom and Britta were sincere about updating it, I wanted to be the first to see their confession.

The Internet connection crashed again.

Restart, reconnect. . . .

Refresh, refresh, REFRESH, goddammit!

Please let the Internet not crash outside Trenton Please please please

And then a new post appeared: "Apology To Readers."

> I never expected this level of attention. While the narrative voice may have been fictional, the facts on this blog are true and not misleading as to the situation on the ground. I do not believe that I have harmed anyone – I feel that I have created an important voice for issues that I feel strongly about.
>
> I only hope that people pay as much attention to the people of the Middle East and their struggles in this year of revolutions. The events there are being shaped by the people living them on a daily basis. I have only tried to illuminate them for a western audience.

> This experience has sadly only confirmed my feelings regarding the often superficial coverage of the Middle East and the pervasiveness of new forms of liberal Orientalism.

> However, I have been deeply touched by the reactions of readers.
>
> Best,
> Tom MacMaster,
> Istanbul, Turkey
> July 12, 2011
> The sole author of all posts on this blog[52]

A rush of adrenaline coursing through my veins, I frantically tweeted:

> And we have a confession: Tom MacMaster is #Amina![53]

It was over. After nearly a week of tireless searching by friends and skeptics alike, Amina Arraf had been outed as a scruffy, 40-year-old American in Scotland. And this wasn't a hoax launched during the Syrian uprising – he masqueraded as Amina *for at least five years.*

I re-read Tom's confession. "I do not believe that I have harmed anyone. . .This experience has sadly only confirmed my feelings regarding the often superficial coverage of the Middle East and the pervasiveness of new forms of liberal Orientalism. . . ."

What on earth was he talking about? This was "an apology to readers?" It sounded more like a smug lecture from an unrepentant brat caught with his hand in the cookie jar.

As word of the blog post spread, my adrenaline rush turned to anger.

> If we could only calculate the sheer number of hours we spent this week on #Amina, each one of which was an hour spent not on Syria itself.[54]
>
> Is it wrong for me to be suddenly getting rather angry about all of this? #Amina #Tom #hoax[55]

The wave of rage spread across Twitter. Online free speech activist Jillian York, who had spent an enormous amount of time trying to help Amina, was livid.

> RT @jilliancyork: No, I'm furious. Wasted my time, wasted my government's time, wasted journalists' time, hurt some vulnerable individuals.[56]
>
> RT @jilliancyork: Whole thing was a hoax perpetuated by some pathetic, attention-needy American man.[57]
>
> RT @jilliancyork: Creating falsehoods about a country when there are real tragedies is not helpful; deception only fuels more distrust.[58]

Tarek Amr, an Egyptian blogger and editor for Global Voices, chimed in.

> RT @gr33ndata: And the media that gave that stupid case all that attention is to be blamed too. Since day one, it was so fishy[59]

Elizabeth Tsurkov, who had known Amina online for months and considered her a friend, didn't mince words about MacMaster.

> RT @Elizrael: He is truly one of the cruelest people I've ever had the misfortune of knowing. He hurt me and others who cared deeply about Amina.[60]

Rami Nakhla, the Syrian activist who had first alerted me to the kidnapping post, took it in stride.

> RT @MalathAumran: i regret nothing & i will do the same thousands time 4 any case likes Amina case & being a Hoax its his problem not ours #freeAmina[61]

But Lobna Darwish, a lesbian Egyptian activist, was unforgiving.

> RT @Lobna: How arrogant is a white man to think he can simply put on the hat of the brown queer woman, fuckin outrageous[62]
>
> RT @Lobna: I don't even want to think about the headlines tomorrow in Syria. The fucker.[63]
>
> RT @Lobna: next time i claim to be an Arab lesbian, I'll be asked to show some proof #A7a #FuckTomMacMaster[64]

Amid the torrents of tweets, the ultimate victim of MacMaster's betrayal – Amina's girlfriend Sandra – tweeted perhaps the most dignified attempt at closure one might imagine.

> RT @sade_la_bag: I'm deeply hurt. But now it's time to take care of the ones that actually fight for freedom and deserve it. #arabspring[65]

The next morning, MacMaster began to give interviews; Eyder managed to get him on the phone.[66] He claimed to have created Amina over five years earlier so he could have honest discussions regarding the Middle East. A Syrian-American woman, he surmised, would be able to participate in more sincere, in-depth conversations than some random American guy would.

Ironically, when he decided to have Amina move to Syria in 2010, he was attempting to take a break from the persona. Then the Arab Spring happened and things heated up in Syria; he decided to launch a blog about her life in Damascus.

The blog became a runaway success – so much so, MacMaster claimed, that he couldn't keep up with it any more. He was concerned his story was unraveling. So he had the character kidnapped, hoping she could just disappear amidst the chaos of the uprising.

"Hopefully everything will blow over," MacMaster told Eyder, "and people can really focus on the real human tragedy of what's really happening in Syria."

It seemed a bit late for that.

Just when I thought the Gay Girl saga couldn't get any stranger, it did. As Liz Henry prognosticated, the final twist was about Paula Brooks. Elizabeth Flock and Melissa Bell of the *Washington Post*, who had doggedly pursued the Amina case from the start, got Paula Brooks to offer a confession of her own.

No, she wasn't Tom MacMaster. She was *yet another American man* pretending to be a lesbian.

> "Paula Brooks," editor of Lez Get Real since its founding in 2008, is actually Bill Graber, 58, who said he is a retired Ohio military man and construction worker that had adopted his wife's identity online. Graber said she was unaware he had been using her name on his site. . .
>
> In the guise of Paula Brooks, Graber corresponded online with Tom MacMaster, thinking he was writing to Amina Arraf. Amina often flirted with Brooks, neither of the men realizing the other was pretending to be a lesbian.[67]

What had started as a desperate search for a missing activist had descended into farce. As one person tweeted:

> RT @TommyGalante: Story of the Internet. Dudes pretending to be chicks from places they aren't at. It happens to the best of us. Unfortunate though[68]

The next 24 hours were a blur. I don't know how many interviews I did. One clip of me even found its way onto *The Daily Show* during a segment about Amina.[69] And a Taiwanese YouTube channel that specializes in creating computer animations about random news stories created one about Gay Girl In Damascus. I had a cameo as a balding Asian version of Seinfeld's George Costanza, magically communicating with Twitter birds fluttering around my head. Then it showed me rushing into Amina's office to rip off her wig, exposing a mortified Tom MacMaster.[70]

This was getting ridiculous.

Within a few days, most people moved on to other news stories. But the consequences of Gay Girl In Damascus would likely be on the minds of Middle Eastern bloggers for a long time, including one from Lebanon named Mustapha. Yes, he's a real blogger; I've met him in person.

Mustapha wrote a blog post titled "Thank You Tom MacMaster."[71]

> I don't know who you are, but I already know that you're a prick.
>
> You say you never expected this kind of attention? Bullshit! A gay girl in Damascus who writes in perfectly good English? A damsel in distress who's easy on the eyes and fights tyranny in her country, only in the end to be kidnapped by regime goons? Can there be a more effective attention grabbing device? A prick and a liar you are Mr. MacMaster.
>
> Thanks for deceiving tens of thousands of people into supporting "Amina", joining Facebook groups and changing our avatars on Twitter.

> Thank you for making us all look like idiots and for diverting our attention from the real people who are being tortured in Syrian jails..
>
> You have forever tarnished the reputation of bloggers in this region who chose to write in English. *One day if I'm kidnapped by my government, many readers won't care because I could turn out to be another Amina.* A fictional entity concocted by a western fool who had good intentions.

From the very moment I heard about Amina's kidnapping, I tried to reiterate that we shouldn't assume Amina was a hoax unless proven otherwise. We had to assume she was real and under grave threat. Calling her a hoax before we were 100 percent sure would have meant the death of Amina.

If Amina had actually been a real gay girl in Damascus.

Raw Footage

The scene is a morgue, and the camera shows the upper body of a cadaver – a young teenage boy. His face is bruised and swollen, showing the hallmarks of a vicious beating. Cigarette burns dot his chest. He is covered in flower petals.

> "Here is another freedom martyr. . .He is 13 years old."

As the camera zooms in on a bullet hole in his chest, a doctor describes innumerable desecrations to the boy's body.

> ". . .He was subjected to extreme torture. . ."

There are bullet holes in each arm; each bullet also penetrated the sides of his chest. The doctor points to another wound.

> "Here is another bullet in his belly."

The camera pans slowly to the boy's face. It is almost swollen beyond recognition.

> "Look at all the bruises on his face; there is evidence that his neck was broken."

Gingerly, the doctor takes hold of the boy's chin, slowly turning his head back and forth. It rotates unnaturally.

The camera pans to his feet. His left calf has an enormous black contusion. Both kneecaps are smashed.

> "As if all this torture was not enough for them, they cut off his penis before they shot him."

The footage goes out of focus as it points to his groin. It's intentionally blurred, but still clear enough to make out the mutilation.

> "Where is Human Rights Watch, the International Criminal Court and freedom activists from what is happening in Syria?!?"

The camera zooms in on the boy's groin and pauses, demanding you bear witness.

It's May 25, 2011. His name was Hamza Al-Khatib.[1]

Of all the Arab Spring revolutions, Syria's has been the longest and most brutal. Initially, it received scant attention, with the media focusing heavily on Libya and elsewhere. Then in March 2011, two months prior to Hamza Al-Khatib's murder, a group of kids in the city of Deraa spray-painted a wall. They scrawled a slogan made popular in Tunisia that now echoed far and wide across the Arab world:

Ash-sha`b. . .yurid. . .isqat an-nizam!

The people. . . demand. . . the fall of the regime!

A policeman caught them in the act and arrested them. It should've resulted in a fine and a dressing-down by officers before releasing them. Instead they were beaten and detained.

Repression isn't new in Syria. Since the 1960s, the country has been ruled by the al-Assad family, members of a minority religious sect called the Alawites. Syria is religiously diverse, but the majority of its citizens are Sunni Muslims – traditional adversaries of Shia Islam, of which the Alawites are an offshoot.

Consolidating their power base, the Assad family appointed Alawites to the country's most important posts. They dominated the military and intelligence services. They controlled a disproportionate amount of the country's major industries. And there was little the rest of Syria's citizens could do about it.

Hafez al-Assad, the first member of the family to serve as Syrian president, had no qualms about using violence to control the population. His security forces routinely arrested and tortured dissidents. In 1982, when the Muslim Brotherhood tried to exert authority over the city of Hama, Assad sent in army tanks. It's estimated that somewhere between 10,000 and 20,000 civilians died amid shelling. It took several weeks for news outlets to begin sorting out what had happened; there was no one in the city during the time of the massacre, professional journalist or otherwise, who had the means to report it live to the world.[2]

When Hafez passed away in June 2000, his son Bashar al-Assad became president. It wasn't supposed to happen this way; Bashar's brother Basil had been groomed for the presidency, but he died in a car accident. Bashar, a seemingly mild-mannered ophthalmologist residing in England, found himself next in line for the job.

While pundits debated Bashar's qualifications to be president, much of the discussion turned to whether this 40-year-old eye surgeon was Syria's best chance for serious political reform. He certainly could talk the talk, openly discussing greater government accountability, free and open elections, legalizing opposition parties. Many Syrians put their hopes on Bashar; perhaps he wouldn't be his father's son after all.

Over the next 10 years, almost nothing happened. No substantial reforms. Lots of promises, committees, lip service. And all the while, opposition members continued to disappear into the bowels of Syria's security apparatus.

In the early days of the Arab Spring, Syrians protested on several occasions; one man even set himself on fire, just like Mohamed Bouazizi in Tunisia.[3] But it wasn't until that day in March when those teenagers were detained by police that the people of Deraa decided they'd had enough. They organized protests on the model of other Arab Spring countries, and posted videos of police cracking down on rallies. As in Tunisia, word began to spread. Protests erupted all over the country.

There was nothing Bashar al-Assad could say to placate the protesters. No more promised reforms, no more dialogues about civil liberties, no more committees. The Syrian people were ready to march in the streets – and die, if necessary – until they toppled their dictator.

Ash-sha`b yurid isqat an-nizam.

The people demanded the fall of the regime.

By April 2011, protests had broken out across Syria. On the 29th of that month, 13-year-old Hamza Al-Khatib and his family made the five-mile walk to a protest rally. The gathering was met with gunfire and tear gas, and Hamza became separated from his parents. Nothing was known about his whereabouts until his body was returned to his parents on May 24.[4]

Within days, a video appeared on YouTube. It was the footage of Hamza's remains in the morgue, a doctor documenting the boy's wounds. Other copies of it spread to multiple YouTube channels, as well as on Facebook and other video-sharing sites.

People also began to circulate a professional portrait photo of Hamza.[5] It shows him in a polo shirt, his dark bangs covering his forehead. He is seated in front of a backdrop, blue on the left and green on the right, adorned with rays of light that appear to emanate from his head. His eyes hint at a smile, but his mouth grimaces with a hint of teenage awkwardness. The picture is not very different than you might find in a typical middle-school yearbook.

Word of Hamza's torture and death spread over several days. Al Jazeera was among the first networks to cover the story. While the most graphic footage wasn't shown, that report made it quite clear how the boy had been violated prior to being killed.[6]

Hamza's death made international headlines. The Syrian opposition and its supporters regarded him as a symbol of the regime's brutality. His face adorned posters alongside other well-known martyrs of the Arab Spring, including Tunisia's Mohamed Bouazizi and Egypt's Khaled Said.[7] At candlelight vigils, children even younger than Hamza carried pictures of him in life and in death.[8] Rallies across the country featured a one-minute moment of silence in remembrance.[9] His photo became the avatar on countless Twitter accounts. And a Facebook page honoring him – "We Are All Hamza Al-Khatib" – quickly surpassed 100,000 fans. Within a year it would grow to more than half a million.[10]

It was a rare moment in the Syrian revolution, when protesters could rally around one person, one symbol. And it wouldn't have been possible if Syrians hadn't taken it upon themselves to risk their lives and record video of what was happening to them, day after day after day.

During the first months of the Syrian revolution, anti-government video channels popped up all over YouTube. Two of the biggest were Shaam News Network (SNN)[11] and Ugarit News.[12] Very quickly they developed reputations for disseminating enormous quantities of video, especially footage of protests and violence targeting civilians. Other channels germinated in individual cities, often associated with Local Coordination Committees (LCCs), clandestine groups of volunteers who organized community protests in conjunction with other LCCs across the country.[13]

Early on, it wasn't unusual for people to upload footage from home computers or Internet cafes. As the regime crackdown became increasingly thorough, doing so became an enormous risk. It didn't necessarily stop protesters – many were willing to die if that's what it took to publish the videos – but over time, many were forced to adopt more clandestine methods to increase their chances of survival, not to mention the successful distribution of their footage.

One of the most straightforward methods was the media center – a nondescript safe house somewhere in town where activists could upload video through satellite Internet access or more traditional means. Citizen journalists brought in USB sticks, memory cards or whatever storage devices they used to hold their footage. These devices often found their way to the media center by way of multiple intermediaries. Activists occasionally relayed footage recorded by Syrian soldiers, who sold them to the opposition for profit. Once footage was secured and uploaded, it could be re-posted across multiple social networks.

There also was the time-honored tradition of smuggling. Syria's borders have always been porous for black-market cigarettes, alcohol and the like. These smuggling routes were now being used for food, medical supplies, weapons, people and video footage. If a particular city lacked Internet access because the government deactivated it, sometimes smuggling the footage across the border was the only option.

Even during the darkest days of 2011, Syrians managed to evade government efforts to silence them. One of the most dramatic incidents occurred in the city of Hama – the same city that experienced the military onslaught by Bashar al-Assad's father in 1982, when thousands of residents were killed.

It was the eve of Ramadan – July 31, 2011. As residents prepared for the holy month known for daytime fasts and nighttime feasts, government tanks rolled into Hama. The city was the epicenter of regional anti-government protests, and there were reports of local defections from the army. The government decided to make an example of Hama for another generation of Syrians.

One of the first reports I saw regarding an assault on Hama came from Iyad El-Baghdadi in Dubai, who already had his hands full documenting the fighting in Libya.

> RT @iyad_elbaghdadi: Eyewitnesses from Hama report random shooting at anything that moves, started at 6 AM in town center. #Syria[14]

Al Jazeera's Rula Amin received word from local sources that many had died in Hama – and it was still early in the day.

> RT @RulaAmin: Syrian activists say at least 50 people killed in #Hama today, 13 in #Deir Alzour, 7 in Hrak near #Deraa as army enters these towns #syria[15]

While keeping an eye on Twitter, I focused my efforts on YouTube. Most Syrian opposition channels posted footage on the site, from large revolutionary outlets like Shaam News Network to individual citizen journalists. Each time I received word through various sources that compelling Syrian footage had been uploaded, the first thing I'd do was check if it was from a new channel. If yes, I'd go through its archive to get a sense of the quality, sometimes sharing links via Twitter for my followers to review clips. If the channel seemed like a potentially useful source, I subscribed. By the time the Syrian government unleashed its assault on Hama, I was subscribed to dozens of opposition YouTube channels.

A pair of videos from SNN showed the lengths to which amateur videographers went to document government-sponsored violence. In the first clip, the cameraman is disturbingly close to a tank. He's near some foliage, but still exposed.[16] In a second clip, he begins his narration, but before he can say much of anything, a loud shot rings out. The picture suddenly swings toward the ground as the cameraman wails in pain; the footage ends abruptly.[17]

New videos surfaced on YouTube day and night. Every time I refreshed my browser, additional clips appeared in my queue. There was literally more footage coming in than I could watch, even if I dedicated all my waking moments to the task. Many of these clips had zero views; someone had uploaded the footage only moments before I found them.

In one dramatic clip from SNN, the cameraman narrates an attack on a residential Hama neighborhood. At first glance it looks like a tank, but it's actually a BMP-1, a heavily armored, Russian-built infantry vehicle sporting a 73mm semi-automatic gun. Bullets fly at a rate of more than one each second, with firepower that can blast through walls or blow a person in half. "Son of a bitch!" the cameraman yells at the vehicle. "If I had an RPG I would've cut you to pieces!"

The camera tilts out of focus as a loud explosion is heard, followed by sustained heavy gunfire. As the cameraman regains focus and zooms in on the soldiers manning the vehicle, dozens of protesters off-camera taunt them and cry out *Allahu Akbar*! They show no fear in the face of such weaponry.[18]

Many of the videos are shockingly graphic. One clip shows volunteers picking up a dead protester. As they lift him, it's clear that almost his entire head has been blown off; all that's left is his neck, part of his stubbled chin, and skin flaps from what used to be his face.[19] A second video filmed at a local hospital shows the same dead protester before moving on to other corpses, taking viewers on a tour of atrocities for several minutes.[20]

While I monitored my collection of Syrian video channels, my Twitter followers did the same, sharing relevant footage throughout the day.

> RT @iyad_elbaghdadi: Mosque destroyed by tank shelling in Hama earlier today. A few hours before the first *tarawih* [Ramadan prayers]. http://t.co/xDaAtco #Syria #RamadanMassacre[21]

The brief video clip shows the interior of a mosque. It's full of rubble. Even the holiest places within the city were under siege.

Edward Dark, the pseudonym of an online Syrian activist I'd followed since the start of the revolution, discovered some of the most disturbing footage that day.

> RT @edwardedark: child in Hama attacked with a knife by security forces http://t.co/9924SZZ #Syria[22]

I didn't want to open the link, but I had to. Earlier in the revolution, I had made the decision to watch every video that I would retweet. If I was going to subject others to the horrors of conflict, I had the responsibility of watching it first. Also, I didn't want my followers to be surprised by the contents of the footage, so I always described it in blunt terms, usually accompanied by the word *graphic*.

This particular video, which was later deleted from YouTube, showed a young child whose face had been slashed, screaming in pain as doctors attempted treatment. I retweeted it, but added a preface making it as clear as possible how I had reacted to it:

> I'm at a loss for words. Go hug your kids.[23]

My emotional response was compounded by the fact that I was with my own children at the time. My wife and I had promised our kids a visit to McDonald's so they could enjoy the play area for a while. The juxtaposition of what I saw offline and online rattled me.

> Sitting in a McDonalds Play Place, back against the wall, watching real-time horrors in Syria, as my kids play & squeal with joy. #paradox[24]

Back against the wall, like a paranoid gunslinger sitting in the corner of a saloon. That had become my default position whenever I used my computer in public, lest I accidentally expose others to the horror of it all.

It was now well past sunset in Syria. According to activists, more than 100 civilians had been killed in Hama that day, though there was no way to verify the total. The violence continued, even though Islam's holiest month had commenced when the sun sank below the horizon. I wished my Twitter followers a blessed Ramadan, and to enjoy breaking their fasts as best they could under such circumstances.

> *Ramadan mubarak*, everyone. May your days be peaceful and your *iftars* joyful.

In Syria, at least, peaceful days were wishful thinking. Things were about to get far worse for the people of Hama.

> RT @tweets4peace: Heavy gunfire near Alqasabashi roundabout in #Hama now, please take care. #Syria #RamadanMassacre #Ramadan2011[25]

It was now past midnight on August 2, and the siege of Hama showed no signs of halting. Footage continued to pour in on YouTube: more damaged mosques, more tanks, more casualties. I received a tweet from Kate Gardiner, a former colleague from PBS Newshour, then working for Al Jazeera English.

> RT @KateGardiner: I'm told this is live picture from Hama City, #Syria tonight. http://bit.ly/pjp4oE[26]

I opened the link; it was a livestream. Given the time of night, you couldn't make out much except city lights in the distance. A steady wind whipped the camera's microphone.

The camera operator began to speak in Arabic. I rushed over to the desk of my coworker Ahmed Al Omran (@ahmed) and asked him to come over to my computer. I unplugged my headphones and flinched when the audio blared from my desktop speakers. Ahmed translated the cameraman's angry, desperate monologue while I took dictation and described the sounds of Hama.

> Audio: There's news of 2 tanks located a park in the city, near the governors palace (? hard to understand fully) #hama #syria[27]
>
> Hama audio: People of Hama tell the people of Syria that we are ready to die for a free Syria. Bashar is a traitor.[28]
>
> Really hard to tell what's going on. Hearing sounds that seem like explosions, but the wind is hammering the mic and it could be nothing.[29]

I increased the volume and heard people chanting, then a gunshot. Then more chanting, another gunshot.[30]

> Hama audio: Security forces are firing on the city of Hama. #syria[31]

> Hama audio: burst of gunfire in the distance. five, maybe 10 shots.[32]

> Hama audio: I just heard what sounded like a shell exploding. #syria[33]

> Hama audio: even more machine gun bursts, getting closer. Cameraman continues to recite Takbeer ["Allahu Akbar"]. #syria[34]

> Hama audio: The attack is coming from four different directions. #syria[35]

The cameraman directed his scorn toward Bashar al-Assad and the Arab world at large.

> Hama audio: To Bashar: keep lying, keep lying. Where are the other Arab rulers? What are you doing with your lives? #syria[36]

> Hama: your wives are being slaughtered, your children are being orphaned. Where are you, secretary of the Arab League?!? #syria[37]

> Hama audio: We won't bow for anyone except God. #syria[38]

> Hama audio: we'll take freedom if you want it or not, you little dog. (Massive machine gun fire in the distance) #syria[39]

> Hama audio: The Arab rulers are sitting at fancy food tables, watching their Arab brothers being slaughtered by Bashar's corrupt regime.[40]

> Hama audio: Where are you, Arabs?!? #syria[41]

> Hama audio: Allahu Akbar from the minarets. We heard a child and a woman scream in the distance. #syria[42]

I paused to admire the tenacity of the people filming the live footage.

> Livestreaming from Hama while bullets are flying takes some serious chutzpah. #syria[43]

As the siege continued through Ramadan, the people running the Hama stream somehow managed to keep it functioning. They'd go offline, sometimes for hours at a time, then reappear without warning. For the next several days, I kept their website open at all times, just in case the livestream returned.

Late one night, the camera operator described the latest violence in Arabic. I needed help with translation again, and suggested we use the hashtag #HamaStream.

> Looks like the Hama livestream is live again: http://qik.com/video/42854249 Anyone want to listen and translate? Use tag #hamastream[44]

> Please listen now: http://qik.com/video/42854249 heard an explosion, people screaming Allahu Akbar. More explosions[45]

The sound of shells and gunfire became increasingly louder.

> Someone PLS translate and tag #hamastream! http://qik.com/video/42854249 #hama #syria[46]
>
> Major machine gun fire and shelling going on http://qik.com/video/42854249 PLS TRANSLATE AND USE #hamastream tag![47]
>
> Significant machine gun fire now. #hamastream #syria[48]

Suddenly, the video stopped.

> The #hamastream ends under extreme duress. I really hope whoever was streaming it is okay. http://qik.com/video/42854249 #syria #hama[49]

Fortunately, the livestream automatically archived each video. My colleague Ahmed, as well as others online who spoke Arabic, started translating.

> RT @ahmed: Audio: the situation is catastrophic, but we will resist. We are humans, not animals to be slaughtered like this.[50]
>
> RT @ahmed: Audio: can you hear the sound of bombing? I'm in this area this getting bombed in Hama. I can't speak, I'm afraid I will be killed.[51]
>
> RT @freesyria74: #hamastream " barbaric attacks by security forces and shabeeha [thugs] on the city" Shelling for 3d straight day"[52]

Then the stream went live again.

> RT @Hasan_Bahraini: Severe lack of food supplies in Hama – interrupted by gunshots and shouts of *Allahu Akbar* #hamastream #hama[53]
>
> RT @ahmed: Audio: most of Hama districts are being bombed, everything, the buildings and unarmed people. #hamastream[54]
>
> RT @ahmed: Audio: Allahu Akbar! Where are the brothers? (gunshots) #hamastream[55]
>
> RT @freesyria74: #hamastream Live from Hama,#Syira " how long the world is going to stay silent" "We are humans too"[56]
>
> RT @Hasan_Bahraini: "#Arabs, your silence has killed us. May God be our aid" #hama #hamastream[57]

> RT @NadiaE: "Your silence has killed us" says a young man from Hama, Syria #hamastream. I'm so ashamed I am one of the silent ones.[58]

Just before the stream stopped, I heard someone yell.

> RT @itsEnas: @acarvin At the end of the video,someone beside the guy that was streaming told him to cut the streaming,yelling:"turn it off, turn it off!"[59]

For Syrians and non-Syrians alike, the 2011 Ramadan assault on Hama was a traumatic flashback to the 1982 siege, with one crucial difference: back then, the world knew nothing about it until it was too late. Now we could watch the horror unfold in real time. But would anyone do anything about it this time?

The outside world had come to rely on these Syrian citizen journalists. While a number of Western journalists entered the country for brief periods, the work of these amateur videographers brought forward the full scope of Syria's violence on a day-to-day basis. Video channels like SNN and Ugarit News served as ever-expanding archives for what was fast becoming a civil war. If you added up all of the Syrian YouTube channels, they probably would have encompassed tens of thousands of video clips.

And sometimes those channels simply vanished.

One morning, I saw a frantic tweet from Hamza Mousa, the Egyptian doctor who spent so much time in Libya.

> RT @Hamzamu: #Syria : Youtube.com closed Syrian Revolution Video Channel more than 8000 Video LOST #youtube Please RT[60]

I didn't know exactly what he was talking about, but it got my attention.

> @hamzamu wait, what? Which channel?[61]

"Ugarit News," he reported.

Ugarit had one of the largest archives of Syrian footage on YouTube. I checked, and its channel had been wiped clean. A message from YouTube said it was shut down for violating the site's rules, or terms of service.

I was absolutely indignant; why would YouTube kill off one of the most important outlets from Syria? I knew some staff at Google, which owns YouTube, so I asked them:

> Why did Youtube remove UgaritNews? It was one of the most important sources of citizen journalism from #Syria. Huge loss.[62]

Meanwhile, I vented:

> UgaritNews removed from Youtube for TOS [Terms Of Service] violation. We've just lost a lifeline into #Syria. Thousands of videos gone. http://bit.ly/mRW2PH[63]

In less than an hour, the channel was restored, thanks to a speedy response by my Google contacts. I asked them what had gone wrong. The channel, apparently, had given too many videos the same name. There was so much footage coming out of Hama, they used the same title on multiple clips for expediency's sake. This triggered YouTube's spam filters, which assumed the videos were violating the site's rules. YouTube's software concluded it was junk.

I was relieved that I had been able to help restore the channel. It made me wonder, though: how many other Syrian channels might have met the same fate without any of us noticing? And how much of that footage was now lost forever?

As the months dragged on, the death toll rose. Initially, it was typical to report a dozen or two killed per day. During the Ramadan massacre that August, you'd routinely see 50, 75 or 100 deaths. By December 2011, more than 100 death counts per day were common. This was probably just what the Assad regime wanted – a slow *drip, drip, drip* of daily casualties that would seem almost routine after a while, making it harder to catch the interest of news organizations. How do you convince news editors to cover a death toll that was the same as the day before and the day before that? Whenever the gears of oppression shifted upward and the toll escalated, it made news. As long as it remained steady, though, Syria would often disappear from the headlines.

This didn't deter Syria's citizen journalists; if anything, it probably strengthened their resolve. Each day they risked their lives, documenting Assad's crimes against civilians, ensuring that the world would know what was happening. Not surprisingly, some of these journalists were killed in the line of duty, but unless someone made a point of memorializing them, their deaths went unnoticed outside of Syria. Just after Christmas, I first heard the name Basil al Sayid, by way of Syrian activist Rami Jarrah, also known online as Alexander Page.[64] Basil was a citizen journalist who had been killed in Baba Amr,[65] an opposition-controlled stronghold in the city of Homs.

> RT @AlexanderPageSY: Today a beautiful person died in #BabaAmro of #Homs he died while filming his last footage RIP Basel al Sayid #Syria[66]
>
> RT @AlexanderPageSY: Outstanding citizen journalist Basil al Sayid who filmed most of the videos in #BabaAmro He dies in this video http://t.co/qozEyX9T[67]

The video begins with the rapid fire of a distant machine gun. Basil's camera is aimed downward, tucked to his chest, as if he's taking a momentary break from filming. You can see his gray sweater, as well as beautiful yellow and red tiles on the floor. The gunfire continues; someone yells *Allahu Akbar*.

There is no sound of the bullet's impact. Basil flinches, then fumbles the camera, which turns directly at his sweater's zipper. It spins 360 degrees; the footage overexposes to nearly completely white before going black.

The gunfire continues; more yelling, more chaos, more panic. *Allahu Akbar, Allahu Akbar, Allahu Akbar, Allahu Akbar*.[68]

I shared the footage with my Twitter followers, CCing the Committee to Protect Journalists.

> Basil Sayid, who shot much of the footage from #Homs, #Syria, reportedly died while filming. Clip: http://t.co/qozEyX9T cc @pressfreedom[69]

Rami, clearly shaken by Basil's death, continued to tweet tributes to his fallen comrade.

> RT @AlexanderPageSY: http://t.co/2keizOfA this is the moment Basel al sayid died in what he did best, basil risked his life every moment documenting assad crimes[70]

> RT @AlexanderPageSY: If everyone knew what Basil al Sayid contributed to #Syria & the endless video documenting he gave us we would be building him a statue now[71]

Others expressed their grief at Basil's passing.

> RT @tweets4peace: Basil El Sayed, wallahi meant the world to us. Should win journalism award of the year. A hero from Baba Amr #Homs.

> RT @BintAlRifai: Basil Al Sayyid, thank you. May you rest in peace. #Syria[72]

Many Syrian citizen journalists operated in the shadows; revealing too much about themselves could get them killed. Almost no one outside of Homs knew Basil's name before his death.

I wanted to learn more about him. Working from home one day, I texted Rami over Skype, asking if he had a few minutes to talk about Basil.

> Do you have any more information on Basil Sayid?

> Was he a member of one of the main video networks, like Ugarit or SNN?

Rami replied cryptically:

> ofcourse
> wiat
> wait
> wait
> please

"Ok, no rush," I wrote back, wondering what he was up to.

A minute or so later, my Skype phone rang. It was Rami, and he had connected me to a house in Homs. Basil's friends and family had gathered there to mourn him. I heard children playing in the background as adults talked quietly among themselves.

I didn't know what to say at first; I had only planned on texting Rami a few questions. Now I was patched in to the people closest to Basil. It was as if they had invited me into their home to join them in their mourning.

I took a deep breath, introduced myself and offered my sincerest condolences. No one spoke English, so Rami served as my translator. He introduced me to a young man who was close friends with Basil and had worked with him throughout the revolution.

I asked him what he could tell me about Basil.

"He was always courageous," Basil's friend said, proudly. "He would do stuff that other people wouldn't do. To film something and be effective, you needed someone courageous, and he actually took on that role."

I was curious about Basil's background as a videographer. It turned out he didn't have one. "He actually was a metal worker – with aluminum," his friend explained. "That's what he used to do. It was when the revolution began that he found that that's what he was better at."

Basil was an independent. Unlike many videographers who report to a specific Local Coordinating Committee or video channel operation, Basil went out on his own and made his footage available to everyone. "He would do this for free," his friend continued. "He never got paid for anything."

Rami then chimed in. "One thing I know about him is Basil had a motorcycle. He would go from one secret newsroom to another, from house to house, passing along any information he'd gotten from the field. Maybe he'd seen someone die, or seen something happen – he would go from network to network, passing on that information."

I asked how Basil passed along his footage. As it happened, he was among those citizen journalists who conveyed their materials through intermediaries to hidden media centers. "He would go on his own, anywhere," his friend continued. "He would go out the whole day and bring back his footage. He would pull out his memory card and hand it to a contact, explain the footage he'd gotten today. The guy would then download the footage, and then Basil would head out to pass it to someone else."

Unsurprisingly, Basil's role in the revolution took its toll on his family, his friend explained:

> The family was obviously always worried about Basil. The fact is, in Homs, everyone is subject to being killed. Given that Basil was filming, he became a government target. Basil used to tell his mother everything that was happening to him. He used to come home and weep to her, telling her that he'd seen someone die, or that he'd been shot at. He always used to feel guilty that it wasn't him. It was assumed that any of them at any moment could die. But Basil was in the most danger because he was filming at the demonstrations and other locations where security forces would open fire.
>
> What Basil and other video journalists do is very important for the revolution. The proof that Basil was so important is the fact that now that he's gone, they're trying to fill in his place, and that's not possible at the moment. They're not finding someone who can do what Basil was doing because he'd actually gotten so good at it. A lot of people depended on the footage he filmed.

I had seen Basil's final video, but wondered if his friend knew more details about his death. There were checkpoints all over Homs, he explained, and some of them were manned by *shabiha* – pro-government thugs who had a reputation for extreme violence. The word literally means "ghosts" in Arabic. Shabiha opened fire on a group of civilians walking through a neighborhood. Basil was nearby and began to film it. He recorded two clips of the incident before he was shot and killed.

I asked Basil's friend one last question: how do you want him to be remembered?

"He was a humanitarian," he said. "He was someone who gave up his life for an idea, for his countrymen. And we want him to be remembered as a hero."

After the interview, my daughter Kayleigh came over and asked what I was doing. I explained I was talking to the friend of a brave man who was a journalist, and he had died trying to show the world the bad things that were happening to people in a country called Syria. Now he was gone, and they want to remember him as a hero.

Kayleigh paused for a moment, apparently recalling a conversation we had after Mohammed Nabbous died in Libya.

She then looked directly at me.

"Does that mean all the heroes have died?"

I was at a loss for words.[73]

Two months later, we received word that another citizen journalist had been killed. He was known as Syria Pioneer, and had bravely streamed hours of footage from Homs, which was now under an even more brutal siege.

In his final video, he sensed the end was near and cursed the world for not coming to Syria's aid.

> Baba Amr is facing a genocide right now. I will never forgive you for your silence. You all have just given us your words but we need actions. . .In a few hours there will be *no* place called Baba Amr and I expect this will be my last message. And *no one* will forgive you who talked but didn't act.[74]

Syria Pioneer's real name was Rami al-Sayed. He was Basil's cousin.

> RT @SyrianIntegrity: @acarvin and he still alive !! Can you even look at this photo ?? #Syria #Homs http://bit.ly/U3Cr6q[75]

In February 2012, around the time Basil's cousin died, the siege of Homs had entered an even uglier stage – a brutal assault that would last for over nine weeks. Ironically – and perhaps intentionally – the start of the operation coincided with the 30th anniversary of the 1982 Hama massacre. The neighborhood of Baba Amr was under constant shelling. Men, women and children died in their homes. Others were shot outside just for crossing the street. The footage coming out of Homs was devastating. So many innocent people maimed, killed, suffering.

After 14 months of monitoring Arab Spring footage, I thought I had seen everything. But there was absolutely nothing that could prepare me for the photo that had just been sent to me.

The image was originally from a Twitter account called @homsi_news. It showed a boy in a hospital room, probably 10 or 12 years old, and his eyes were closed tightly. But his face – I can barely begin to describe it. His entire jaw was gone, blown off in a sudden, sickening moment of violence. Strands of pulpy, bloody flesh hung from where his mouth once was. And somehow he had survived this ungodly mutilation.[76]

I didn't know if I should retweet it. For the moment I just replied to the sender.

> Awful; just awful.[77]

Later, I received a video of the same boy.[78] I wasn't sure I could stomach watching it. I went into another room of my house, making sure no one would accidentally see it, even momentarily. I knew the photo of the boy would haunt me for the rest of my life, and the video was probably much, much worse.

I put on my headphones, took a deep breath and clicked play.

As the video begins you can see blood on the floor and hear the moans of the boy. The moans don't sound human – normally a person screaming in pain would have a lower jaw to help articulate the sound.

The camera pans to a table. The boy's feet are arched, his toes curling in agony. The camera pulls out for a wider angle; he's on his back, struggling to sit up. A man helps him rise. The boy cries out again, the same blood-curdling howl, the worst sound you can imagine. His jaw and right cheek are completely missing, leaving nothing but a bloody cavern that was once his mouth. The remaining flesh around his face is shredded into ribbons.

The man standing next to him is yelling, calling out to God, full of rage against President al-Assad. He walks to an adjacent table, revealing another boy, even younger than the first. He's flat on his back; his left leg below the knee has been blown off. All that remains is a shaft of exposed bone and bloody rags of skin and muscle. The camera pans his face. He looks afraid but doesn't make a sound. The other boy, however, continues to wail like a wounded animal. His blood drips all over the floor.

I could barely comprehend the horror of what I had just seen. As repellent as the footage was, I knew I had to share it with my Twitter followers. Its utter savagery captured the human toll of the siege of Homs in ways no other footage could.

I tried to type but struggled to hit the keys, as if the blood had drained from my hands. And I couldn't just write, "Graphic video of two injured boys." Hundreds of times over the previous year, I had tweeted gory footage with the word *graphic* attached to it. But *graphic* wouldn't suffice; this was so much worse.

> 2 boys: one w/ his jaw blown off; the other his foot. Worse than graphic; an abomination. My hands are shaking. http://t.co/kFkRGHqZ #syria[79, 80]

Indeed, an abomination, a crime that no living thing should ever experience.

This wasn't the first time I had responded to a video with such anger. Previous footage of wounded civilians, particularly children, made my blood boil with rage. But I always let the footage speak for itself. I never asked people to do something about it or get involved. As a journalist it wasn't my job to tell people to take action when it came to these revolutions. But as the fury swelled inside me, I couldn't help but wish that I could go to Homs and bring that poor boy to safety.

> If I could airlift that child to a trauma center specializing in radical plastic surgery. I would do so right now. #syria[81]

London-based writer Steven Maclean was one of the first to respond.

> RT @Steven_Maclean: @acarvin Can't believe the kid missing his jaw is just sat there. Must be in deep shock. Awful images.[82]

Ruwayda Mustafa, a Kurdish human rights activist in Britain, seemed as shaken as I was.

> RT @RuwaydaMustafah: there are only a handful of images from the last 12 months that will haunt me. That will be one of them. #syria[83]

Ali Abunimah of ElectronicIntifada.net, who had proved so instrumental during the Gay Girl In Damascus investigation, wasn't optimistic about the boy's chances.

> RT @AliAbunimah: @acarvin horrible. It is difficult to imagine the prospects for the first boy.[84]

I replied, still holding out hope that some way he'd make it.

> @AliAbunimah: I can't think of a more horrific survivable wound. And one of the hardest to repair. He's disfigured for life. #syria #crimes[85]

I kept thinking about options for the boy. Clearly he wasn't going to get the treatment he needed in Homs. But war veterans have survived similar wounds going back at least to the U.S. Civil War. There had to be some way of saving him – and hopefully repairing some of the damage as well.

> There's gotta be some way to evac that kid to a plastic surgery center somewhere. No survivable wound is more disfiguring. #syria[86]
>
> I don't know it is at CNN who makes decisions to adopt wounded kids and get them help but someone should show them that video. Now. #syria[87]

Um Farouk, the alias of a Syrian doctor based in Cairo, had little hope for him.

> RT @Mou2amara: if it's the face injury we're talking about then don't think he could make it out or the room [alive][88]

Perhaps I was being naïve, but I was convinced the boy could make it. I'd seen too many clips of people who had lost their jaws due to war and accidents. It was a grave wound, but not necessarily a death sentence.

> @Mou2amara It's a survivable wound. Trust me, I've seen footage of people who've had plastic surgery to deal with such devastation.[89]

A Syrian activist who goes by the pseudonym @itsenas was incredulous.

> RT @itsenas: @acarvin Andy there is no mean of sending this boy to a plastic surgeon.He's in a field hospital. It's indescribable.[90]

I was still convinced that someone had to at least make the effort to save him.

> @itsEnas Is there any way to get him to the border? Of course he needs to be stabilized but at some point he will need surgery.[91]

No one had an answer. My Twitter followers included doctors, nurses and other health professionals, but this was new territory for us. Desperate, I tweeted relief organizations working in Syria, including the Global Medical Relief Fund.

> Dear @GMRFChildren: this boy in Syria had his jaw blown off. We're trying to find out if he's still alive. http://t.co/MqcJEZcw[92]

Meanwhile, I received a note from CNN producer Christine Theodoru; her team was aware of the video.

> RT @ChristineCNN: We've seen the video; we're trying to find out more ourselves. . .[93]

"Thanks Christine," I replied. "will let you know if I learn more."[94]

I desperately wanted to find a way to help the boy. Unless he received proper treatment soon, he probably wouldn't survive due to blood loss and infection.

Offline, I reached out to people I knew were either in Homs or had contacts in the city. All of them were equally worried about the boy, so they began checking with their own sources to see if they could determine his name and condition. Initial reports suggested he was in the main field hospital and being stabilized. In very grave condition, no doubt, but apparently still alive. We spent hours messaging each other, coordinating as best we could, which was difficult given some of them were not in a position to reveal their exact names or locations to me or each other.

While I waited to see if any of those contacts would pay off, I received a direct message from someone I followed online, but did not know personally. This person had gone to school with a Beirut-based reconstructive surgeon who might be able to help.

I immediately replied via email.

> Thanks so much for reaching out – I truly appreciate it. I have several people working on identifying him. It appears that he is still alive and still in Homs, but it may take a while to convince them to give us his name.

> Assuming we can ID him, how might this work? Would someone have to evac him to the Lebanese border?

This person, I learned, had connections with volunteers on the ground in Lebanon who smuggled supplies across the Syrian border. If I could ID the boy and get him out of Homs to the Syrian frontier, this person's contacts could get him to Lebanon, where a reconstructive surgery team would be waiting for him. The team would need about six hours' notice once we confirmed he was en route. Beyond that, though, the doctors were ready and willing to do the surgery, pro bono.

Publicly, I continued to ask if anyone was having any luck identifying the injured boy.

> Has anyone made any progress IDing the boy in Homs whose jaw was blown off? I have a lead re: medical treatment. #Syria[95]

> @tweets4peace: do you know anyone who can help me get the name of the boy in Homs whose jaw was blown off?[96]

> @BintAlRifai I have a medical lead. . . I now need his name and his location.[97]

Privately, we were making progress. At least two of my sources contacted people at the field hospital who confirmed he'd been stabilized. These contacts would coordinate with the Free Syrian Army – the Syrian opposition's semi-official military force – to get him across the Lebanese border. And we now knew his first name: Hamza, just like the boy who had been tortured to death nine months earlier.

This wasn't going to be easy. Free Syrian Army sources reported that mountain roads had iced over, which meant transport would be impossible until they thawed after sunrise. Then there was the issue of getting permission from his family. The surgery team would need a parent or family proxy to make the trip with him. This was totally understandable – I mean, we were talking about transporting a seriously wounded minor through a war zone and across national borders for medical treatment.

We soon learned the boy's parents were terrified about having him transported anywhere. As bleak as the situation was in Homs, transport meant putting their son's life into the hands of complete strangers. How would they know we were sincere? How would they know we wouldn't abandon the boy? How would they know that a medical team was indeed waiting for him across the border? It would take time to gain their trust – and time was running short.

That evening, a number of Twitter contacts reported a rumor that Hamza had passed away.

> RT @itsEnas: @tweets4peace @acarvin Received news that the guy with the jaw had died 2 hours post his injury.[98]

"I truly hope you're wrong," I said. "Getting some additional confirmation."[99]

Another contact from Homs, @BigAlBrand, also heard the boy had died.

> RT @BigAlBrand: I got news that the kid I'm looking for died. Please someone deny or confirm ASAP. Thank you.[100]

I replied:

> @BigAlBrand Is this the boy shot in the jaw? I have several people working to confirm his status right now. Contradictory info so far.[101]

Offline, I heard back from several sources. They were still convinced Hamza was alive.

The back-and-forth continued into the evening. Until we heard directly from sources at the field hospital, we would keep working under the assumption he was still alive.

The waiting was agonizing; I spent hours staring at my laptop, hoping good news would suddenly materialize.

> Sitting by the inbox can be just awful sometimes. #syria[102]
>
> Trying to explain to my 5-year-old why I can't play with her right now. This is harder than usual. #syria[103]
>
> btw re: the boy in Homs please don't expect an answer from me shortly. This will take a while. Just know that we're working on it. #syria[104]

As the hours dragged on, word came out of Homs that the shelling had resumed. Rose Alhomsi (@tweets4peace), who was in constant contact with relatives there, was among the first to report the news.

> RT @tweets4peace: Breaking: Baba Amr now: Bombs can be heard followed by heavy gunfire. Prayers. #homs #syria[105]
>
> RT @tweets4peace: Tonights bombs on Baba Amr have affected the graveyard. Even the dead can't be at peace with Assad. #homs #homsattack[106]
>
> RT @tweets4peace: Shelling on Baba Amr is intensifying. It is night time with no electricity. This is a nightmare. #HOMSATTACK[107]
>
> RT @tweets4peace: Baba Amr being shelled heavily now. I don't know what to say. #homs #homsattack[108]

"Do people have basements in Homs?" I asked my followers.[109]

Katherine Maher, a D.C. colleague who has worked extensively in the Arab world, wrote back:

> RT @krmaher: @acarvin most houses in Syria slab foundation construction. Historically basements are rootcellars, in warmer climes not attached to house[110]

Others relayed details about the attack. Rami Jarrah was in contact with his own sources on the ground.

> RT @AlexanderPageSY: BREAKING Right now heavy shelling from tanks and gunfire as regime forces pound the #BabaAmr area of #Homs #Syria[111]

Omar Shakir, the pseudonym of a citizen journalist inside Homs, reaffirmed these reports.

> RT @OmarShakir91: #Syria #Homs #BabaAmr is being shelled by T-72 tanks[112]
>
> RT @OmarShakir91: Pray for us, we are being bombarded from every direction #Syria #Homs #Babaamr[113]

Over in Beirut, Shakeeb Al-Jabri grimly commented:

> RT @LeShaque: They're set to finish off Hamza, even if they have to flatten Bab Amro to get to him. #Syria[114]

A Twitter contact using the alias @DamascusTweets wrote:

> RT @DamascusTweets: OH MY GOD! VERY VERY VERY Heavy shelling on #BabaAmr #Homs from 4 sides. This is going to be bad, very bad. #Syria[115]
>
> RT @DamascusTweets: #SOSHoms #SOSHoms #SOSHoms #SOSHoms #SOSHoms #SOSHoms #SOSHoms #SOSHoms #SOSHoms #SOSHoms #SOSHoms #SOSHoms #SOSHoms . . .[116]

Rose Alhomsi was still in contact with her family.

> RT @tweets4peace: Baba Amr being hit from all sides at this current point in time. #homs #soshoms #syria #homsattack[117]

> RT @tweets4peace: bomb. . .bomb................. bombbombbomb.. bomb..... bomb....bombbomb...bomb.......bombbombbombbomb #soshoms #homsattack[118]

> RT @tweets4peace: For God's sake the bombs are intensifying on Baba Amr, we lost children today, how many more!!! #SOSHOMS #homsattack[119]

It was absolutely numbing. Even if Hamza had indeed survived, it would still be hours before he could be moved; the roads were probably just beginning to thaw. I had been sitting in front of my computer for 12 hours. I had to get some rest.

> I'm going to call it a night soon. Will give an update on the boy from Homs as soon as I can tomorrow morning. Stay safe, everyone.[120]

The first tweet I saw the next morning felt like a punch in the gut:

> RT @apk222: @acarvin@ rqskye RIP Hamza Kabbour, the boy who lost lower half of his face yesterday. #Homs #Syria #BasharCrimes #Bashar yfrog.com/ocdk9sjkj[121]

I clicked the photo; it showed Hamza lying down, his face wrapped in gauze. I couldn't tell if he was unconscious or dead.

I wrote back:

> @apk222 @rqskye I'm still confirming. His death was already reported incorrectly once before. Hope for the best but prepare for the worst.[122]

Others tweeted reports of Hamza's death. Most didn't cite any sources, and the ones that did pointed to a Facebook post that lacked any details. Perhaps I was just in denial, but I needed to hear it from my sources organizing the rescue. One of them emailed me and said Hamza was dead, but referenced the same Facebook post. I needed more. I needed to be sure.

About an hour later, I received a direct message from one of my contacts involved in the rescue attempt.

> May God rest his soul. Maybe death in his case was the most merciful thing that could happen. God bless.

My other sources confirmed it via their contacts at the field hospital. There had been so many complications – stabilizing him with limited medical supplies, the blood loss, the weather, getting permission from his parents, the renewed shelling – that there was never a chance to evacuate him from the field hospital. Hamza had simply lost too much blood; nothing could've been done to stop it.

I felt empty, blank, defeated. Even though I'd tweeted we should hope for the best but prepare for the worst, I wasn't anywhere close to being prepared. In more than a year of covering the Arab revolutions online, this was the first time I'd attempted to get involved directly. And it hadn't made a damn bit of difference.

I collected myself as best I could and went back online.

> Sad news: all of my sources are reporting that Hamza, the boy whose jaw was shot off in Homs, passed away before we could evacuate him.[123]
>
> We had successfully arranged transport for him across the border, where a reconstructive surgery team was waiting. But he never stabilized.[124]
>
> Roads across the mountains were also icy last night, which complicated matters further.[125]
>
> I'd like to thank all of you who offered your support & assistance. I can't name those directly involved, but you have my deepest gratitude.[126]
>
> RIP Hamza; I'm sorry we couldn't help you. We did our very best. #homs #syria[127]

Before the day was out, there would be more videos of dead and injured children in Homs. I tried to watch them all, tried to bear witness; it was the least I could do to honor them. But I finally reached a point where I had to shut my laptop and close my eyes. I recalled that first image of Hamza sitting there in agony, bloody rags of flesh hanging from his face, his eyes squeezed closed in pain.

And then I felt those eyes open and stare at me.

I'm sorry, Hamza. I truly am.

EPILOGUE

The Tear Gas Club

The enormous clouds of dust and car exhaust began to make me cough – and I hadn't even arrived in downtown Cairo yet. I was standing along the edge of a highway in 6th of October City – an exurb about an hour west of Egypt's capital. It's not the type of place that most non-Cairenes have heard of, let alone visited, but I was staying at a hotel there to help conduct a journalism workshop at a university down the road.

It was my first time back in Egypt in over 15 years – and my first time since the revolution.

My work finished for the day, I waited for my ride to Cairo: Mosa'ab Elshamy, the pharmacy student I followed so closely during the Egyptian revolution. He'd become one of my favorite Egyptian tweeps and go-to sources. He was side-splittingly funny and always placed himself at the front lines of any confrontation, whether to take photos, throw rocks or both.

He was one of the best examples of a citizen journalist/activist I'd gotten to know in 2011. While directly engaged in the revolution, he was dead serious about documenting it as accurately as possible, whether through his camera lens or by tweeting on his Blackberry. I'd never forget being on the edge of my seat as he tweeted from the front lines near Cairo's Egyptian Museum during that battle in Tahrir Square, as Molotov cocktails flew over his head. The man was fearless.

A car pulled up and a guy got out of the passenger seat. My God, he was young. I knew Mosa'ab was a college student, but seeing him in person, I realized he was probably just 20 years old. He was thin, with dark hair but a light complexion.

We greeted each other warmly before getting into the car. Mosa'ab was joined by Amr El Beleidy, whom I also followed on Twitter. The three of us were off to a "tweetup" – one of those unnecessary social media words that essentially means a face-to-face social gathering organized via Twitter. When some of my Egyptian contacts heard I was planning to visit Cairo, several began plotting a get-together so I could meet as many of them as possible in one setting. It was scheduled to start at 9ish at a rooftop café about half a mile east of Tahrir Square. Given Cairo's famously congested traffic, we were probably going to be at least 30 or 40 minutes late – which in Egypt is equivalent to arriving a little early.

Just before we arrived, the car swerved into a giant traffic circle surrounded by hotels, travel agencies and other businesses. There was a KFC along the other side of the circle. I immediately recognized it.

We had reached Tahrir Square – the center of the revolutionary universe, birthplace of the Egyptian uprising.

Tahrir is a sprawling urban roundabout where people ignore sidewalks and walk straight through the dense onslaught of traffic, like the old Frogger arcade game,[1] with a defiance that presumes no one would dare run over them. It was hard to believe that for 18 days that past January and February, this was ground zero for the Arab Spring.

Unable to resist the urge, I pulled out my phone and opened up Foursquare, the social network that lets you document your whereabouts:

> I finally made it here. (@ Tahrir Square) http://4sq.com/jXtiFL[2]

Yes, it was a little silly. I was checking in on Foursquare even though I wasn't going to get out of the car; we had an appointment to keep. But this was my first sighting of Tahrir since the revolution – I had so many memories, so many emotions.[3]

At the rooftop café, I was surprised to see at least 25 people already there, spread out along a deck, some standing around sipping non-alcoholic beers, others hunched around a table, debating furiously as they lighted their third or fourth cigarettes of the conversation.

I was instantly overwhelmed. These were people I knew intimately, had spent countless, nail-biting hours with, and stayed up nights worrying about. Yet if I passed most of them on the street, I wouldn't have recognized most of them. Slowly, one by one, their identities came into focus. . .Mohammed el Dahshan, a warm, scruffy-faced young economist and writer then known on Twitter as @TravellerW.[4] Alaa Abd El-Fattah (@alaa), the first person from Egypt I'd gotten to know online. Gigi Ibrahim (@GSquare86), the socialist activist who participated in countless protests. Tarek Shalaby (@TarekShalaby), who live-tweeted his own arrest. Sarah Carr (@sarahcarr), the British-Egyptian writer whose incisive wit was apparent whether she was tweeting or researching an article. We also had another special guest, Dima Khatib of Al Jazeera, who was visiting from South America.

Just as I was hoping to grab a drink, a strange popping sound burst out in the distance: *pop, pop, POP, pop, POP*. Everyone stopped talking. Then it happened again: *Pop, pop, POP.* Instinctively, they reached into their pockets and pulled out their phones. A handful of mobiles beeped at once. Then a few more beeped. And then more.

"What was that popping noise?" I asked one of them.

"Tear gas," she replied.

Something was going down at Tahrir Square.

Within a minute or two, a dozen of them rushed out the door in the direction of Tahrir, including Mosa'ab. There wasn't a particular plan or anything, as best I could tell. People in Tahrir likely needed their help – and people everywhere needed to know what was happening.

As the first wave of people departed the café, more messages came in describing what was going on. The families of protesters killed in the revolution had scheduled a memorial service at a nearby theater, but apparently the police prevented them from entering the building. It had escalated into a confrontation. Among the Egyptian activist community, these families are treated with the utmost respect – they're the mothers and fathers of martyrs. And now they were under attack.

A second wave of people left the café. In less than five minutes, a group of nearly 40 people had dwindled to just a handful. And they were all looking at me.

"So?" I asked.

"Well, what do you want to do?" replied Amr El Beleidy.

"I'd like to see what's going on, if that's okay," I said.

"Are you sure?" jumped in Tarek Amr, aka @gr33ndata, a contributor to Global Voices Online.

"I'm sure. Let's just start heading over and play it by ear."

It was an awkward situation. There hadn't been a major dust-up in Tahrir that summer, and I certainly never planned to get involved in one. But I couldn't just retreat into a car and head back to my hotel. I desperately wanted to experience Tahrir, even if this were a relatively minor confrontation. I wanted to experience what they had experienced, even if just a hint of it.

I took out my phone and sent out a tweet, half jokingly yet somewhat ominously:

> Famous last words: I hear tear gas being fired in Tahrir; gonna check it out.[5]

We left the café and began walking toward Tahrir. Block by block, the sound of tear gas canisters got louder and louder. Several young men walked in our direction, apparently coming from the scene. They were holding vinegar-soaked rags over their mouths and noses.

Then I got my first whiff of tear gas.

While we were still a number of blocks away from Tahrir, the wind shifted directions just enough to bring a trace of the chemical agent in our direction. It first affected my eyes, as if I'd just pureed a large onion and stuck my head into the food processer. *I guess that's why they call it tear gas*, I thought. Then I began to feel it in my sinuses, like I'd intentionally snorted a line of wasabi powder. The wind shifted again and it was gone, though I could still feel its residual effects. I coughed several times and felt its metallic taste in my mouth.

"Welcome to the tear gas club," someone said. "So what do you want to do now?"

I was asking myself the same question. The closer we got to Tahrir, the more we realized that something big was happening. But what, we weren't sure. I wanted to get closer, but cautiously; clearly the activists didn't want anything to happen to me on their watch. "Let's keep going, but play it by ear," I replied. "If things look hairy we can always turn around."

And run like hell, I thought.

Approaching Tahrir from the east proved to be difficult; the wind brought wave after wave of tear gas, each worse than the last. We decided to cut through some side streets and approach the square from the southeast. If I had been online back at home, I would have had a mental map of the entire situation: where the safest entry points were, what territory was under government control, where the pressure was growing. But here on the ground, coughing up tear gas, I only knew as much as I could see.

We turned another corner and saw a mass of uniforms about a block ahead of us. They were riot police, and their backs were facing us. Somewhere beyond them was a large crowd, but we couldn't tell how large. We could only hear the commotion. Tear gas hung in the air just beyond the police, but at least it wasn't wafting continuously in our direction. Across the street from us, several police vehicles assembled. Behind us, a contingent of riot police sat on the curb, waiting for orders.

Somehow, we had managed to get stuck behind police lines, smack dab into the middle of the security perimeter. I glanced at everyone else, and they all had the same expression on their faces.

Oh shit.

"What do we do?" I asked.

"Nothing," Amr cautioned. "We wait and see. And don't take out your camera unless you want to be arrested."

We were caught in a tense limbo. We couldn't go forward without getting hit by rocks thrown at the police in front of us, and we couldn't get through the platoon of reinforcements behind us. There were several other men standing around – mostly local shop owners – and the police weren't bothering them. As long as we didn't do anything stupid, the police would probably just ignore us, too.

"Can I take out my phone?" I asked.

"Sure, but don't use it for too long," I was told.

I tried to access my Twitter timeline, but it wasn't reloading. The local 3G network was probably overloaded by everyone using phones in Tahrir. I figured I'd at least try to send out a few tweets from the scene.

> A block away from Tahir. Hear stun grenades, taste tear gas. Dont plan on getting any closer than this.[6]

> Yes, I'm fine. I'm in safe company- dudes who don't want to take unnecessary chances. #Tahrir[7]

> More police sirens. Eyes and sinuses sting. I can taste it on the roof of my mouth. #Tahrir[8]

> More tear gas. Boom, boom, Boom[9]

To our left, additional reinforcements arrived on foot. Several more police vehicles appeared from around the corner and headed toward the main skirmish line.

> Armored police van just drove by. Looks like a post-appcalyptic ice cream truck. Probably not good humor men, though. #Tahrir #EGYPT[10]

I had to remind myself to pause for a minute or two between each tweet. If I stared at my phone for much longer than a few moments at a time, I was probably asking for trouble. The Internet reception improved, and I could see my Twitter timeline again. One person after another asked me a variation on the same question: *Are you ok?*

> @KathrynHallPR @sarrahsworld I'm two blocks from Tahrir, keeping a safe distance. #egypt[11]

At least I thought I was two blocks away. I couldn't be exactly sure. There wasn't enough of a 3G signal for me to pull up a GPS map, and the way we had zig-zagged toward the square I could only guess roughly where we were. Nothing like tear gas and sound grenades to throw off your inner compass.

All around me was action, tension, confusion. A sensory overload. Something big was happening, right then and there. I could see it, hear it, feel it, smell it, even taste it.

Yet I had absolutely no idea what was going on. I felt completely overwhelmed.

Conserving my phone's power, I put it back in my pocket and soaked in my surroundings with as much mindfulness as I could muster. I was on the edge of what appeared to be a major battle in Tahrir Square, though from my particular position it was impossible to get a sense of the breadth, the magnitude or the aggressiveness of the battle. The police line in front of me seemed to be holding firm, but I didn't know how many people deep it was. Perhaps the police were winning; perhaps the protesters had actually advanced and pushed the police into their current position. And how many protesters were just beyond the skirmish line? Perhaps 500? Or maybe 5,000? Were many people hurt? Even killed? I just didn't know.

There I was, on the scene of a melee in Tahrir Square. Yes, I was physically present, but I couldn't get a handle on the tactics being used almost right in front of me. From the comfort of my home or office, I could monitor multiple Twitter streams, piecing together whatever happened to be going on in Tahrir. Sometimes I'd know dozens of people on the scene at any given time. They acted as an array of human sensors, reporting out snippets of information all across the square in real time.

The activists on the ground, by way of Twitter, had always provided me with slices of information that, when pulled together, gave me a bird's eye view of the event – that sense of situational awareness. Being there in person, though, was a whole other matter. It was a visceral, dramatic experience, yet I could only assess what was going on right in front of me. What was occurring just 50 or 100 meters beyond police lines was a complete mystery.

I quickly snapped out of my thoughts when a woman in her forties came toward us from across the street, having somehow walked through the police reinforcements. She was elegant and graceful; her orange silk scarf appeared to be the only hint of color within a haze of gray. She looked strangely familiar.

The woman stopped directly in front of us and said something to my travel companions. I couldn't understand what they were saying to each other, but it was very brief. She then left us and walked about 20 meters closer to the police lines – much closer than we had been willing to go up until that point.

"What was that all about?" I asked.

"It was very strange," Amr replied. "She just came over and asked, 'Thugs or martyrs?'"

"Thugs or martyrs?" I said, confused.

"Yes, thugs or martyrs," he continued. "She wanted to know who the police were up against – whether it was against the families of martyrs who had assembled earlier, or if a group of thugs had shown up to cause trouble."[12]

"What did you tell her?" I asked.

"Martyrs, as far as I know," he said.

Tarek then chimed in. "Did she look familiar to you?"

We all nodded.

"I think that was Bouthaina Kamel," he continued.

"Bouthaina Kamel?" I repeated. "The first woman to declare her intention to run for president?"

"Yes, that's her," Tarek said.

As soon as it clicked, we went forward to chat with her a bit more. She didn't seem to mind, though I still didn't know what they were talking about. Amr then switched from Arabic to English.

"Do you know @acarvin, the journalist on Twitter?" he asked.

"Yes," she said, casually shrugging in agreement.

"Please meet Andy Carvin," he continued, pointing at me.

A warm smile appeared on her face. "How do you do?" she said, offering a firm handshake.[13]

They switched back to Arabic for a moment or two, then she said goodbye. Bouthaina continued her path toward the skirmish line, further and further away from us until she disappeared through the tear gas into Tahrir.

What balls, I thought to myself.

We had now been stuck for about 30 minutes. The front line was wavering; we had to run when a group of police suddenly turned around and chased some protesters in our direction. Once we were able to get out of the way, I caught my breath resting on a car door, then tweeted.

> Just ran for our lives. False alarm. Have no idea why we ran except the guys in front of us ran towards us. Dodged a guy w/ a broom #Tahrir[14]
>
> Three dozen riot police just assembled to our left. Protesters far to our right, blocked by more police. Impending pincer movement? #Tahrir[15]
>
> Meanwhile, I'm leaning again a car with three old guys and a sleeping cat. Oh, the days that they have seen. #Tahrir #jan25 #EGYPT[16]

It was time to leave. The pressure building up between the police and the protesters was reaching its breaking point, and we didn't want to be there when it ruptured. We retraced our way back down the side street. Just when we thought we were in the clear, we were greeted by a formation of riot police. There were so many of them. Column by column, I discreetly counted: exactly 200 policemen with shields, helmets and batons.

"Walk faster, but not too fast," Amr said.

"Could you hear what any of the officers were saying?" I asked.

"One of them said, 'There are too many of them. We need to act now or they will double in size.'"[17]

I swallowed hard, then tweeted.

> Taking our leave. This'll get worse before it gets better. Time to find our car and figure out how to circumvent police blockade.[18]
>
> The traffic-mapping function on Google Maps is neat, but tonight we could use one that maps riot police perimeters. #Tahrir[19]

An old man came out of nowhere and started shouting anti-Mubarak slogans at us. One of the plain-clothes officers appeared to take notice.[20]

Keep walking, keep walking.

We finally reached our car and began the arduous process of driving around the police perimeter. I took out my phone again and caught up on my Twitter timeline. Within a minute or two, I felt I had a better understanding of what was going on than I did the entire time I was actually there. Tarek Shalaby, as always, was live-streaming from inside the melee.[21] Some of the others who had been at the tweetup, including Mosa'ab Elshamy and Mohammed El Dahshan, were caught in the thick of it.

> RT @TravellerW: hit in the chest with a ricocheting canister. Luckily bounced on grass 1st so blow minor. More fright than pain. Alhamdulillah [God be praised] #tahrir[22]

> RT @mosaaberizing: http://twitpic.com/5ibwqy – Protesters running away from tear gas. Highly potent & way worse than any I've inhaled before[23]

> RT @mosaaberizing: Agh fuck this, my mum has found out from TV that I'm in the square.[24]

Tweet after tweet, they gave me a taste of the situational awareness I had back in D.C. – that virtual helicopter allowing me to visualize the entire field of battle.

> RT @occupiedcairo: Now firing gas into Talat harb [street][25]

> RT @Egyptocracy: Some people are making Molotov bombs. #Egypt #Jun28 #Tahrir[26]

> RT @Repent11: On side streets tear gas being fired on side streets many injured.[27]

> RT @Rouelshimi: Its getting intense. People running. The police forces are moving into the square. #tahrir #egypt[28]

> RT @3arabawy: fucking hell too much tear gas[29]

> MT @sarrahsworld: I'm with @NoorNoor1 noor in the ambulence #Egypt #Jan25[30]

> RT @NoorNoor1: Im well no one worry.[31]

> RT @3arabawy: what a tweet up ! Many friends are here. People breaking rocks, throwing at police[32]

Mosa'ab then added:

> RT @mosaaberizing: On a side note, it feels oddly amazing to have @acarvin and @dima_khatib live tweet from Tahrir.[33]

"You and me both, dude," I tweeted back.[34]

A Revolution's Legacy

I shuffled off the plane amid a long queue of Libyans. At the bottom of the stairs, they split off into tight formations of four, six, eight people, wrangling their children and luggage. From the looks of things, I was one of the few people traveling alone.

Entering the airport terminal, we were greeted by a pair of immigration lines: one for Libyans and the other non-Libyans. The Libyan line stretched the length of the arrivals hall. The non-Libyan line was deserted, apart from an indifferent immigration officer, sitting behind an oversized wooden desk and reading a newspaper, apparently not expecting any business.

As I approached the desk he looked up, surprised and mildly annoyed. Without saying a word, he put out his hand impatiently, glaring up at me for the inconvenience. I gave him my passport and waited for him to stamp it.

He scrutinized my documents, page by page, rapidly flipping each sheet with his thumbs as if he were counting money. When he reached my Libyan visa, he squinted and clicked his tongue disapprovingly.

I suddenly wondered what it's like to be deported.

That wasn't supposed to happen, of course. While I managed to have my Libyan visa expedited – I knew a guy who knew a guy – everything should've been in order. And after flying all the way from the U.S. to Jordan, then backtracking here to Benghazi, the last thing I wanted was to be escorted to a plane and forced out of Libya just one day shy of their revolution's first anniversary.

My fate was in the hands of this grim-faced inspector.

After staring at my visa for what felt like an eternity, he looked around and patted his shirt pocket, searching for a pen. He placed my passport on his enormous wooden table, crossed something out and began to write very, very slowly.

The man glanced up at me and handed over my passport, waiting for me to look at it.

At the top of the visa, he had scratched out the elaborate Arabic calligraphy. The redacted words spelled out *Great Socialist People's Libyan Arab Jamahiriya,* a mouthful of a title that Gaddafi had insisted on using for the country. But Gaddafi was gone now, buried in a secret desert location, redacted by his own people.

Just below the excised calligraphy, the immigration officer had written something else in English, carefully lettered just as a penmanship student would:

L I B Y A

"Welcome, welcome," he exclaimed, then waved me through to retrieve my luggage.

It was February 16, 2012, and I had finally made it to Libya – just in time for the first anniversary of the revolution the next day. At the start of the Arab revolutions, I promised my family I wouldn't travel anywhere while bullets were still flying. I was no combat reporter, and I wasn't going to pretend I was. But now Gaddafi had been dead for nearly four months. And while no one would necessarily describe Libya as secure, it was stable enough.

I didn't know what to expect of Benghazi, or Libya generally. I'd travelled to its neighbors, Tunisia and Egypt, but Libya had been closed to most Americans for a long time. I didn't know if there would be any similarities to those other countries. I also didn't know what to expect from all the contacts I had established in Libya over the previous year. I had an idea who some of them were, especially those who had opened up about themselves after the revolution. But others remained a mystery: men, and presumably some women, who did their part in the civil war behind online pseudonyms. I hoped to see their faces for the first time.

Strangely, my initial impression was that Benghazi was like Havana. Like the capital of Cuba, Benghazi is a coastal city with a history of European colonization. While Spanish architecture graces Havana, here Italian architecture evokes that same continental flair. And as in Cuba, Benghazi's beautiful buildings are crumbling after decades of neglect. It is a fading beauty, but a proud one.

My host in Benghazi was known on Twitter as @LibyaSupreme,[1] and was one of the first people to supply me with footage of the protests. Raised in the U.S. in a family of Libyan dissidents, he came to Benghazi not long after the revolution began to supply the opposition with computer servers. He'd been here ever since. Today, he's known locally as a rapper who goes by Malik L – the L stands for Libya.

The next day, February 17 – the first anniversary of the revolution – we walked to the city's courthouse, where Mohammed Nabbous sent out his first livestreams. The courthouse has become the spiritual center of the revolution – Benghazi's Tahrir Square. Over the course of the day, Libyans assembled in front of a stage adjacent to the courthouse. There were the usual speeches, remarks, prayers – not that different than many other political rallies.

But all that changed once the sun went down.

As dusk approached, people from all over Benghazi and surrounding areas made their way toward the courthouse. The streets were in gridlock – a traffic jam stretched for miles. Yet no one was fazed. Car after car barely crawled by, packed with families – parents, children, grandparents – blaring patriotic music and waving Libyan independence flags. Young people with flags leaned out the windows as far as they could reach without actually falling out of their cars; the more adventurous rode on the hood or roof. In some spots, teenagers carried portable stereos into the middle of traffic and began dancing. No one in the cars seemed to mind.

For every vehicle, 20 or 30 people made their way toward the courthouse on foot. Fathers lofted their sons and daughters onto their shoulders. The children waved sparklers. Militia members, their AK-47s slung over their backs, high-fived and embraced friends and strangers alike. Some congregated around *technicals* – pickup trucks mounted with heavy guns. Every so often, a *thuwwar* – a militiaman – would spin in the gunner's seat, rotating his gun in quick circles until it appeared he might pass out from dizziness.

The sounds were as extraordinary as the sight of all those joyous people. There was no break from the noise – an endless cacophony of music, honking horns, chanting, cheering, singing and the occasional celebratory gunfire. City officials had asked people to refrain from firing weapons, and most people seemed pleased with the results. Every so often, though, *thuwwar* would fire off their heavy guns, sending high-caliber tracer bullets soaring overhead and into the Mediterranean. I hoped no fishermen were out on their boats.

Everywhere we went, people stopped to talk with us. As a local rapper, Malik was easily recognizable, especially by young people, but folks of all ages came over to shake our hands, give us hugs and share a moment of celebration. A surprising number spoke English, but even those who didn't inevitably had a similar exchange with me:

"Where you from?"

"*Amrika*," I responded.

"America! Welcome to Libya – free Libya!"

The celebrations in Benghazi lasted well into the night. This was a family affair, and kids were everywhere. Groups of teenagers set off fireworks and held matches in front of spray paint canisters, turning them into makeshift flamethrowers. Away from the gridlock, young men with muscle cars did donuts in intersections, their tires screaming and emitting trails of smoke. Onlookers watched approvingly, standing as close as possible without actually getting run over.

Next to the courthouse, groups of people assembled hot-air balloon lanterns – the same type of lanterns that Free Generation Movement used to launch a giant Libyan independence flag during Gaddafi's occupation of Tripoli. Some teams were more successful than others, as the stiff Mediterranean breeze constantly blew out candles designed to fill the lanterns with hot air. The ones that did launch flew almost horizontally, blown hard by the sea winds. One lantern crashed into me, almost setting my coat on fire. A handful of them floated above rooftops and vanished into the beyond, hundreds of onlookers cheering them higher and higher until they were faint embers glowing in the distance.

Malik also took me to the courthouse itself, which had been unlocked for the public. Inside, we were greeted by young men and women, clapping, chanting revolutionary slogans, singing. The walls were covered with poster-sized images of people who died during the civil war. Most of the pictures were of men; there were a few women as well. An adjacent room served as a makeshift memorial to children who been killed, with candles, framed pictures of kids, even their favorite toys and clothes. Some were mere infants.

Exiting the children's memorial, we returned to the main hall of the courthouse, where a young man was leading in a call-and-response song. As I stood there, tapping my feet and clapping along with everyone, I looked up at the wall across from me. Like all the other walls, it featured posters of martyrs. One poster was larger than many others. It was a portrait of a young man in front of a Libyan independence flag, his head turned toward the camera, his eyes thoughtful, his face dignified.

It was Mohammed Nabbous.

"Mohammed's grave isn't too far; we just keep walking."

I was at a cemetery on the southern side of Benghazi, not far from where Mohammed Nabbous was killed in the hours prior to NATO's first bombing raids. There was very little vegetation; most of the graveyard was hardscrabble and scrub brush. A cool mist cut through this swath of desert. It settled on my forehead like cold sweat.

Each grave was a bed of dirt surrounded by a concrete rectangle frame, approximately the length and width of a coffin. Some of the graves were decorated with flowers, small plants, Libyan independence flags or family mementos; others bore no sign of visitation or upkeep. The graves had been dug in chronological order. The further we walked, the earlier the dates: March 22, March 21, March 20. Each day had 10 or more graves. When we reached the March 19 graves, we stopped.

"This is Mohammed's grave," his friend Zuhair al-Barasi said, pointing to the headstone. "This one here."

The burial plot was on my right. It was adorned with several decorative plants, as well as a number of roses in varying stages of wilt. A small plastic bowl sat directly in front of the headstone; I had noticed them on other graves, too.

"They put water out for the birds," Zuhair explained. "Seeds sometimes."

I pointed to the headstone. "So what does it say there?"

"It has the number of the grave, then his name, Martyr Mohammed Nabbous, date of birth, and the date of his death," he said, grimly.

We stood there for a few moments. The chilly mist had turned into a light rain.

"It really feels like it was just yesterday in some ways," I said, thinking of that awful day, exactly 11 months earlier.

Zuhair nodded his head, grimaced and let out a sigh.

"The funeral was on the 19th – around this time of day, actually," he recalled.

"Was it a large funeral?" I asked.

"No, because it was a complete mess here in Benghazi. There was a battle close by – the [Gaddafi] army coming, the shooting – so when we buried him, there were battles going on. We didn't know what was happening because NATO had just started to bomb. I remember just to get to the hospital, after I was told Mohammed was injured, there was a battle in front of it."

"So what do you know about what happened when he died?" I asked. "I remember hearing that day that he went out one more time in a pickup truck, after getting a lot of footage and bringing it back to the house."

"Yes," he replied. "Mohammed was in the. . .the trunk?"

"The back of the pickup truck? The truck bed," I explained.

"Yeah, the truck bed," Zuhair responded. "There was one kind of big gun in the back. I don't know which one it was, but it wasn't working. But that's where Mohammed was. He wanted to film some guys as they shoot a tank with RPGs. And you know, when there are tanks, there are snipers. And a sniper shot him."

"Do you think they knew who he was, or was he just some guy with a camera?" I asked.

"This I cannot tell. We can never know."

Zuhair grimaced and shook his head.

"And that day, we could hear the bombs. It was like a big giant coming – *stomp, stomp, stomp*. So we took our families wherever we could. Some of the houses, they had a basement."

He paused for another moment and quietly laughed. "You know, one or two days before [he died], I was hiding his camera."

"To prevent him from going back out?"

"Yeah. And he came to my house, but I had hidden it, just so he would stay home. Because I know Mohammed. But he came into my house, and he started screaming, 'I want my camera! I have [recorded] *nothing* of this revolution – I want to shoot it myself!' And he started opening the drawers in my house, and I finally said, 'Come on, take it. Just take it.'"

"I remember the hours before he died," I recalled. "He was driving around with a camera in one hand and his phone sitting in his lap. It was absolutely extraordinary how he was just winging it."

Zuhair nodded silently. I noticed a grieving woman at another grave, a dozen or so headstones away from us. She appeared to be praying, but she couldn't stop weeping.

"You know, this is something I've never told anybody," Zuhair said. "But Mohammed wanted to go to the bathroom, he never stood up. He used bottles."

"Bottles?" I replied, surprised.

"Yes, water bottles," he said, laughing.

"So he must have worked nonstop each day," I said.

"From around 10 in the morning to five in the morning."

The rain was beginning to pick up. I looked around the grave for small stones. I placed one on the concrete perimeter for myself, and then other stones for friends of Mo who had asked me to do the same.

"Why did you do that?" Zuhair asked, puzzled.

"It's a tradition in my family," I explained. "It's a way of saying that we've been here, we remember you. And I imagine you could say the stones represent the permanence of that bond."

"That seems like a good tradition," he replied.

As we prepared to leave, I approached Mo's grave one last time to say *Kaddish*, the Jewish prayer of mourning. As I finished, I contemplated the irony of me performing a Jewish prayer at a Muslim cemetery in Libya – and got the distinct feeling it would've made Mo smile.

If Benghazi is Libya's Havana, Tripoli is its Miami. I was surprised at the enormous contrast between the two cities. Then again, Gaddafi hated Benghazi and the rest of the eastern part of the country because of its wealth and influence before he came to power. He allowed Benghazi to stagnate, while making significant investments in Tripoli. Better hotels, better roads, better highways; it was his way of reminding people in the East that they would never advance as long as he remained in charge of the country.

I had arranged to meet Ali Tweel and some of the other people I had been in touch with before Gaddafi cut off Internet access in Tripoli in March 2011. We decided to meet for coffee at the local Radisson, since its café didn't segregate men and women.

At the hotel, I didn't know what to expect. My contacts in Tripoli had been so cautious about what info they put online, I didn't know what they looked like, how old they were – and in some cases, even their gender. For a long time I thought @flyingbirdies was a woman, until Ali Tweel called him *he* online.

Half a dozen people were waiting at the café. They all recognized me. I didn't recognize one of them.

"Welcome to Tripoli," one said. He smiled, realizing I didn't know who he was.

"I'm Ali Tweel."

"Ali, so good to finally meet you!" I exclaimed.

Next to Ali was a thin man, probably in his late 20s or early 30s. "My name is Akram Elsadawie," he said. It didn't ring a bell.

"I'm @flyingbirdies," he added, smiling.

"You're @flyingbirdies?" I said, laughing. "I honestly had no idea what you would look like."

Another young man was quiet, with dark hair and glasses. I stared at him for a moment, looking into his eyes.

"Mustafa Abukhit," he said softly, shaking my hand.

"If you took off your glasses and arched your eyebrow, I would've recognized you immediately," I said, joking about his avatar, which showed a closeup of one eye.

We talked for two hours, reviewing life in Tripoli during the revolution. Prices for basic goods had skyrocketed: a loaf of bread cost several times more than before the revolution. And despite Libya's international status as a major oil producer, gasoline lines stretched for miles. People queued their cars sometimes for days.

And then there were the mercenaries. Gaddafi had a force of mercenary soldiers patrolling the streets of Tripoli during the months of the revolution. Sometimes they fired at people or into buildings for no apparent reason. And just as terrifying, secret police hunted down whatever opposition remained in the city. Arrests were often arbitrary. Everyone feared that they, too, might disappear.

Now, after the revolution, they were optimistic. Yes, Libya had many obstacles to overcome – many armed militias were still beyond government control; corruption was rampant, and there were tensions between the East and West of the country. But they all wanted to look forward. They were young, educated, multilingual. They were exactly the kind of people it would take to rebuild the country.

At the same café the next day, I saw a woman, thin, probably in her thirties, a headscarf wrapped tightly around her hair and chin. I could tell she was eager to talk to me, but I didn't recognize her.

She approached and introduced herself. "My name is Mervat; Mervat Mhani."

"Very nice to meet you," I replied, still trying to put together who she was.

"I am one of the founders of Free Generation Movement. Niz Ben-Essa is my brother."

An enormous smile overtook my face. I had hoped to meet Niz and the co-founders of FGM, but he had returned to Wales and his medical practice soon after the liberation of Tripoli. While Niz never mentioned his sister during the revolution, there was often a woman in FGM videos, delivering messages of solidarity to Libyans around the country. It never occurred to me that the woman might be his sister.

We sat down and talked a long time about FGM and those bold, defiant videos. "It all started when protests began in Benghazi, when people first came out," Mervat began. "And my brother Niz came in from Cardiff. He just hopped on a plane, sent an email to his bosses, saying 'Libya is calling; I have to go back to my country.'"

"Niz came up with the idea of doing civil disobedience acts, like distributing independence flags," she continued. "We had to print them at home, so we could only do a couple of hundreds of them at a time. That was the first thing we did, and it was very scary, because we needed to distribute them on the streets. What happened was they would go in their cars, open the door and put a small stack of them on the street, and the wind would blow them around.

"Then we moved from there to hanging the independence flag in various places," Mervat said. "But then the Internet got cut off, so the guys got a satellite dish, and we reconnected again."

"We kept filming; one of the things we did was burn Gaddafi's largest poster in the city. We designed the large FGM banner, made the video of it, and as a present, we then burned Gaddafi's poster."

"What about the video where someone brought a PA system and started playing it?" I asked.

"The national anthem?" she responded.

"Yeah, how did they get away with that?"

"It was in a bag, and Niz just took it. It had a speaker inside with a remote control and USB. It was on the steps of the mosque at Algeria Square; he put it there, walked beside it and turned it on. And it just blasted. We did the same thing in the neighborhood of Fashloum, but at that time we put the speakers into rubbish bins, and put them in various areas across Fashloum, from beginning to end. The guys organized it so they would first place five or 10 minutes of static, nothing. It wasn't feasible to use remote control for all of them."

"So you needed an audio fuse, essentially," I responded.

"Exactly," she continued. "And nobody knew where it was coming from. You'd never think it would come from a rubbish bin. And it was amazing; the expression on peoples' faces, they were mouthing the words to it. Just amazing. . .It's pretty scary to film, though, to actually go out and do that."

"Well that's what was so remarkable about them," I commented. "I kept wondering how on earth you were getting away with this."

"It was very carefully planned," she explained. "They would go over it, over and over again. It was only among Free Generation Movement members. Family members, and only very, very close friends. In total there were 19 of us."

"If I remember at one point Niz had to go underground."

"Yes, that was when we were arrested," she said. "Myself, my husband, my cousin. We actually had a place where we would take reporters – a safe house – and do interviews. And I don't know how, but they were able to locate that house. When they stormed the house, they thought they were going to find a [guerilla] cell there. The amount of men that turned up – that was really scary. They knew something was happening, they had footage of the Free Generation Movement that they picked up from the Internet. But they couldn't connect it with our family.

"Then 10 days later, that's when Niz moved from my parents' house – that was just a precautionary thing – and moved into my dad's farm. He removed the satellite dish from on top of my parents' house and moved to the farm. So that time, they were in hiding but we could go see them."

"I was picked up [by the police] from my parents' house after it had been searched, then they took me to my apartment and searched that," Mervat continued. "They took our passports, our phones, our laptops, but we weren't arrested. They left a surveillance car outside and said, 'Tomorrow you have to come to us.' So the next day we went. My husband and I were very lucky, because my father-in-law called everyone he knew [in the government] and begged them. He begged, 'Let them go; they're not involved in anything.' And by midnight, we were released. But we had surveillance from that time; they never returned our passports."

"That same day, Niz went into hiding and didn't come out until the liberation of Tripoli. But they continued their work, because they still had their satellite dish. I think they claimed they were in Tunis at the time. We would send them information through another member of FGM. He was the only one who knew where they were. We would write notes on food packets. Or my sister in the U.K. would call, and we'd talk in code, and then she would call him."

"So when the time came for the liberation of Tripoli," I continued, "did you and Niz have any idea that it was about to start?"

"Yes, yes. Niz knew that zero hour would be on the 20th. A lot of Tripoli residents did; I did as well. It was generally by word-of-mouth; that's how I found out. But Niz had official information that it was going to be the 20th. My husband was ready with guns and everything. It was supposed to begin at the last prayer of the day, but people were so excited that it really started after they broke their Ramadan fast for the day. Everybody went out; there was gunfire galore."

"The 20th of August is a holy day for us," Mervat added. "The day of the conquest of Mecca. We thought that would be perfect timing. I don't know how Gaddafi supporters didn't figure it out."

"So what is FGM doing now?"

"We're doing civil society work, basically. We have many projects, including one that works on the missing in Libya. There's another that adopts families and helps their needs, like a charity. We have a centralized database for all the martyrs. And we have a literacy awareness campaign that's going to be launched very soon. We're trying to encourage Libyans to establish libraries and encourage them to read. Not literacy as in educating them, but as in broadening their horizons. We don't have funding, though; we're funding ourselves, using our own resources on all these projects."

"Do you think Free Generation Movement will eventually become an NGO?"

"It *is* an NGO," she replied, proudly. "It's official and registered. And hopefully it will expand, *insha'allah*."

"Before I leave," she added, "I want to give you something." She reached into her purse and pulled out a small cellophane packet. Inside it was a round piece of cardboard decorated red, black and green, with a star and crescent adorning the center.

"Is that what I think it is?" I asked.

"You've seen the video then?" Mervat replied. "Yes, this is one of Libyan independence flag buttons we distributed across Tripoli. They were hand-made. We had to print them out at home, cut them out and make them into buttons. This is one of the very last ones I have, and I want you to have it."

I almost didn't know what to say. "Thank you, I'm honored."

"And don't lose it," she added, laughing. "Like I said, it is one of the very last ones I have."

"Don't worry; I'll find an appropriate place to keep it. I wouldn't want to lose a piece of history."

"This must be the new *souq* they've been talking about."

It was early afternoon on a Friday in Tripoli, and I was touring the city with a friend of a friend named Emad. He was an enormous, burly fellow, but soft-spoken and a good local guide.

We had driven from the center of the capital to an enormous compound, the size of a large urban park or a zoo. The compound was surrounded by concrete walls, many of them covered in graffiti and damaged by NATO air strikes. Boys raced each other to the top of one wall that was leaning at a 45-degree angle. At the southwest corner of the compound was the *souq* – a community market. Six months earlier, there was no *souq* nearby. There generally weren't any people, either; at least not civilians. If you walked by the compound or were unfortunate enough to have your car break down there, you'd probably end up getting shot.

This was Bab al Aziziya, Muammar Gaddafi's compound, his personal fortress, with high walls, parade grounds, villas and military barracks. Now it was a disheveled ruin. When opposition forces captured the compound the previous August, wave after wave of people came in to loot and vandalize it. Whatever opulence might have existed had been stripped clean, like the denuded skeleton of an animal attacked by piranhas.

Emad and I walked toward the compound gate, weaving our way through the souq. It reeked of rotting fruit, fermenting garbage and fresh barbecue. People hawked all kinds of merchandise: socks, dry goods, coat hangers, cooking pots, blood oranges, roasted chickens, brass fittings. "They took those from inside Bab al Aziziya," Emad noted, pointing to the brass.

We climbed over a concrete barrier and made our way into the compound. It was so much more expansive than I had imagined, an abandoned city within a city. A promenade leading to the heart of the complex had become a huge garbage dump. Along with the usual trash you'd expect in any big city, there were computer parts, office equipment and broken TVs from when the compound was sacked. An extraordinary number of tuna cans littered the roadside.

A bit of fabric, jutting out of a pile of trash, caught my attention. At first I wondered if it was an abandoned prayer rug. I grabbed a stick to force it out of the pile, raised it in front of me and shook off a layer of grime.

It was a small decorative rug, intended to serve as a wall hanging, with a man's grinning portrait on it.

"Is that who I think it is?" I said.

"Yes, that's Gaddafi," Emad responded. "But as a younger man. And you get two Gaddafis for the price of one – he's on the other side of the rug, too."

I stared at the rug. It was one of the ugliest portraits I'd ever seen. I imagined the photo that inspired it must have been nice enough – a smiling Muammar Gaddafi in his prime, sporting his military uniform and ever-present colonel's hat. But when the picture was interpreted on a synthetic pile rug, it made him look like a burn victim, a Stage 1 zombie before the worst of the decomposition set in. I pitied the poor bureaucrat who had it hanging over his desk in his Bab al Aziziya office.

Given how visitors had scavenged the compound for months, I was surprised at finding any Gaddafi memorabilia. Then it occurred to me that from a Libyan perspective, the rug had no value at all. It was the face of a man who demanded homage from more than two generations of Libyans. For them, it was garbage that should've been burned a long time ago. It was as worthless as the man himself.

I rolled it up and brought it with us.

We reached a small hill with a wall stretching its entire length. In the middle of the wall was a green gate, made of corrugated metal.

"No one could enter here," Emad said as we passed through the gate. "Even very important people. This was for Gaddafi and his guests only."

It was Gaddafi's private residence, a split-level structure that reeked of the worst of 1970s American architecture, with flawed geometric experimentation and a quasi-postmodern use of space – basically Frank Lloyd Wright's worst nightmare. We explored the abandoned home; nothing was left standing, except the occasional electrical wire jutting out of a corner. The walls were covered in graffiti and bullet holes; the floor was a tetanus shot waiting to happen. The smell of charred wood and melted plastic hung in the air like a fog. I found it suffocating.

An exit on the top floor led us to a swimming pool, which retained a couple inches of brackish water and broken glass.

"Did you ever imagine that in your lifetime that you would be able to visit inside here?" I asked Emad.

"No, I never did," he said. "I live a 10-minute walk from here and I never thought I would ever even get close to it."

We backtracked out of the compound. I was still carrying the Gaddafi rug portrait and couldn't wait to wash my hands. I looked over the expanse of the ruined complex; an entire district of Tripoli dedicated to one man's greed and megalomania.

"Will any of this be preserved as a museum?" I asked Emad.

"No, I don't think so. They are working on plans to turn this into a park."

"Isn't some of it worth preserving, for future generations of Libyans to remember their history?" I said, pressing him.

"We don't need to preserve anything," Emad shrugged. "How will anyone ever forget what he did to us? This entire place should be wiped clean."

I turned on the heat lamp in my hotel bathroom and ran the shower at its highest temperature to fill the space with steam. I poured miniature bottles of shampoo over the Gaddafi rug: his colonel's hat, his uniform, his frizzy hair, his smug, sociopathic smile. Reaching for a toilet brush, I scoured him, hard. Six months' worth of dirt and mold slowly washed away from his face. He emitted a noxious odor, like a latrine that had been tear-gassed.

Shampoo bottle after shampoo bottle, I scourged Gaddafi, the toilet brush finding every corner, every crevice. There was nowhere for him to hide. I aimed the showerhead at his face. The brown, stinking liquid that had been draining out of the rug for more than 10 minutes soon became translucent water. Eventually, it ran clear.

I rolled up Gaddafi as tightly as I could and pounded him with my shoe to force out the remaining water. That didn't do the job, so I put on my shoes and stomped him. I then unrolled Gaddafi, inspected him, and pounded him some more.

When I was through with him, I hung Gaddafi in the bathroom on a towel rack. He was completely drained. Yet he still smiled back at me, cheerily.

I left the bathroom and closed the door, leaving him in darkness for a time. In the interim, I rummaged through my backpack, looking for a small cellophane packet.

I went back into the bathroom, turning up the dial on the heat lamp. Gaddafi was still smiling at me. I inspected his uniform, looking for the right spot. I opened the cellophane packet and removed the cardboard Libyan independence button from Niz Ben-Essa's sister. During the revolution, Gaddafi's thugs might have killed you if you were caught carrying one, let alone wearing it.

I leaned toward Gaddafi and pinned the button on his lapel.

I had one final appointment in Libya. It was in the lobby of the Corinthia, an absurd, cavernous palace of a hotel in Tripoli. I arrived early and waited, out of place, contemplating the previous 14 months. So much had happened since that day in December 2010, when a young Tunisian named Mohamed Bouazizi set himself on fire to protest the seizure of his produce cart.

Egyptians overthrew Hosni Mubarak in just 18 days, yet they continue to struggle over their country's destiny and place in the world. The protests in Bahrain have faded, but a core group of activists continue to press forward, against the odds. Hundreds of Yemenis died in the year it took to force out Saleh, and then saw him skate away with immunity. Syria's downward spiral is far from over, with no way to predict how deep the abyss. And here in Libya, everything seems like tempered chaos; a place where militias toting anti-aircraft guns serve as traffic cops for cars that ignore them anyway.

What was I was doing here – in Libya, of all places? I never set out to become a journalist, let alone one involved in the Arab world. I was merely a guy who happened to work for a mainstream media organization, whose heart was online, within the many online communities I considered a second home.

As I became enthralled with tales of revolution from North Africa and the Middle East, I became more entwined with those communities. They weren't just a passive audience of complete strangers. The people I got to know online became my editor, my translator, my rabbi, my muse. For years I've worked to tap the bottomless well of online generosity as a way to understand the world better, and give back to it by sharing the results of their benevolence far and wide. I never expected that well to erupt with so many stories of bravery, selflessness and sacrifice – stories that might have fallen through the cracks of history without the tools and collective determination to preserve them.

These stories are far from over, of course. The so-called Arab Spring is merely the beginning of a process that could easily take an entire generation. And nothing captured that sentiment more than the two people I was about to meet.

A young, pretty woman with piercing blue eyes entered the lobby, pushing a stroller, an ornate headscarf with pink and white flowers wrapped around her face. Inside the stroller was a brown-haired baby, not even nine months old. She wore a cute pink jumpsuit, and was playing with a stuffed bunny rabbit.

Her name was Maya, and she had her father's smile.

Eleven months earlier, Mohammed Nabbous sacrificed his life while proving to the world that Gaddafi had violated yet another ceasefire. He never lived to see the NATO jets bomb Gaddafi forces. He never saw the countless citizen journalists who followed him – in Libya, Syria and across in the region. He never saw the Libyan independence flag unfurled over Green Square in Tripoli – now called Martyrs Square – or the shaky camera phone videos that captured the final hours of Muammar Gaddafi's life.

I wondered if he would have given up seeing all of that and more, to see his young daughter, born three months after his death.

I sat at the hotel café, chatting with Mo's wife over coffee and fruit juice. She insisted I call her Sam – "Perditta" was just a name made up by Mo and his friends for her own protection during the revolution. I remembered hearing Mo say the name Sam in his livestream – it never occurred to me he was referring to his wife.

Her infectious smile belied that she was still in mourning, just as so many other people in Libya and across the Arab world were mourning their own spouses, siblings, parents and children. Mo had made the ultimate sacrifice for his country. Now it was up to his fellow Libyans to prove it was all worth it.

Like so many other people I had met in Libya, Sam was optimistic. She was exploring a variety of projects to help the country's transition to democracy and civil society. She had done her part during the revolution, but she was by no means finished. There was still so much work to be done.

As we talked, Maya cooed at her toy bunny. Giggling, she tossed me the stuffed animal and we played peekaboo.

"Would you like to hold her?" Sam asked.

"Of course I would."

I leaned down to pick up Maya. She gave me a broad, anticipating smile. As I lifted her from the stroller, I found myself raising her upward. There I was in the middle of a Tripoli hotel lobby, and I began to spin clockwise. As we picked up speed, Maya's legs flew outward, her hair flying wildly. She began to laugh, as if to say *faster, faster*, elated, ecstatic, our eyes locked in the moment.

Mo would have adored her.

END NOTES

Prologue

1 https://twitter.com/acarvin/status/32857553494872064

The Fire Spreads

1 For a detailed account of the Bouazizi incident: http://www.foreignpolicy.com/articles/2011/12/16/the_real_mohamed_bouazizi?page=full
2 http://www.cbsnews.com/stories/2011/02/20/60minutes/main20033404.shtml
3 http://www.guardian.co.uk/world/2011/jan/20/tunisian-fruit-seller-mohammed-bouazizi
4 http://24sur24.posterous.com/36701582
5 http://www.foreignpolicy.com/articles/2012/05/25/the_godfathers_of_tunis
6 http://tnleaks.org/2008/06/23/08tunis679-corruption-in-tunisia-whats-yours-is-mine/
7 http://www.state.gov/r/pa/ei/bgn/5439.htm
8 http://www.amnesty.org/en/library/info/MDE30/021/2003
9 http://www.hrw.org/reports/2010/03/24/larger-prison-0
10 http://www.amnesty.org/en/region/tunisia/report-2008
11 http://www.andycarvin.com/?p=1021
12 http://www.andycarvin.com/?p=1021
13 http://af.reuters.com/article/topNews/idAFJOE6BI06U20101219
14 For more on media restrictions in Tunisia prior to the revolution, read this report by the Open Source Center: http://publicintelligence.net/ufouo-open-source-center-tunisian-government-severely-restricts-media-freedoms/
15 http://globalvoicesonline.org/2007/11/12/access-denied-map-mapping-web-20-censorship/
16 http://globalvoicesonline.org/2008/08/20/silencing-online-speech-in-tunisia/
17 International Telecommunications Union data sheet, percentage of individuals using the Internet by country, 2011 data. http://www.itu.int/ITU-D/ict/statistics/material/excel/Individuals%20using%20the%20Internet2000-2011.xls
18 http://interactiveme.com/index.php/2011/06/facebook-statistics-in-the-mena-middle-east-q1-2011/
19 http://publicintelligence.net/ufouo-open-source-center-tunisian-government-severely-restricts-media-freedoms/
20 http://24sur24.posterous.com/36701582
21 http://www.facebook.com/photo.php?v=157295397649745
22 http://24sur24.posterous.com/36701582
23 http://www.facebook.com/video/video.php?v=1248420386917
24 http://www.facebook.com/video/video.php?v=132433530151270
25 http://www.facebook.com/photo.php?v=157289277650357
26 Among the earliest sightings of the video on Twitter is this series of tweets from December 18, 2011, preserved in a screengrab. See http://lockerz.com/s/231957469.

27 http://www.facebook.com/pages/%D8%B4%D8%B9%D8%A8-%D8%AA%D9%88%D9%86%D8%B3-%D9%8A%D8%AD%D8%B1%D9%82-%D9%81%D9%8A-%D8%B1%D9%88%D8%AD%D9%88-%D9%8A%D8%A7-%D8%B3%D9%8A%D8%A7%D8%AF%D8%A9-%D8%A7%D9%84%D8%B1%D8%A6%D9%8A%D8%B3/137969316260836
28 http://globalvoicesonline.org/2010/12/23/tunisia-unemployed-mans-suicide-attempt-sparks-riots/
29 See https://tunileaks.appspot.com/
30 https://twitter.com/chrismessina/status/223115412
31 https://twitter.com/chady2009/status/16229141321883648
32 http://lockerz.com/s/231957469
33 http://globalvoicesonline.org
34 http://globalvoicesonline.org/author/andycarvin/
35 https://tunileaks.appspot.com/
36 http://24sur24.posterous.com/
37 http://globalvoicesonline.org/2010/12/23/tunisia-unemployed-mans-suicide-attempt-sparks-riots/
38 http://www.aljazeera.com/news/africa/2010/12/2010122682433751904.html
39 http://www.aljazeera.com/indepth/opinion/2010/12/20101227142811755739.html
40 https://twitter.com/acarvin/status/19926141645103104
41 https://twitter.com/acarvin/status/25198268686270465
42 https://twitter.com/acarvin/status/25200216755929089
43 https://twitter.com/acarvin/status/25206243844956160
44 https://twitter.com/acarvin/status/25209277257875456
45 http://www.foreignpolicy.com/articles/2011/12/16/he_real_mohamed_bouazizi?page=full
46 http://www.aljazeera.com/indepth/features/2011/02/2011215123229922898.html
47 http://www.youtube.com/watch?v=bwyHRC6nH8c
48 http://www.storify.com
49 http://storify.com/acarvin/rep-gifford
50 http://storify.com/acarvin/sidi-bou-zid-a-jasmine-revolution-in-tunisia/
51 https://twitter.com/acarvin/status/25226839521763328. I also began using another tool, Curated.by, to compare the results with Storify, but it wasn't turning out the way I had hoped. I quickly abandoned the effort and focused my energies on Storify instead.
52 https://twitter.com/acarvin/status/25267262919278592
53 https://twitter.com/acarvin/status/25271261793886208
54 https://twitter.com/acarvin/status/25379272659046400. The #wjchat hashtag is a reference to the Web journalism chat that takes place on Twitter each Wednesday evening.
55 http://bit.ly/dM9tfn
56 https://twitter.com/acarvin/status/25225326678245377
57 https://twitter.com/tuntweet/status/25227486920974336
58 http://www.youtube.com/watch?v=Bg8BqRk5944
59 https://twitter.com/MarieNeigeG/status/25625942374223872
60 http://www.npr.org/blogs/thetwo-way/2011/01/13/132888992/tunisia-protests-social-media
61 https://twitter.com/acarvin/status/25947271807897600
62 https://twitter.com/acarvin/status/25947703640854528
63 https://twitter.com/acarvin/status/25958404786753536
64 https://twitter.com/acarvin/status/25959924668309504

65 https://twitter.com/acarvin/status/25961852412370944
66 https://twitter.com/acarvin/status/25964751754362881
67 https://twitter.com/acarvin/status/25950602454376448
68 https://twitter.com/acarvin/status/25962535765151744
69 https://twitter.com/acarvin/status/25967001008607232
70 https://twitter.com/acarvin/status/25967656012095488
71 https://twitter.com/acarvin/status/25968345786351616
72 https://twitter.com/acarvin/status/25969350162784256
73 https://twitter.com/acarvin/status/25971557968904194
74 https://twitter.com/acarvin/status/25971863989522433
75 https://twitter.com/acarvin/status/25974040866848769
76 https://twitter.com/acarvin/status/25987028608880641
77 https://twitter.com/acarvin/status/37597574965760001
78 https://twitter.com/MMM/status/25996287702728704

The Fire Spreads

1 http://news.bbc.co.uk/2/hi/middle_east/7332929.stm
2 http://www.nytimes.com/2008/04/07/world/middleeast/07egypt.html?_r=1
3 http://www.slate.com/articles/news_and_politics/jurisprudence/2007/05/big_brothers.html
4 http://abcnews.go.com/Blotter/egypt-face-launched-revolution/story?id=12841488&page=1#.UCf7ZuaSDMs
5 http://www.aljazeera.com/news/middleeast/2010/06/201061415530298271.html
6 http://articles.cnn.com/2010-06-25/world/egypt.police.beating_1_brutality-mohamed-elbaradei-egyptian?_s=PM:WORLD
7 http://en.wikipedia.org/wiki/File:Khalid-Saeed.jpg
8 http://www.facebook.com/elshaheeed.co.uk
9 http://www.thenational.ae/news/world/africa/undercover-police-arrested-over-beating-death-of-egyptian-man
10 http://www.egyptindependent.com/news/activists-hope-25-january-protest-will-be-start-something-big
11 http://boingboing.net/2011/02/02/egypt-the-viral-vlog.html
12 http://www.democracynow.org/2011/2/8/asmaa_mahfouz_the_youtube_video_that
13 https://twitter.com/alya1989262/status/26353718601449472
14 http://techcrunch.com/2011/02/16/jan25-twitter-egypt/
15 http://web.archive.org/web/20110314134636/http://www.almasryalyoum.com/en/node/304368
16 The original Facebook RSVP no longer exists, but this was the URL: http://www.facebook.com/events/115372325200575/
17 http://www.amnesty.org/en/news-and-updates/feature-stories/human-rights-defender-egypt-ahmed-seif-el-islam-20081209
18 http://www.ahdafsoueif.com/about.htm
19 http://www.manalaa.net
20 http://www.hrw.org/en/news/2006/05/05/egypt-troops-smother-protests-detain-activists
21 http://www.ethanzuckerman.com/blog/2006/05/08/egyptian-blogger-detained-for-participating-in-peaceful-protest/
22 http://globalvoicesonline.org/2006/05/12/egypt-blogging-behind-bars/
23 http://web.archive.org/web/20060528184010/http://freealaa.blogspot.com/

24 http://web.archive.org/web/20060520175414/http://www.andycarvin.com/archives/2006/05/vlogging_for_alaa.html
25 http://globalvoicesonline.org/2006/06/22/alaa-is-free/
26 https://twitter.com/#!/alaa/following

The Battle for Tahrir Square

1 http://twitter.com/yasmineelrafie/status/32786543508721664
2 https://twitter.com/acarvin/status/32572040984662016
3 https://twitter.com/acarvin/status/32609843990757376
4 https://twitter.com/acarvin/status/32609937712484352
5 https://twitter.com/acarvin/status/32632907629600768
6 https://twitter.com/acarvin/status/32814552152276992
7 http://twitter.com/TravellerW/status/32765378853601280
8 http://twitter.com/TravellerW/status/32765378853601280
9 http://twitter.com/TravellerW/status/32766893215449088
10 http://twitter.com/BloggerSeif/status/32773334898835457
11 https://twitter.com/acarvin/status/32815241901375489
12 https://twitter.com/acarvin/status/32933396783038464
13 http://twitter.com/yasmineelrafie/status/32787056568565760
14 http://twitter.com/yasmineelrafie/status/32787669918425088
15 https://twitter.com/acarvin/status/32815731137585152
16 https://twitter.com/acarvin/status/32815979562008576
17 https://twitter.com/acarvin/status/32816122180935680
18 https://twitter.com/acarvin/status/32816298446561280
19 https://twitter.com/acarvin/status/32816543070945280
20 https://twitter.com/acarvin/status/32819730154786816
21 https://twitter.com/acarvin/status/32819808588275712
22 https://twitter.com/acarvin/status/32819851470839809
23 https://twitter.com/acarvin/status/32820179268276225
24 https://twitter.com/acarvin/status/32821125025112064
25 https://twitter.com/acarvin/status/32821240435580928
26 https://twitter.com/acarvin/status/32820714440499201
27 https://twitter.com/acarvin/status/32822626778882050
28 https://twitter.com/acarvin/status/32823314569240576
29 https://twitter.com/acarvin/status/32823107957817345
30 https://twitter.com/acarvin/status/32823982168219648
31 https://twitter.com/acarvin/status/32825861572927488
32 https://twitter.com/acarvin/status/32826674072518656
33 https://twitter.com/acarvin/status/32825930812493824
34 https://twitter.com/acarvin/status/32836414051717122
35 https://twitter.com/acarvin/status/32932278959083520
36 https://twitter.com/acarvin/status/32824928759713793
37 https://twitter.com/acarvin/status/32825149254279168
38 https://twitter.com/acarvin/status/32825566080012288
39 https://twitter.com/acarvin/status/32827342929793024
40 https://twitter.com/acarvin/status/32832334847803392
41 https://twitter.com/acarvin/status/32832610170310656
42 https://twitter.com/acarvin/status/32835207757303809
43 https://twitter.com/acarvin/status/32832641271070721
44 https://twitter.com/acarvin/status/32832902311976960
45 https://twitter.com/acarvin/status/32838086652071936;

46 https://twitter.com/acarvin/status/32833211033714688
47 https://twitter.com/acarvin/status/32857147498827777
48 https://twitter.com/acarvin/status/32833457511993345
49 https://twitter.com/acarvin/status/32842839507337218
50 https://twitter.com/acarvin/status/32846789266640896
51 https://twitter.com/acarvin/status/32847775100051457
52 https://twitter.com/acarvin/status/32848088204845056
53 https://twitter.com/acarvin/status/32854695793922048
54 https://twitter.com/acarvin/status/32855527197249538
55 https://twitter.com/acarvin/status/32855610659704832
56 https://twitter.com/acarvin/status/32855802247127040
57 https://twitter.com/acarvin/status/32857401925304320
58 https://twitter.com/acarvin/status/32857991770275840
59 https://twitter.com/acarvin/status/32857553494872064
60 https://twitter.com/acarvin/status/32862107305246721
61 https://twitter.com/acarvin/status/32861111426486273
62 https://twitter.com/acarvin/status/32899794221400064
63 https://twitter.com/acarvin/status/32904562478157824
64 https://twitter.com/acarvin/status/32905780512428032
65 https://twitter.com/acarvin/status/32901249233846272
66 https://twitter.com/acarvin/status/32901871987331072
67 https://twitter.com/acarvin/status/32902578115182593
68 https://twitter.com/acarvin/status/32905639063724033
69 https://twitter.com/acarvin/status/32905457232252929
70 https://twitter.com/acarvin/status/32906447851356160
71 https://twitter.com/acarvin/status/32906447851356160
72 https://twitter.com/acarvin/status/32908152194203648
73 https://twitter.com/acarvin/status/32908741057712128
74 https://twitter.com/acarvin/status/32909193014935553
75 https://twitter.com/acarvin/status/32909852804120576
76 https://twitter.com/acarvin/status/32910461095649280
77 https://twitter.com/acarvin/status/32910993608675328
78 https://twitter.com/acarvin/status/32911084646047744
79 https://twitter.com/acarvin/status/32913815939055616
80 https://twitter.com/acarvin/status/32913711232458752
81 https://twitter.com/acarvin/status/32915740596109312
82 https://twitter.com/acarvin/status/32914335483297792
83 https://twitter.com/acarvin/status/32915091145883648
84 https://twitter.com/acarvin/status/32915091145883648
85 https://twitter.com/acarvin/status/32915875531063296
86 https://twitter.com/acarvin/status/32929662548054016
87 https://twitter.com/acarvin/status/32931828788625410
88 https://twitter.com/acarvin/status/32910813832417281
89 https://twitter.com/acarvin/status/32948226545942528
90 https://twitter.com/acarvin/status/32952032432234497
91 https://twitter.com/acarvin/status/32964082013306880
92 https://twitter.com/acarvin/status/32965048305451008
93 https://twitter.com/acarvin/status/32964325350047744
94 https://twitter.com/acarvin/status/32965304623566848
95 https://twitter.com/acarvin/status/32965448765022208
96 https://twitter.com/acarvin/status/32962597376499712

97 https://twitter.com/acarvin/status/32966662105862146
98 https://twitter.com/acarvin/status/32980399437119488
99 https://twitter.com/acarvin/status/32980399437119488
100 https://twitter.com/acarvin/status/32980965458444288
101 https://twitter.com/acarvin/status/32980903948984320
102 https://twitter.com/acarvin/status/32980980545363968
103 https://twitter.com/acarvin/status/32983869309329409
104 https://twitter.com/acarvin/status/32983789663813632
105 https://twitter.com/acarvin/status/32984476174782464
106 https://twitter.com/acarvin/status/32984695000006656
107 https://twitter.com/acarvin/status/32984565488295936
108 https://twitter.com/acarvin/status/32986438832357376
109 https://twitter.com/acarvin/status/32987143722766336
110 https://twitter.com/acarvin/status/32985596485967872
111 https://twitter.com/acarvin/status/32985738131808256
112 https://twitter.com/acarvin/status/32990733959049216
113 https://twitter.com/acarvin/status/32994053788409856
114 https://twitter.com/acarvin/status/32993222477365248
115 https://twitter.com/acarvin/status/33000289070096384
116 https://twitter.com/acarvin/status/33001247435014144
117 https://twitter.com/acarvin/status/33006448476823552
118 https://twitter.com/acarvin/status/33012906094366720
119 https://twitter.com/acarvin/status/33013152375373824
120 https://twitter.com/acarvin/status/33012733729308672
121 https://twitter.com/acarvin/status/33012108941598720
122 https://twitter.com/acarvin/status/33013316611735552
123 https://twitter.com/acarvin/status/33013048985915392
124 https://twitter.com/acarvin/status/33017209810849792
125 https://twitter.com/acarvin/status/33018192561442816
126 https://twitter.com/acarvin/status/33023669756231680
127 https://twitter.com/acarvin/status/33025985037340672
128 https://twitter.com/acarvin/status/33022120707629056
129 https://twitter.com/acarvin/status/33035313957834753
130 https://twitter.com/acarvin/status/33036145558429696
131 http://thetweetwatch.com/Detail/Status/33057779535052800
132 https://twitter.com/acarvin/status/33037903059755008
133 https://twitter.com/acarvin/status/33035476294176769

The People Demand

1 http://twitter.com/Ghonim/status/30748650980249600
2 https://twitter.com/acarvin/status/32409122041237504
3 https://twitter.com/acarvin/status/33653930244186112
4 https://twitter.com/acarvin/status/34621624451866624
5 https://twitter.com/acarvin/status/34627153140125696
6 https://twitter.com/acarvin/status/34636017185062913
7 https://twitter.com/acarvin/status/34644995998744576
8 https://twitter.com/acarvin/status/34658698148323328
9 https://twitter.com/acarvin/status/34650478780354560
10 https://twitter.com/acarvin/status/34675249979064320
11 http://twitpic.com/3xhapn

12 https://twitter.com/acarvin/status/34729910232813568
13 https://twitter.com/acarvin/status/34730020685484032
14 https://twitter.com/acarvin/status/34730084447289344
15 https://twitter.com/acarvin/status/34730705871306752
16 http://twitter.com/bencnn/status/34721683029884928
17 https://twitter.com/acarvin/status/34965517643026433
18 http://twitter.com/IvanCNN/status/34997652705775617
19 https://twitter.com/acarvin/status/34992924043386881
20 https://twitter.com/acarvin/status/34995215894974464
21 https://twitter.com/acarvin/status/34995700051869696
22 https://twitter.com/acarvin/status/34997473382645760
23 http://www.mcclatchydc.com/2011/02/12/v-print/108637/text-of-egyptian-military-communique.html
24 https://twitter.com/acarvin/status/35779661510213632
25 https://twitter.com/acarvin/status/35761237325389824
26 https://twitter.com/acarvin/status/35789278134931456
27 https://twitter.com/acarvin/status/35789278134931456
28 https://twitter.com/acarvin/status/35802317416566785
29 https://twitter.com/acarvin/status/35802402095497216
30 https://twitter.com/acarvin/status/35802527597330432
31 https://twitter.com/acarvin/status/35802603904307200
32 https://twitter.com/acarvin/status/35802807508402176
33 https://twitter.com/acarvin/status/35803585233027073
34 https://twitter.com/acarvin/status/35805945397248000
35 https://twitter.com/acarvin/status/35805991161303040
36 https://twitter.com/acarvin/status/35806780718202880
37 https://twitter.com/acarvin/status/35806541625958400
38 https://twitter.com/acarvin/status/35806978320113665
39 https://twitter.com/acarvin/status/35817437073121280
40 https://twitter.com/acarvin/status/36043791186137088
41 https://twitter.com/acarvin/status/36043791186137088
42 https://twitter.com/acarvin/status/36044512593715201
43 https://twitter.com/acarvin/status/36044634924777473
44 https://twitter.com/acarvin/status/36044743985209344
45 https://twitter.com/acarvin/status/36051501281452032
46 https://twitter.com/acarvin/status/36044882976059392
47 https://twitter.com/acarvin/status/36070744651862016
48 https://twitter.com/acarvin/status/36071767931883521
49 https://twitter.com/acarvin/status/36077279876616192
50 https://twitter.com/acarvin/status/36072624736043008
51 https://twitter.com/acarvin/status/36044960738451456
52 https://twitter.com/acarvin/status/36052112303464448
53 https://twitter.com/acarvin/status/36052351982899200
54 https://twitter.com/acarvin/status/36070893163651072
55 https://twitter.com/acarvin/status/36083582216704000
56 https://twitter.com/acarvin/status/36080348932603904
57 https://twitter.com/acarvin/status/36093126531756032
58 https://twitter.com/acarvin/status/36093191262441472
59 https://twitter.com/acarvin/status/36094068404518912
60 https://twitter.com/acarvin/status/36094784938573824

61 https://twitter.com/acarvin/status/36095450683539457
62 https://twitter.com/acarvin/status/36103976197963776
63 https://twitter.com/acarvin/status/36099123824295937
64 https://twitter.com/acarvin/status/36096116474773504
65 https://twitter.com/acarvin/status/36093869254774785
66 https://twitter.com/acarvin/status/36094344821739520
67 https://twitter.com/acarvin/status/36094680726896640
68 https://twitter.com/acarvin/status/36094397124706304
69 https://twitter.com/acarvin/status/36110728603779072
70 https://twitter.com/acarvin/status/36095916708601856
71 https://twitter.com/acarvin/status/ 36103874330759169
72 https://twitter.com/acarvin/status/36103963979943936
73 https://twitter.com/acarvin/status/36095350657908736
74 https://twitter.com/acarvin/status/36095604346064896
75 https://twitter.com/acarvin/status/36097977508433920
76 https://twitter.com/acarvin/status/36094465122766849
77 https://twitter.com/acarvin/status/36094965469683712
78 https://twitter.com/acarvin/status/36096359752798209
79 https://twitter.com/acarvin/status/36097287155359744
80 https://twitter.com/acarvin/status/36104734800609282
81 https://twitter.com/acarvin/status/36097865625505792
82 https://twitter.com/acarvin/status/36100144894058496

Arrested Development

1 http://www.egyptindependent.com/news/tens-thousands-tahrir-some-threasten-extend-protests
2 For a detailed accounts of tweets from the Israeli embassy that night, please see this excellent Storify collection put together by @asteris of Global Voices Online: http://storify.com/asteris/egypt-brutal-crackdown-against-protesters-in-front-1
3 http://twitter.com/mosaaberizing/status/69785077466415104
4 http://twitter.com/Gsquare86/status/69803509364699136
5 http://twitter.com/mosaaberizing/status/69810386517508096
6 http://twitter.com/mosaaberizing/status/69813664387055616
7 http://twitter.com/Gsquare86/status/69856602060111872
8 https://twitter.com/acarvin/status/69861861234970624
9 https://twitter.com/acarvin/status/69863267522187264
10 https://twitter.com/acarvin/status/69863338173 60384
11 https://twitter.com/acarvin/status/69878452626530305
12 http://twitter.com/Gsquare86/status/69863310635446272
13 http://twitter.com/Gsquare86/status/69863719424892928
14 http://twitter.com/mosaaberizing/status/69899232680742912
15 http://twitter.com/mosaaberizing/status/69900048158310401
16 https://twitter.com/acarvin/status/69879876949262336
17 https://twitter.com/acarvin/status/69884174839971840
18 https://twitter.com/acarvin/status/69886389008875520
19 https://twitter.com/acarvin/status/69920742254448641
20 https://twitter.com/acarvin/status/69881911773888512
21 https://twitter.com/tarekshalaby/status/69901129550544897
22 https://twitter.com/acarvin/status/69908323956301825
23 https://twitter.com/acarvin/status/69908160667844608

24 http://twitter.com/mosaaberizing/status/69902190227111937
25 http://twitter.com/mosaaberizing/status/69903408437538817
26 https://twitter.com/acarvin/status/69909591319773184
27 https://twitter.com/acarvin/status/69916914884935680
28 https://twitter.com/acarvin/status/69921484897918976
29 http://twitter.com/Gsquare86/status/69923599477248001
30 https://twitter.com/acarvin/status/69921641844588544
31 https://twitter.com/acarvin/status/69921754948177920
32 https://twitter.com/acarvin/status/69927443665915904
33 https://twitter.com/acarvin/status/69928058068545536
34 https://twitter.com/acarvin/status/69923023502852096
35 https://twitter.com/acarvin/status/69922004777713664
36 https://twitter.com/acarvin/status/69921900733792256
37 https://twitter.com/acarvin/status/69922168951160832
38 https://twitter.com/acarvin/status/69923449400852480
39 https://twitter.com/acarvin/status/69924000276561920
40 https://twitter.com/norashalaby/status/69923133922095104
41 https://twitter.com/acarvin/status/69924085353816064
42 https://twitter.com/acarvin/status/69924163711803392
43 https://twitter.com/acarvin/status/69924496668233728
44 https://twitter.com/acarvin/status/69924735756144642
45 https://twitter.com/acarvin/status/69924833961590784
46 https://twitter.com/acarvin/status/69924864575799296
47 https://twitter.com/acarvin/status/69933041182715904
48 https://twitter.com/acarvin/status/9926358091968512
49 https://twitter.com/acarvin/status/69926403675652096
50 https://twitter.com/acarvin/status/69929086981648384
51 https://twitter.com/acarvin/status/69929170565726208
52 https://twitter.com/acarvin/status/69929256628649984
53 https://twitter.com/acarvin/status/69929295442755584
54 http://twitter.com/mxbw/status/69922561911296000
55 https://twitter.com/acarvin/status/69926547418660864
56 https://twitter.com/acarvin/status/69929575857131521
57 https://twitter.com/acarvin/status/69945567622594560
58 https://twitter.com/acarvin/status/69930121368322049
59 https://twitter.com/acarvin/status/69937223268704258
60 https://twitter.com/acarvin/status/69937563149938689
61 https://twitter.com/acarvin/status/69935771532017664
62 https://twitter.com/acarvin/status/69930684990492673
63 https://twitter.com/acarvin/status/69957754051244032
64 https://twitter.com/acarvin/status/70628434187001858
65 https://twitter.com/acarvin/status/71234199067164672
66 https://twitter.com/acarvin/status/71331763259052032
67 https://twitter.com/acarvin/status/71578283279527936
68 http://en.nomiltrials.com/p/about-us.html

U Cant Break Us

1 http://www.hrw.org/reports/1997/bahrain/
2 http://www.hrw.org/legacy/worldreport99/mideast/Bahrain.html

3 http://dosfan.lib.uic.edu/ERC/democracy/1995_hrp_report/95hrp_report_nea/Bahrain.html
4 http://www.state.gov/www/global/human_rights/1996_hrp_report/bahrain.html
5 http://www.unhcr.org/refworld/country,,AMNESTY,,BHR,,3ae6aa05c,0.html
6 http://en.wikisource.org/wiki/National_Action_Charter_of_Bahrain
7 http://www.aljazeera.com/news/middleeast/2011/02/201121318555638811 7.html
8 https://twitter.com/acarvin/status/38030626070204416
9 https://twitter.com/acarvin/status/38031117911064576
10 https://twitter.com/acarvin/status/38031152258220032
11 https://twitter.com/acarvin/status/38031192024416256
12 https://twitter.com/acarvin/status/38031232767893504
13 https://twitter.com/acarvin/status/38031318726098944
14 https://twitter.com/acarvin/status/38031358211272704
15 https://twitter.com/acarvin/status/38031517389307904
16 https://twitter.com/acarvin/status/38031763024523264
17 https://twitter.com/acarvin/status/38031842338807808
18 https://twitter.com/acarvin/status/38031912958300160
19 https://twitter.com/acarvin/status/38032017799135233
20 https://twitter.com/acarvin/status/38033078945464321
21 https://twitter.com/acarvin/status/38032701156102144
22 https://twitter.com/acarvin/status/38034212883927040
23 https://twitter.com/acarvin/status/38034320119562240
24 https://twitter.com/acarvin/status/38034363148935168
25 https://twitter.com/acarvin/status/38034529163804672
26 https://twitter.com/acarvin/status/38034725910233088
27 https://twitter.com/acarvin/status/38037097428287488
28 https://twitter.com/acarvin/status/38037293247905792
29 https://twitter.com/acarvin/status/38037836561260545
30 https://twitter.com/acarvin/status/38038180867346432
31 https://twitter.com/acarvin/status/38037643300306944
32 https://twitter.com/acarvin/status/38034613368659969
33 https://twitter.com/acarvin/status/38034703562964993
34 https://twitter.com/acarvin/status/38069793114292224
35 https://twitter.com/acarvin/status/38069819215585280
36 https://twitter.com/acarvin/status/38069866653163520
37 https://twitter.com/acarvin/status/38069919522373632
38 https://twitter.com/acarvin/status/56517364140867584
39 https://twitter.com/acarvin/status/56517402636189696
40 https://twitter.com/acarvin/status/56517439625764864
41 https://twitter.com/acarvin/status/56517468822323201
42 https://twitter.com/acarvin/status/56517495938498560
43 https://twitter.com/acarvin/status/56517522882707457
44 https://twitter.com/acarvin/status/56517581095452672
45 https://twitter.com/acarvin/status/56517614213672961
46 https://twitter.com/acarvin/status/56517822246944768
47 https://twitter.com/acarvin/status/56517878920384512
48 https://twitter.com/acarvin/status/56517989113147392
49 https://twitter.com/acarvin/status/56518064199569408
50 https://twitter.com/acarvin/status/56518137281134592
51 https://twitter.com/acarvin/status/56518190993379329
52 https://twitter.com/acarvin/status/56518200535420928

53 https://twitter.com/acarvin/status/56518599631835137
54 http://www.twitlonger.com/show/9oh1i7
55 https://twitter.com/acarvin/status/56723466988171264
56 https://twitter.com/acarvin/status/56742492527280128
57 https://twitter.com/acarvin/status/56742520146763777
58 https://twitter.com/acarvin/status/56742534747140096
59 https://twitter.com/acarvin/status/56742958183088129
60 https://twitter.com/acarvin/status/57461910836232192
61 http://angryarabiya.blogspot.com/2011/04/letter-to-president-obama.html
62 https://twitter.com/acarvin/status/57461827398934528
63 https://twitter.com/acarvin/status/57465708895940608
64 https://twitter.com/acarvin/status/57486766277525504
65 https://twitter.com/acarvin/status/57486853846220800
66 https://twitter.com/acarvin/status/57486896045105152
67 https://twitter.com/acarvin/status/57486896045105152
68 https://twitter.com/acarvin/status/57487015280787456
69 https://twitter.com/acarvin/status/57542181002555394
70 https://twitter.com/acarvin/status/57915074806951936
71 https://twitter.com/acarvin/status/57541782312992769
72 https://twitter.com/acarvin/status/57769476355137536
73 https://twitter.com/acarvin/status/58626820521738240
74 https://twitter.com/acarvin/status/57491649198161920
75 https://twitter.com/acarvin/status/57491851418157057
76 https://twitter.com/acarvin/status/57492048814682117
77 https://twitter.com/acarvin/status/57492303404728320
78 https://twitter.com/acarvin/status/57493559477141504
79 https://twitter.com/acarvin/status/57526233541517312
80 https://twitter.com/acarvin/status/57528438306775040
81 https://twitter.com/acarvin/status/57860096885145600
82 https://twitter.com/acarvin/status/58613656493113344
83 https://twitter.com/acarvin/status/58618025158524928
84 https://twitter.com/acarvin/status/58987364948770817
85 https://twitter.com/acarvin/status/58987486919135232
86 https://twitter.com/acarvin/status/58990744446304256
87 https://twitter.com/acarvin/status/59336134890762241
88 http://angryarabiya.blogspot.com/2011/04/update-from-zainabs-mother.html
89 https://twitter.com/acarvin/status/60832987981418497
90 https://twitter.com/acarvin/status/60833052250750976
91 https://twitter.com/acarvin/status/60833074677682176
92 https://twitter.com/ONLINEBAHRAIN/status/140431716727795712
93 https://twitter.com/MARYAMALKHAWAJA/status/140437951820726272
94 https://twitter.com/Mo7ammedMirza/status/140443318726307840/photo/1
95 http://www.youtube.com/watch?v=baVhDKhXyfU
96 https://twitter.com/angryarabiya/status/140472182219358208
97 https://twitter.com/angryarabiya/status/140473834976448512
98 https://twitter.com/angryarabiya/status/140474819920662529
99 https://twitter.com/angryarabiya/status/140476779927306240
100 https://twitter.com/angryarabiya/status/140479546016272384
101 https://twitter.com/angryarabiya/status/140480345907793920
102 https://twitter.com/angryarabiya/status/140481207535284225
103 https://twitter.com/angryarabiya/status/140488271166836736

104 https://twitter.com/acarvin/status/140489400864866304
105 https://twitter.com/angryarabiya/status/140490351919104000
106 https://twitter.com/angryarabiya/status/140490351919104000
107 https://twitter.com/angryarabiya/status/140491205908758528
108 https://twitter.com/angryarabiya/status/140497104186511360
109 https://twitter.com/angryarabiya/status/140502994188906496
110 https://twitter.com/angryarabiya/status/140503785243017217
111 For a full accounting of all of her tweets, visit Jim Early's excellent Storify page documenting the event. http://storify.com/mkearley2008/at-angryarabiya-s-brave-act
112 https://twitter.com/acarvin/status/147337555522756609
113 https://twitter.com/acarvin/status/147338766892277760
114 https://twitter.com/acarvin/status/147338827701301249
115 http://t.co/WuO4DY1W
116 https://twitter.com/acarvin/status/147359901683953665
117 https://twitter.com/acarvin/status/147382849601941504
118 http://mypict.me/index.php?id=331539961
119 https://twitter.com/acarvin/status/147382301276372993
120 http://mypict.me/index.php?id=331540082
121 https://twitter.com/acarvin/status/147382378984259585
122 http://mypict.me/index.php?id=331540105
123 https://twitter.com/acarvin/status/147394791099994113
124 https://twitter.com/acarvin/status/147402231229067264
125 https://twitter.com/acarvin/status/147402259272179713
126 https://twitter.com/acarvin/status/147403169708773376
127 http://www.telly.com/QUQGF?fromtwitvid=1
128 http://t.co/uwzjHnpj
129 http://www.frontlinedefenders.org/files/abdulhadi_letter.pdf
130 http://www.amnesty.org.uk/news_details.asp?NewsID=20033
131 https://twitter.com/acarvin/status/188058784088850432
132 https://twitter.com/acarvin/status/147382849601941504

Long Shot

1 If you ever want to start a fight between rival copyeditors, ask them to spell Muammar Gaddafi's name. Given the vagaries of transliteration from Libyan Arabic into English, there are more than 100 possible ways to spell it. I've selected the one that I saw used most often by Libyan activists. When I hear Libyans say his name, the most common pronunciation seems to be something like gih-DEHHFY., extending the D sound.
2 http://www.facebook.com/groups/libyan17feb/
3 http://www.asharq-e.com/news.asp?section=1&id=24095
4 http://www.aljazeera.com/news/middleeast/2011/02/201122171649677912.html
5 http://www.libya-nclo.com/%D8%A7%D8%AE%D8%A8%D8%A7%D8%B1/%D8%AF%D8%B9%D9%88%D8%A9%D9%85%D9%86%D9%85%D9%88%D8%A7%D8%B7%D9%86%D9%8A%D9%86%D9%84%D9%8A%D8%A8%D9%8A%D9%8A%D9%86.aspx
6 http://www.libya-nclo.com/%D8%A7%D8%AE%D8%A8%D8%A7%D8%B1/%D9%84%D9%8A%D8%A8%D9%8A%D8%A7%D8%A3%D9%86%D8%A8%D8%A7%D8%A1%D8%B9%D9%86%D8%AC%D9%87%D9%88%D8%AF%D9%84%D8%AA%D8%B4%D9%83%D9%8A%D9%84%D8%AD%D9%83%D9%88%D9%85%D8%A9%D8%AC%D8%AF%D9%8A%D8%AF%D8%A9%D8%A8%D9%88%D8%AC%D9%88%D9%87%D9%85%D9%86%D8%A7.aspx

7 https://twitter.com/acarvin/status/34054385445109760
8 International Telecommunications Union data sheet, percentage of individuals using the Internet by country, 2011 data. http://www.itu.int/ITU-D/ict/statistics/material/excel/Individuals%20using%20the%20Internet2000-2011.xls
9 https://twitter.com/acarvin/status/37581723826917376
10 https://twitter.com/acarvin/status/37697951316975616
11 https://twitter.com/acarvin/status/37966625298710528
12 https://twitter.com/acarvin/status/37689061762285568
13 https://twitter.com/acarvin/status/37968021381189632
14 https://twitter.com/acarvin/status/37978139879538688
15 https://twitter.com/malikLofficial/status/38015067006042112 After the civil war, @LibyaSupreme changed his Twitter name to @MalikLofficial.
16 https://twitter.com/acarvin/status/38018846073819137
17 https://twitter.com/acarvin/status/38035678998700032
18 Al Bayda, it turns out, is approximately 120 miles east of Benghazi. See https://maps.google.com/maps?q=Al+Bayda,+Al+Jabal+al+Akhdar,+Libya&hl=en&ll=32.759562,21.741943&spn=4.50792,7.701416&sll=38.804821,-77.236966&sspn=2.088942,3.850708&oq=al+bayda&doflg=ptk&hnear=Al+Bayda,+Al+Jabal+al+Akhdar,+Libya&t=m&z=7
19 https://twitter.com/acarvin/status/38028832523030528
20 https://twitter.com/acarvin/status/38240338137186304
21 https://twitter.com/acarvin/status/38254878228750336
22 https://twitter.com/acarvin/status/38259872856276992
23 https://twitter.com/acarvin/status/38259872856276992
24 https://twitter.com/acarvin/status/38260980467109888
25 https://twitter.com/acarvin/status/38293775877029888
26 https://twitter.com/acarvin/status/38294880262434816
27 https://twitter.com/acarvin/status/38295112480071680
28 https://twitter.com/acarvin/status/38295382668742656
29 https://twitter.com/acarvin/status/38324760844697600
30 https://twitter.com/acarvin/status/38328322815565824
31 https://twitter.com/acarvin/status/38328351982764032
32 https://twitter.com/acarvin/status/38338097972387840
33 https://twitter.com/acarvin/status/38340577661689857
34 https://twitter.com/acarvin/status/38340721337573376
35 https://twitter.com/acarvin/status/38298692234641409
36 https://twitter.com/acarvin/status/38345461546885120
37 At the time of writing, the original URL for this video, http://www.libyafeb17.com/?p=405, was unavailable, but a copy of it can be found in the Internet Archive: http://web.archive.org/web/20110223031520/http://www.libyafeb17.com/?p=405
38 https://twitter.com/acarvin/status/38341702808768512
39 https://twitter.com/acarvin/status/38350460733751296
40 https://twitter.com/Abukhit/status/23292894962006425б/photo/1
41 http://a1.twimg.com/profile_images/1244998192/loading_animation_bigger.gif
42 https://twimg0-a.akamaihd.net/profile_images/404925089/koki.jpg
43 https://twitter.com/acarvin/status/39723435890454528
44 https://twitter.com/acarvin/status/39723545466646528
45 https://twitter.com/acarvin/status/39725721635000320
46 https://twitter.com/acarvin/status/39724009570570240
47 https://twitter.com/acarvin/status/39735178498818048

48 https://twitter.com/acarvin/status/39737103474630656
49 https://twitter.com/acarvin/status/39758830451699712
50 https://twitter.com/acarvin/status/40031853280903168
51 https://twitter.com/acarvin/status/40031927314546688
52 https://twitter.com/acarvin/status/40032007274770432
53 https://twitter.com/acarvin/status/40039719098126336
54 https://twitter.com/acarvin/status/40095683188883456
55 https://twitter.com/acarvin/status/40101310975975425
56 https://twitter.com/acarvin/status/40128092580089856
57 https://twitter.com/acarvin/status/40128132900069376
58 https://twitter.com/acarvin/status/40812697029320704
59 http://www.time.com/time/world/article/0,8599,2052978,00.html
60 For examples, see the following. Be forewarned that they are extremely graphic, including footage of people who have literally been blown to pieces by heavy weaponry. Please consider carefully before viewing them. http://yfrog.com/h4oacietj http://yfrog.com/h7ucplxj
61 http://www.youtube.com/watch?v=rh2mZ3G6-B4&feature=player_embedded
62 https://twitter.com/acarvin/status/40037327942332416
63 https://twitter.com/acarvin/status/40042105728405504
64 https://twitter.com/acarvin/status/40042105728405504
65 https://twitter.com/acarvin/status/40042575230406656
66 https://twitter.com/acarvin/status/41152437930835969
67 https://twitter.com/acarvin/status/41152463151185920
68 https://twitter.com/acarvin/status/41152500442730497
69 https://twitter.com/acarvin/status/41152562367430656
70 https://twitter.com/acarvin/status/41152716294066176
71 https://twitter.com/acarvin/status/41152763039580160
72 https://twitter.com/acarvin/status/41152824339341312
73 https://twitter.com/acarvin/status/41152857570811904
74 https://twitter.com/acarvin/status/41155217353490432
75 https://twitter.com/acarvin/status/41155261016047616
76 https://twitter.com/acarvin/status/41156127429361664
77 https://twitter.com/acarvin/status/41160531578597381
78 https://twitter.com/acarvin/status/41160531578597381
79 https://twitter.com/acarvin/status/41164201485545472
80 https://twitter.com/acarvin/status/41164241159467008
81 https://twitter.com/acarvin/status/41164345220136961
82 https://twitter.com/acarvin/status/41164370595688449
83 https://twitter.com/acarvin/status/41178909093539840
84 https://twitter.com/acarvin/status/41178194572873728
85 https://twitter.com/acarvin/status/41179304725458944
86 https://twitter.com/acarvin/status/41179332491747328
87 https://twitter.com/acarvin/status/41179350342709248
88 https://twitter.com/acarvin/status/41179492705771520
89 https://twitter.com/acarvin/status/41179555695828992
90 https://twitter.com/acarvin/status/41179715423174656
91 https://twitter.com/acarvin/status/41179639640498176
92 https://twitter.com/acarvin/status/41180237605781504
93 https://twitter.com/acarvin/status/41180319780569088
94 https://twitter.com/acarvin/status/41184511005822976

95 https://twitter.com/acarvin/status/41187097180119040
96 https://twitter.com/acarvin/status/41180130470674432
97 https://twitter.com/acarvin/status/41180130470674432
98 https://twitter.com/acarvin/status/39104268480950272
99 https://twitter.com/acarvin/status/39110675175456768
100 https://twitter.com/acarvin/status/39110958827843585
101 Private direct message, Feb 19, 2011 23:55:30
102 CNN International interview, February 19, 2011, as archived on YouTube: http://www.youtube.com/watch?v=38EXALI60hg
103 CNN International interview, February 19, 2011, as archived on YouTube: http://www.youtube.com/watch?v=38EXALI60hg
104 Chat log from private Skype text exchange with the author, February 21, 2011, 9 a.m.

A Candle Loses Nothing

1 Unless otherwise noted, these quotes from Mohamed Nabbous come from a livestream video that is no longer archived on Livestream.com. One of the admins of the livestream channel was kind enough to send me a copy of the original video, which I have archived on YouTube and transcribed using the tool Amara, formerly known as Universal Subtitles. See http://www.youtube.com/watch?v=f5yyZa5bRXc and http://www.universalsubtitles.org/en/videos/naGduAWFHqL7/en/209937/
2 http://www.foxnews.com/world/2011/03/04/libya-shuts-internet-service-ahead-planned-anti-government-protests/
3 http://www.un.org/News/Press/docs/2011/sc10200.doc.htm#Resolution
4 http://web.archive.org/web/20110318224707/http://www.bbc.co.uk/news/world-middle-east-12787056
5 https://twitter.com/acarvin/status/48930399421865984
6 https://twitter.com/acarvin/status/48950186399117312
7 http://www.universalsubtitles.org/en/videos/naGduAWFHqL7/en/209937/
8 http://www.universalsubtitles.org/en/videos/naGduAWFHqL7/en/209937/
9 http://www.universalsubtitles.org/en/videos/naGduAWFHqL7/en/209937/
10 http://www.universalsubtitles.org/en/videos/naGduAWFHqL7/en/209937/
11 http://www.universalsubtitles.org/en/videos/naGduAWFHqL7/en/209937/
12 http://www.universalsubtitles.org/en/videos/naGduAWFHqL7/en/209937/
13 http://www.universalsubtitles.org/en/videos/naGduAWFHqL7/en/209937/
14 http://www.universalsubtitles.org/en/videos/naGduAWFHqL7/en/209937/
15 http://www.universalsubtitles.org/en/videos/naGduAWFHqL7/en/209937/
16 http://www.universalsubtitles.org/en/videos/naGduAWFHqL7/en/209937/
17 http://www.universalsubtitles.org/en/videos/naGduAWFHqL7/en/209937/
18 http://www.universalsubtitles.org/en/videos/naGduAWFHqL7/en/209937/
19 http://www.universalsubtitles.org/en/videos/naGduAWFHqL7/en/209937/
20 http://www.universalsubtitles.org/en/videos/naGduAWFHqL7/en/209937/
21 http://www.universalsubtitles.org/en/videos/naGduAWFHqL7/en/209937/
22 http://www.universalsubtitles.org/en/videos/naGduAWFHqL7/en/209937/
23 http://www.universalsubtitles.org/en/videos/naGduAWFHqL7/en/209937/
24 Transcript of chatroom, transcribed by the author from screen shots supplied by chatroom administrators.
25 http://www.universalsubtitles.org/en/videos/naGduAWFHqL7/en/209937/
26 https://twitter.com/acarvin/status/48959262906515457
27 http://www.universalsubtitles.org/en/videos/naGduAWFHqL7/en/209937/
28 http://www.universalsubtitles.org/en/videos/naGduAWFHqL7/en/209937/

29 http://www.livestream.com/libya17feb/video?clipId=pla_e13a2505-305a-46ba-b3bd-3173ad75fa6c
30 Like many other members of the opposition, Perditta referred to Muammar Gaddafi as Gerdaffi. This isn't one of the many alternative ways of spelling his surname; it's actually a pun that utilizes the Arabic word for "monkey."
31 Screen shot from the chatroom, supplied to the author.
32 https://twitter.com/acarvin/status/48965628903694336
33 http://www.livestream.com/libya17feb/video?clipId=pla_e13a2505-305a-46ba-b3bd-3173ad75fa6c
34 Chat log supplied to the author.
35 Chat log supplied to the author.
36 Chat log supplied to the author.
37 http://goo.gl/maps/yvPZn
38 Chat log supplied to the author.
39 http://www.livestream.com/libya17feb/video?clipId=pla_e13a2505-305a-46ba-b3bd-3173ad75fa6c
40 http://www.livestream.com/libya17feb/video?clipId=pla_e13a2505-305a-46ba-b3bd-3173ad75fa6c
41 http://www.livestream.com/libya17feb/video?clipId=pla_e13a2505-305a-46ba-b3bd-3173ad75fa6c
42 https://twitter.com/acarvin/status/48963084009750528
43 http://www.livestream.com/libya17feb/video?clipId=pla_e13a2505-305a-46ba-b3bd-3173ad75fa6c
44 http://www.livestream.com/libya17feb/video?clipId=pla_e13a2505-305a-46ba-b3bd-3173ad75fa6c
45 http://www.livestream.com/libya17feb/video?clipId=pla_e13a2505-305a-46ba-b3bd-3173ad75fa6c
46 https://twitter.com/acarvin/status/48973570214346752
47 https://twitter.com/acarvin/status/49067509869051904
48 http://www.livestream.com/libya17feb/video?clipId=pla_0dd5342d-9f76-49d7-b2b4-4c915ca3ee88
49 http://www.livestream.com/libya17feb/video?clipId=pla_0dd5342d-9f76-49d7-b2b4-4c915ca3ee88
50 http://www.livestream.com/libya17feb/video?clipId=pla_0dd5342d-9f76-49d7-b2b4-4c915ca3ee88
51 http://www.livestream.com/libya17feb/video?clipId=pla_0dd5342d-9f76-49d7-b2b4-4c915ca3ee88
52 http://www.livestream.com/libya17feb/video?clipId=pla_0dd5342d-9f76-49d7-b2b4-4c915ca3ee88
53 http://www.livestream.com/libya17feb/video?clipId=pla_0dd5342d-9f76-49d7-b2b4-4c915ca3ee88
54 http://www.livestream.com/libya17feb/video?clipId=pla_0dd5342d-9f76-49d7-b2b4-4c915ca3ee88
55 Email sent to the author, March 19, 2011.
56 http://www.livestream.com/libya17feb/video?clipId=pla_6d651483-94e1-41c0-bc94-9913c48ef38e
57 http://www.livestream.com/libya17feb/video?clipId=pla_6d651483-94e1-41c0-bc94-9913c48ef38e
58 http://www.livestream.com/libya17feb/video?clipId=pla_6d651483-94e1-41c0-bc94-9913c48ef38e

59 Skype text sent to the author, March 19, 2011.
60 Direct message to the author, March 19, 2011.
61 Email sent to the author, March 19, 2011.
62 Email sent by the author, March 19, 2011.
63 Email sent to the author, March 19, 2011.
64 Email sent to the author, March 19, 2011.
65 Email sent to the author, March 19, 2011.
66 http://www.livestream.com/libya17feb/video?clipId=pla_ad4fc39a-1de6-4b6b-85cf-f7c762140630
67 http://www.livestream.com/libya17feb/video?clipId=pla_ad4fc39a-1de6-4b6b-85cf-f7c762140630
68 Direct message to the author, March 19, 2011.
69 Email sent to the author, March 19, 2011.
70 Direct message sent to the author.
71 Chat logs from the livestream sent to the author by chat administrators.
72 http://www.livestream.com/libya17feb/video?clipId=pla_413c69cd-9914-493e-a77d-7e22c7c019c8
72 http://www.livestream.com/libya17feb/video?clipId=pla_413c69cd-9914-493e-a77d-7e22c7c019c8
73 http://www.livestream.com/libya17feb/video?clipId=pla_413c69cd-9914-493e-a77d-7e22c7c019c8
74 http://www.livestream.com/libya17feb/video?clipId=pla_413c69cd-9914-493e-a77d-7e22c7c019c8
75 http://www.livestream.com/libya17feb/video?clipId=pla_413c69cd-9914-493e-a77d-7e22c7c019c8
76 http://www.livestream.com/libya17feb/video?clipId=pla_413c69cd-9914-493e-a77d-7e22c7c019c8
77 http://www.livestream.com/libya17feb/video?clipId=pla_413c69cd-9914-493e-a77d-7e22c7c019c8
78 http://www.livestream.com/libya17feb/video?clipId=pla_413c69cd-9914-493e-a77d-7e22c7c019c8
79 http://www.livestream.com/libya17feb/video?clipId=pla_413c69cd-9914-493e-a77d-7e22c7c019c8
80 Chat logs supplied to the author by chat administrators.
81 Chat logs supplied to the author by chat administrators.
82 Chat logs supplied to the author by chat administrators.
83 http://www.livestream.com/libya17feb/video?clipId=pla_9745ec21-c64d-440f-abe7-a412e7db456d
84 http://www.livestream.com/libya17feb/video?clipId=pla_9745ec21-c64d-440f-abe7-a412e7db456d
85 https://twitter.com/acarvin/status/49121176441720832
86 https://twitter.com/acarvin/status/49123816458301440
87 https://twitter.com/acarvin/status/49124094091870208
88 https://twitter.com/acarvin/status/49124442739179520
89 https://twitter.com/acarvin/status/49124792921620480
90 https://twitter.com/acarvin/status/49124870533029888
91 https://twitter.com/acarvin/status/49125360620679168
92 https://twitter.com/acarvin/status/49125543534272512
93 https://twitter.com/acarvin/status/49127653143363584
94 https://twitter.com/acarvin/status/49128175250313216

95 https://twitter.com/xeni/status/49130092240179200
96 https://twitter.com/acarvin/status/49134478567804929
97 https://twitter.com/acarvin/status/49134717710245889
98 https://twitter.com/xeni/status/49130463704530945
99 https://twitter.com/acarvin/status/49134990885269504
100 https://twitter.com/bencnn/status/49178664629321729
101 https://twitter.com/bencnn/status/49179447538094080
102 https://twitter.com/LibyaInMe/status/49184023557324801
103 https://twitter.com/iyad_elbaghdadi/status/49192094178357248
104 https://twitter.com/acarvin/status/49137113513459712
105 https://twitter.com/acarvin/status/49142632257028097
106 https://twitter.com/BiancaJagger/status/49135646895386624
107 https://twitter.com/ThePinebox/status/49177743094595584
108 https://twitter.com/acarvin/status/49183282008563712
109 @Hamzamu, the Egyptian doctor who first reported Mo's death on Twitter, has put together a collection of video tributes to Mo, which can be found here: http://storify.com/hamzamu/mouhamed-nabbous-mo-youtube-videos
110 https://twitter.com/acarvin/status/49133983707054080
111 https://twitter.com/acarvin/status/49162825091907584
112 https://twitter.com/acarvin/status/49154445740740609
113 https://twitter.com/acarvin/status/49135524635615232
114 https://twitter.com/acarvin/status/49142944015462400
115 https://twitter.com/acarvin/status/49149531207647232
116 https://twitter.com/acarvin/status/49297917986619392

Tilting at Rumor Mills

1 https://twitter.com/acarvin/status/47714980849664000
2 https://twitter.com/acarvin/status/47724657259982848
3 https://twitter.com/acarvin/status/47748405660884992
4 http://www.aliveinbaghdad.org
5 https://twitter.com/acarvin/status/47749663436193792
6 https://twitter.com/BaghdadBrian/status/47750155251879937
7 https://twitter.com/acarvin/status/47744883326324736
8 https://twitter.com/acarvin/status/47778447027744768
9 https://twitter.com/acarvin/status/47778322788257792
10 https://twitter.com/acarvin/status/47778392711495680
11 https://twitter.com/acarvin/status/47778533140996096
12 https://twitter.com/acarvin/status/47778560659832833
13 https://twitter.com/acarvin/status/47779294042267648
14 https://twitter.com/acarvin/status/47808832172339201
15 https://twitter.com/acarvin/status/47809460827205632
16 https://twitter.com/acarvin/status/47809908959215616
17 https://twitter.com/acarvin/status/47813208353947648
18 https://twitter.com/acarvin/status/47851875869007873
19 https://twitter.com/acarvin/status/47858887575085056
20 https://twitter.com/acarvin/status/47858887575085056
21 https://twitter.com/DougPologe/status/47859551604711424
22 https://twitter.com/acarvin/status/47860476834615296
23 https://twitter.com/acarvin/status/49541843641303041
24 https://twitter.com/acarvin/status/49542272718606336

25 https://twitter.com/acarvin/status/49629487524093952
26 https://twitter.com/blogdiva/status/49629308402151426
27 https://twitter.com/blogdiva/status/49629308402151426
28 https://twitter.com/acarvin/status/49635419322716160
29 https://twitter.com/acarvin/status/49655707338936320
30 https://twitter.com/acarvin/status/51290775278981121
31 https://twitter.com/acarvin/status/51451279695806464
32 https://twitter.com/acarvin/status/51451013785321472
33 https://twitter.com/jan15egy/status/46641931073228800
34 https://twitter.com/acarvin/status/46642649075171328
35 http://www.facebook.com/pages/%D8%A7%D9%84%D9%85%D9%86%D8%A7%D8%B1%D8%A9%D9%84%D9%84%D8%A5%D8%B9%D9%84%D8%A7%D9%85-%D8%A7%D9%84%D8%B1%D8%A6%D9%8A%D8%B3%D9%8A%D8%A9/179449562095105?sk=info
36 https://twitter.com/acarvin/status/46648197946425344
37 https://twitter.com/acarvin/status/46644628774072320
38 https://twitter.com/HarisAlisic/status/46643704345272320
39 https://twitter.com/acarvin/status/46643993282482176
40 https://twitter.com/acarvin/status/46647677370380290
41 https://twitter.com/sonomadiver/status/46649219888590848
42 https://twitter.com/jasonhansman/status/46648286735646720
43 https://twitter.com/shorepatrol/status/46688466934841344
44 https://twitter.com/acarvin/status/46647562400305152
45 https://twitter.com/brhone/status/46649445198209024
46 http://commons.wikimedia.org/wiki/File:BL10pounderStarShellMkII.jpg
47 https://twitter.com/LeShaque/status/46647995873234944
48 http://www.weaponsindia.com/bm81illum.htm
49 http://www.weaponsindia.com/bm81illum.htm
50 https://twitter.com/LeShaque/status/46648306213994496
51 https://twitter.com/LeShaque/status/46649108198457344
52 http://www.militaryphotos.net/forums/showthread.php?174374-Defexpo-India-2010/page9
53 http://img411.imageshack.us/img411/3180/dsc00465k.jpg
54 https://twitter.com/LeShaque/status/53191753938903042
55 http://www.youtube.com/watch?v=1qI2HYHysnU
56 https://twitter.com/acarvin/status/53560315748696064
57 http://storify.com/acarvin/how-to-debunk-a-geopolitical-rumor-with-your-twitt2
58 https://twitter.com/acarvin/status/53567519453216769
59 https://twitter.com/ingefl/status/53578322944344064
60 http://www.flickr.com/photos/andycarvin/5581189990
61 http://www.flickr.com/photos/andycarvin/5581189998
62 https://twitter.com/MadcapMagician/status/53574265097818112
63 https://twitter.com/AminElShelhi/statuses/53577483123032064
64 http://www.scribd.com/doc/34065603/NATO-AOP-2-C-The-Identification-of-Ammunition-2008
65 https://twitter.com/acarvin/statuses/53580503734951936
66 https://twitter.com/acarvin/status/53575475372625920
67 http://edition.presstv.ir/detail/172525.html
68 https://twitter.com/acarvin/status/53645137531768833
69 http://www.flickr.com/photos/libyaalhurratv/5693673320

70 http://www.flickr.com/photos/libyaalhurratv/5693674234
71 http://www.universalsubtitles.org/sv/videos/TMwJ92hKYhVh/en/86723/
72 https://twitter.com/cjchivers/status/66584847312891905
73 https://twitter.com/acarvin/status/66598136570847232#432
74 http://bit.ly/MleEgG
75 https://twitter.com/der_bluthund/status/66601681290412033
76 https://twitter.com/shava23/status/66601081764974592
77 https://twitter.com/ProfdelaPaz/status/66604267028488192
78 https://twitter.com/cultauthor/status/66601429846065152
79 https://twitter.com/acarvin/status/66602031284101120
80 https://twitter.com/cultauthor/status/66602471795068928
81 https://twitter.com/cultauthor/status/66602879473037312
82 https://twitter.com/acarvin/status/66606353896062976
83 https://twitter.com/tetreaultaj/status/66607882879242240
84 https://twitter.com/acarvin/status/66607198830202880#415
85 https://twitter.com/nolesfan2011/status/66607945609256963
86 https://twitter.com/nolesfan2011/status/66609098556321792
87 https://twitter.com/nolesfan2011/status/66610146096328704
88 https://twitter.com/der_bluthund/status/66611973588123648#303
89 https://twitter.com/acarvin/status/66616016297394177
90 https://twitter.com/UrbanMilkmaid/status/66616435568422912
91 https://twitter.com/cjchivers/status/66617839519416320
92 https://twitter.com/der_bluthund/status/66622663111622657#848
93 https://twitter.com/Papakila/status/66621414278565888
94 http://www.nytimes.com/2011/05/07/world/africa/07libya.html
95 https://twitter.com/BCubbison/status/66663520997081088

The Road to Liberation

1 https://twitter.com/acarvin/status/75592923114258432
2 https://twitter.com/acarvin/status/75654010278903808
3 https://twitter.com/acarvin/status/77171474863108096
4 https://twitter.com/acarvin/status/77175538397089792
5 https://twitter.com/acarvin/status/78175948993859585
6 http://www.youtube.com/watch?v=xCVQ9LqRw-k
7 http://www.youtube.com/watch?v=jCSGLcehLmg
8 http://www.youtube.com/watch?v=XpqQ4ttPSfo
9 http://www.youtube.com/watch?v=VUys_sztVFM
10 http://www.youtube.com/watch?v=tOUrRUEd4X8
11 http://www.youtube.com/watch?v=TcNMHnLiD8g
12 http://www.youtube.com/watch?v=htPn-9Yt4Z4
13 https://twitter.com/acarvin/status/91604033290248193
14 https://twitter.com/acarvin/status/100312585982840832
15 http://nationalinterest.org/commentary/headfirst-the-libyan-quagmire-5155
16 http://www.nypost.com/p/news/opinion/opedcolumnists/obama_quagmire_Tg5HRatNCf72nxhK17RmzO
17 http://swampland.time.com/2011/04/20/obamas-libya-quagmire/
18 http://www.sfgate.com/world/article/Libya-campaign-risks-becoming-quagmire-for-NATO-2370709.php
19 http://www.usatoday.com/news/washington/2011-07-30-libya-syria-NATO-america_n.htm

20 http://www.technologyreview.com/web/40214/
21 https://twitter.com/liberty4libya/status/102390937912750080
22 https://twitter.com/acarvin/status/104675595325157376
23 https://twitter.com/acarvin/status/104675970614697984
24 http://twitter.com/justindlong/status/104692510512775168
25 http://twitter.com/acarvin/status/104693867424645120
26 http://twitter.com/justindlong/status/104705369988796416
27 http://twitter.com/acarvin/status/104708359499948033
28 https://twitter.com/acarvin/status/104695301352337408
29 https://twitter.com/acarvin/status/104697838675558402
30 https://twitter.com/acarvin/status/104698729075978240
31 https://twitter.com/acarvin/status/104700317756702721
32 http://twitter.com/Tripoli_Latest/status/104715969863233536
33 http://twitter.com/acarvin/status/104721192132419584
34 http://twitter.com/Tripoli_Latest/status/104722104355782656
35 http://twitter.com/acarvin/status/104724244327432192
36 https://twitter.com/acarvin/status/104701513284329472
37 https://twitter.com/acarvin/status/104733409552769024
38 https://twitter.com/acarvin/status/104701876511059968
39 https://twitter.com/acarvin/status/104724755696975872
40 https://twitter.com/acarvin/status/104724494307962881
41 https://twitter.com/acarvin/status/104714256250970112
42 https://twitter.com/acarvin/status/104726335645155328
43 https://twitter.com/acarvin/status/104931005974056960
44 https://twitter.com/acarvin/status/105004083240370176
45 https://twitter.com/acarvin/status/105006314605912064
46 https://twitter.com/acarvin/status/105007155786153984
47 https://twitter.com/acarvin/status/105009829801758720
48 https://twitter.com/acarvin/status/105015667736068096
49 https://twitter.com/acarvin/status/105088381809197056
50 https://twitter.com/acarvin/status/105088416454152193
51 https://twitter.com/acarvin/status/105250559845605376
52 https://twitter.com/acarvin/status/105251494814679041
53 https://twitter.com/acarvin/status/105281013344768000
54 https://twitter.com/acarvin/status/105281025348866050
55 https://twitter.com/acarvin/status/105281045406040064
56 https://twitter.com/acarvin/status/105306003075112960
57 https://twitter.com/acarvin/status/105340830637760512
58 https://twitter.com/acarvin/status/105341161903898624
59 https://twitter.com/acarvin/status/105351369057239040
60 https://twitter.com/acarvin/status/105351387122118656
61 https://twitter.com/acarvin/status/105352996824694784
62 https://twitter.com/acarvin/status/105353516209545216
63 https://twitter.com/acarvin/status/105353463050936320
64 https://twitter.com/acarvin/status/105357166537490432
65 https://twitter.com/acarvin/status/105434249070526464
66 https://twitter.com/acarvin/status/105434326606426112
67 https://twitter.com/acarvin/status/105450328777965568
68 https://twitter.com/acarvin/status/105434433796046848
69 https://twitter.com/acarvin/status/105451091419860992

70 https://twitter.com/acarvin/status/105355029992570880
71 https://twitter.com/acarvin/status/105357558935601152
72 https://twitter.com/acarvin/status/105357917464694785
73 https://twitter.com/acarvin/status/105358905806303233
74 https://twitter.com/acarvin/status/105361675900817408
75 https://twitter.com/acarvin/status/105358775308918784
76 https://twitter.com/acarvin/status/105358832758308864
77 https://twitter.com/acarvin/status/105369542557044736
78 https://twitter.com/acarvin/status/105369703408615424
79 https://twitter.com/acarvin/status/105374172879921152
80 https://twitter.com/acarvin/status/105370797949980673
81 https://twitter.com/acarvin/status/105373422758019072
82 https://twitter.com/acarvin/status/105381471174410240
83 https://twitter.com/acarvin/status/105376611272101888
84 https://twitter.com/acarvin/status/105376611272101888
85 https://twitter.com/acarvin/status/105441935833055232
86 https://twitter.com/acarvin/status/105367908682698752
87 https://twitter.com/acarvin/status/105373406257618944
88 https://twitter.com/acarvin/status/105377530864869376
89 https://twitter.com/acarvin/status/105401838395854849
90 https://twitter.com/acarvin/status/105402401929953280
91 https://twitter.com/acarvin/status/105441759986843648
92 https://twitter.com/acarvin/status/105394213939712001
93 https://twitter.com/acarvin/status/105406916095787009
94 http://twitter.com/nolesfan2011/status/105381810665570304
95 http://twitter.com/acarvin/status/105382038537908224
96 https://twitter.com/acarvin/status/105378760869675008
97 https://twitter.com/acarvin/status/105378760869675008
98 https://twitter.com/acarvin/status/1105380037162827776
99 https://twitter.com/acarvin/status/105381142106091520
100 https://twitter.com/acarvin/status/105381142106091520
101 https://twitter.com/acarvin/status/105381346872008704

The L-Team

1 http://www.washingtonpost.com/world/hunted-by-regime-tripoli-activist-kept-flame-of-protest-burning/2011/08/29/gIQAVvNToJ_story.html
2 https://twitter.com/acarvin/status/115862648058425344
3 https://twitter.com/acarvin/status/116188453208719361
4 https://twitter.com/nolesfan2011/status/106371525732610049

Multi-Camera Shoot

1 https://twitter.com/acarvin/status/126975671623876608
2 https://twitter.com/acarvin/status/126975883964719104
3 https://twitter.com/acarvin/status/126978028399108097
4 https://twitter.com/acarvin/status/126980857759150081
5 https://twitter.com/acarvin/status/126980857759150081
6 https://twitter.com/acarvin/status/126981047668846592
7 https://twitter.com/acarvin/status/126982517369749504
8 https://twitter.com/acarvin/status/126982529696808960

9 https://twitter.com/acarvin/status/126983279701274624
10 https://twitter.com/acarvin/status/126984294546669568
11 https://twitter.com/acarvin/status/126984804209131520
12 https://twitter.com/acarvin/status/126984804209131520
13 https://twitter.com/acarvin/status/126985305390714880
14 https://twitter.com/acarvin/status/126985538635956226
15 https://twitter.com/acarvin/status/126985745591312384
16 https://twitter.com/acarvin/status/126986590974263297
17 https://twitter.com/acarvin/status/126988291873579009
18 https://twitter.com/acarvin/status/126988693155229698
19 https://twitter.com/acarvin/status/126989099948195841
20 https://twitter.com/acarvin/status/126990192371433472
21 https://twitter.com/acarvin/status/126996080545107969
22 https://twitter.com/acarvin/status/126996080545107969
23 https://twitter.com/acarvin/status/127004562010800128
24 https://twitter.com/acarvin/status/127004312944648192
25 https://twitter.com/acarvin/status/127002083110031362
26 https://twitter.com/acarvin/status/127002266807959555
27 https://twitter.com/acarvin/status/127004244980137984
28 https://twitter.com/acarvin/status/127006518318080000
29 https://twitter.com/acarvin/status/127006671892525057
30 https://twitter.com/acarvin/status/127008086413152256
31 https://twitter.com/acarvin/status/127008384955322368
32 https://twitter.com/acarvin/status/127009033612836864
33 http://www.youtube.com/watch?v=HFHsX7xl-uE
34 https://twitter.com/acarvin/status/127027103957925888
35 https://twitter.com/acarvin/status/127028516939235329
36 https://twitter.com/acarvin/status/127028321576951808
37 https://twitter.com/acarvin/status/127098887642152960
38 https://twitter.com/acarvin/status/127109776789352448
39 https://twitter.com/acarvin/status/127192123563966464
40 https://twitter.com/acarvin/status/127103663004061696
41 https://twitter.com/acarvin/status/127013940185149440
42 https://twitter.com/acarvin/status/127073892517953536
43 https://twitter.com/acarvin/status/127073916790390784
44 https://twitter.com/acarvin/status/127085246716968961
45 https://twitter.com/acarvin/status/127085267592028160
46 http://www.youtube.com/watch?v=NVIkck02qao&feature=share
47 https://twitter.com/acarvin/status/127082006134796288
48 http://feb17.info/news/breaking-video-gaddafis-body-arrives-in-misrata/
49 http://www.nytimes.com/video/2011/10/20/world/africa/100000001124288/video-of-muammar-qaddafis-body.html
50 http://www.globalpost.com/dispatch/news/regions/middle-east/111024/gaddafi-sodomized-video-gaddafi-sodomy
51 http://www.globalpost.com/dispatches/globalpost-blogs/the-casbah/gaddafi-dead-video-initial-capture-exclusive
52 http://www.liveleak.com/view?i=1ed_1319161563&comments=1
53 https://twitter.com/solbutterfly/status/127165570830446593
54 https://twitter.com/acarvin/status/127166728391245824
55 https://twitter.com/acarvin/status/127166747882168320

56 https://twitter.com/acarvin/status/127171194045730816
57 https://twitter.com/acarvin/status/127080818974797824
58 https://twitter.com/acarvin/status/127097763182804992
59 https://twitter.com/acarvin/status/127119908101292033
60 http://www.youtube.com/watch?v=Wm4yHU6HPro
61 http://www.globalpost.com/dispatch/news/regions/middle-east/111024/gaddafi-sodomized-video-gaddafi-sodomy
62 http://www.huffingtonpost.com/2011/10/24/gaddafi-sodomized-video_n_1028970.html

Conflicting Reports

1 https://twitter.com/acarvin/status/76632266041868288
2 http://www.csmonitor.com/World/Middle-East/2011/0218/Yemen-awash-in-guns-wary-about-unrest
3 https://twitter.com/#!/ArabRevolution/yemen
4 https://twitter.com/#!/habibahamid/yemen
5 http://www.armiesofliberation.com/
6 http://www.nytimes.com/2008/05/20/world/middleeast/20blogger.html?pagewanted=all
7 https://twitter.com/acarvin/status/37542142414946304
8 https://twitter.com/acarvin/status/38298180860919808
9 https://twitter.com/acarvin/status/38699883707760640
10 https://twitter.com/acarvin/status/40399589542461440
11 https://twitter.com/acarvin/status/41356062489575424
12 https://twitter.com/acarvin/status/48733882316632064
13 https://twitter.com/acarvin/status/48735640774381568
14 https://twitter.com/acarvin/status/48737991413346305
15 https://twitter.com/acarvin/status/48741186323742720
16 https://twitter.com/acarvin/status/http://yfrog.com/h2k9qbej
17 https://twitter.com/acarvin/status/48741409771102208
18 https://twitter.com/acarvin/status/48767935220682753
19 https://twitter.com/acarvin/status/48769953574293505
20 http://www.youtube.com/watch?v=wcOqLeRsEq8
22 https://twitter.com/acarvin/status/48897501754953728
23 http://www.youtube.com/watch?v=0WQ0T6aqBxc
24 https://twitter.com/acarvin/status/48897776163110912
25 http://www.mciis.org/former_intel_student_beauty_pageant_controversy
26 https://twitter.com/acarvin/status/50928244983205888
27 http://yemenrightsmonitor.blogspot.com/
28 https://twitter.com/acarvin/status/49528366788911104
29 https://twitter.com/acarvin/status/49528613745332225
30 https://twitter.com/acarvin/status/49772119260794880
31 https://twitter.com/acarvin/status/49818027323162624
32 https://twitter.com/acarvin/status/49946554219499520
33 https://twitter.com/acarvin/status/49946510707785728
34 https://twitter.com/acarvin/status/51252531657064448
35 https://twitter.com/acarvin/status/51261667350294528
36 https://twitter.com/acarvin/status/51678824164884480
37 https://twitter.com/acarvin/status/51678704178434049
38 https://twitter.com/acarvin/status/51835895250296832
39 https://twitter.com/acarvin/status/51679072845176832

40 https://twitter.com/acarvin/status/57411461835796481
41 http://www.youtube.com/user/surgicalx?feature=watch
42 http://www.youtube.com/watch?v=9QE6XBAUuh0
43 https://twitter.com/acarvin/status/55263729503313920
44 https://twitter.com/acarvin/status/55264149202141187
45 https://twitter.com/acarvin/status/55264477335126016
46 https://twitter.com/acarvin/status/55264717635194880
47 https://twitter.com/acarvin/status/55271388059152385
48 https://twitter.com/acarvin/status/55271825147576320
49 https://twitter.com/acarvin/status/55279499788562433
50 https://twitter.com/acarvin/status/68386082781265920
51 https://twitter.com/acarvin/status/68386123302436864
52 https://twitter.com/acarvin/status/68387082250362880
53 https://twitter.com/acarvin/status/68386459291369472
54 https://twitter.com/acarvin/status/68390466672009216
55 https://twitter.com/acarvin/status/68390466672009216
56 https://twitter.com/acarvin/status/68393519714279424
57 https://twitter.com/acarvin/status/74858856420868096
58 https://twitter.com/acarvin/status/74859072343642112
59 https://twitter.com/acarvin/status/74859114538336257
60 https://twitter.com/acarvin/status/74859706816004096
61 https://twitter.com/acarvin/status/74859723689701376
62 https://twitter.com/acarvin/status/75211809744891904
63 https://twitter.com/acarvin/status/74998761809657857
64 https://twitter.com/acarvin/status/75212347022655488
65 https://twitter.com/acarvin/status/75212607312760832
66 https://twitter.com/acarvin/status/75212607312760832
67 https://twitter.com/alguneid/status/75213953789202432
68 https://twitter.com/acarvin/status/75215248809930753
69 http://youtu.be/k7cNOFJ5Lj4
70 http://www.youtube.com/watch?v=WcfPzVhn41U
71 https://twitter.com/acarvin/status/75213702638473216
72 http://www.youtube.com/watch?v=dIV8aQp3JAA
73 https://twitter.com/acarvin/status/75216106176004097
74 https://twitter.com/acarvin/status/75239595389890560
75 https://twitter.com/acarvin/status/75239627698614273
76 https://twitter.com/acarvin/status/75340419201908736
77 https://twitter.com/acarvin/status/75341942296285185
78 https://twitter.com/acarvin/status/75342045866237952
79 https://twitter.com/acarvin/status/75342402910556161
80 https://twitter.com/acarvin/status/75342603742228481
81 https://twitter.com/acarvin/status/75343871516737536
82 https://twitter.com/acarvin/status/75343791439101952
83 https://twitter.com/acarvin/status/75394495537094656
84 https://twitter.com/acarvin/status/75346082468593664
85 This tweet and the following one used an online service to extend the length of the tweets by posting them on a website, which is why the tweets exceed the standard 140 characters.
86 https://twitter.com/acarvin/status/75347237907070976
87 https://twitter.com/acarvin/status/75359174661390336

88 https://twitter.com/acarvin/status/75359211701272577
89 https://twitter.com/acarvin/status/75365915398647808
90 https://twitter.com/acarvin/status/75387039545176064
91 https://twitter.com/acarvin/status/75388884283961345
92 https://twitter.com/acarvin/status/75391679779188736
93 https://twitter.com/acarvin/status/75390168470781954
94 https://twitter.com/acarvin/status/75392073162952704
95 https://twitter.com/acarvin/status/75392105412956160
96 https://twitter.com/acarvin/status/75392172354043904
97 https://twitter.com/acarvin/status/75398958897299457
98 https://twitter.com/acarvin/status/76626695012098048
99 https://twitter.com/acarvin/status/76626725236256768
100 https://twitter.com/acarvin/status/76627606665039872
101 https://twitter.com/acarvin/status/76627741105065984
102 https://twitter.com/acarvin/status/76627580354183170
103 https://twitter.com/acarvin/status/76627478982041600
104 https://twitter.com/acarvin/status/76626809839562754
105 https://twitter.com/acarvin/status/76627363043090432
106 https://twitter.com/acarvin/status/76658943836958720
107 https://twitter.com/acarvin/status/76659219243352064
108 https://twitter.com/acarvin/status/76627275260506113
109 https://twitter.com/acarvin/status/76628053442297856
110 https://twitter.com/acarvin/status/76628053442297856
111 https://twitter.com/acarvin/status/76628098778537984
112 https://twitter.com/acarvin/status/76628171700703233
113 https://twitter.com/acarvin/status/76628228218961921
114 https://twitter.com/acarvin/status/76628778071240705
115 https://twitter.com/acarvin/status/76654444414115841
116 https://twitter.com/acarvin/status/76629060347887616
117 https://twitter.com/acarvin/status/76634296789630976
118 https://twitter.com/acarvin/status/76629379249225728
119 https://twitter.com/acarvin/status/76629653225353217
120 https://twitter.com/acarvin/status/76630782956929025
121 https://twitter.com/acarvin/status/76631054491979777
122 https://twitter.com/acarvin/status/76631091255050240
123 https://twitter.com/acarvin/status/76631286378278912
124 https://twitter.com/acarvin/status/76632266041868288
125 https://twitter.com/acarvin/status/76633828625629184
126 https://twitter.com/acarvin/status/76634533239328768
127 https://twitter.com/acarvin/status/76659275778371584
128 https://twitter.com/acarvin/status/76641494500524032
129 https://twitter.com/acarvin/status/76654264537194496
130 https://twitter.com/acarvin/status/76654767325192192
131 https://twitter.com/acarvin/status/76654997017858049
132 https://twitter.com/acarvin/status/76657626410254336
133 https://twitter.com/acarvin/status/76658162714951681
134 https://twitter.com/acarvin/status/76658017042563072
135 https://twitter.com/acarvin/status/76657551181234177
136 https://twitter.com/acarvin/status/76657652238794752
137 https://twitter.com/acarvin/status/76699455314857984

138 https://twitter.com/acarvin/status/76700380439904256
139 https://twitter.com/acarvin/status/76700540427436032
140 https://twitter.com/acarvin/status/76701398313598976
141 https://twitter.com/acarvin/status/76701707010183168
142 https://twitter.com/acarvin/status/76728850087809024
143 https://twitter.com/acarvin/status/76728880622342144
144 https://twitter.com/acarvin/status/76728978148306944
145 https://twitter.com/acarvin/status/76729075116421120
146 https://twitter.com/acarvin/status/76730293721116673
147 https://twitter.com/acarvin/status/76730763122442240
148 https://twitter.com/acarvin/status/76743076269404160
149 http://www.aljazeera.com/news/middleeast/2011/06/201164164346765100.html
150 https://twitter.com/menablog/status/77189267666898944
151 http://www.alhasela.com/cms/node/2559?sms_ss=twitter&at_xt=4deace83b73000a3,0
152 https://twitter.com/acarvin/status/77197420294971392
153 https://twitter.com/NasserElMasri/status/77203158547431424
154 http://twitter.com/warpafx/status/77201417714139136
156 http://twitter.com/MaxDReinhardt/status/77200983662395392
157 http://twitter.com/acarvin/status/77198684600807424
158 http://twitter.com/toea/status/77198579684491264#647
159 http://twitter.com/menablog/status/77199137472397312
160 http://twitter.com/GypsyDesert/status/77199566415470592
161 http://twitter.com/franniefabian/status/77200715025625088#531
162 http://twitter.com/danjukic/status/77202641855328256
163 http://twitter.com/volks/status/77200323004993536
164 http://twitter.com/GypsyDesert/status/77202326070366208
165 http://twitter.com/SubMedina/status/77206742995443712
166 http://twitter.com/sandymaxey/status/77201374001115136
167 http://twitter.com/sandymaxey/status/77211292200468480
168 http://twitter.com/sandymaxey/statuses/77211365751791616
169 http://twitter.com/sandymaxey/status/77206504461172736
170 http://twitter.com/sandymaxey/statuses/77212082927435777
171 http://twitter.com/MoMustafaMD/status/77207411999506432
172 http://edition.cnn.com/2011/WORLD/meast/06/07/yemen.unrest/
173 http://www.npr.org/blogs/thetwo-way/2011/10/06/141138381/a-nobel-peace-prize-for-the-arab-spring-who-would-that-go-to

Outing a Gay Girl in Damascus

1 Quote from blog post on the disappearance of Amina Arraf; post deleted when the blog was removed from public view in the summer of 2011.
2 Archived by the author prior to the deletion of the blog, summer of 2011.
3 http://www.guardian.co.uk/world/2011/may/06/gay-girl-damascus-syria-blog
4 https://twitter.com/acarvin/status/77804332778659841
5 Archived by the author prior to the deletion of the blog, summer of 2011.
6 https://twitter.com/acarvin/status/77804332778659841
7 https://twitter.com/acarvin/status/77804671200280576
8 https://twitter.com/fionamoon/statuses/77835987228692480
9 https://twitter.com/Razaniyat/status/77858005072359424
10 http://twitter.com/sade_la_bag/status/77816306669330433
11 https://twitter.com/Houeida/statuses/78078136943788032

12 https://twitter.com/BSyria/status/77828114306174976
13 https://twitter.com/acarvin/status/77840644894240768
14 https://twitter.com/BSyria/statuses/77840931927244800
15 https://twitter.com/acarvin/status/77841296282226688
16 https://twitter.com/sade_la_bag/status/77912358219022336
17 https://twitter.com/sade_la_bag/status/77875019623055361
18 Direct message exchange with @DannySeesIt, June 7, 2011
19 https://twitter.com/acarvin/status/78130192538808321
20 https://twitter.com/acarvin/status/78133801980669953
21 At the request of my Syrian contact, I am not going to identify him in order to protect his safety.
22 https://twitter.com/acarvin/status/78129181107560449
23 *Ya habibti* is Arabic for "Oh, darling."
24 https://twitter.com/acarvin/status/78168761747775488
25 https://twitter.com/shoofs/status/78189841094942720
26 https://twitter.com/acarvin/status/78190784188395520
27 https://twitter.com/shoofs/status/78191966671736832
28 https://twitter.com/acarvin/status/78192543279484928
29 https://twitter.com/shoofs/status/78198027675893760
30 https://twitter.com/lezgetreal/status/78266990518734848
31 http://thelede.blogs.nytimes.com/2011/06/07/syrian-american-blogger-detained/
32 http://aminaarraf.blogspot.com/2007/09/this-blog-what-it-is-and-what-it-is-not.html
33 https://twitter.com/acarvin/status/78282879876075520. I originally posted this on Twitter using a service deck.ly, which allows you to write tweets longer than 140 characters. The service has since shut down, but I retained a copy of my post.
34 https://twitter.com/acarvin/status/78285091536764929
35 https://twitter.com/acarvin/status/78285607985614848
36 https://twitter.com/GypsyDesert/status/78288853072482304
37 https://twitter.com/acarvin/status/78289432268128257
38 https://twitter.com/acarvin/status/78290017050558481
39 https://twitter.com/oemasoso/status/78401215851008000
40 https://twitter.com/oemasoso/status/78400326700507136
41 https://twitter.com/acarvin/status/78437174944608256
42 https://twitter.com/acarvin/status/78479234078744576
43 https://twitter.com/monaeltahawy/status/78458369144393728
44 https://twitter.com/monaeltahawy/status/78458741061730304
45 https://twitter.com/acarvin/status/78459689830055936
46 https://twitter.com/monaeltahawy/status/78460249983553536
47 https://twitter.com/monaeltahawy/status/78463237888290816
48 https://twitter.com/acarvin/status/78489265377517568
49 Private direct messages sent to the author.
50 http://electronicintifada.net/comment/397
51 http://www.blogher.com/gay-girl-damascus-blogging-hoax-chasing-amina
52 Originally posted on the Gay Girl in Damascus blog, but deleted when the blog was removed by its author during the summer of 2011.
53 https://twitter.com/acarvin/status/79990768126791680
54 https://twitter.com/acarvin/status/79993447771152384
55 https://twitter.com/acarvin/status/79999306345611265
56 https://twitter.com/jilliancyork/status/79999453725073408
57 https://twitter.com/jilliancyork/status/79993850990575616

58 https://twitter.com/jilliancyork/status/80002708664369152
59 https://twitter.com/gr33ndata/status/79994346111385600
60 https://twitter.com/Elizrael/status/80003166397153281
61 https://twitter.com/MalathAumran/status/80336299659243522
62 https://twitter.com/lobna/status/80020609299525633
63 https://twitter.com/lobna/status/80019597692121089
64 https://twitter.com/lobna/status/80027579159035904
65 https://twitter.com/sade_la_bag/status/80086497654611968
66 http://www.npr.org/blogs/thetwo-way/2011/06/14/137148644/man-behind-syrian-blogger-hoax-something-innocent-got-out-of-hand
67 http://www.washingtonpost.com/blogs/blogpost/post/paula-brooks-editor-of-lez-get-real-also-a-man/2011/06/13/AGld2ZTH_blog.html
68 https://twitter.com/TommyGalante/status/80014718189838336
69 http://www.thedailyshow.com/watch/wed-june-15-2011/we-re-here--we-re-queer--get-newsed-to-it---ny-marriage-equality---gay-blogger-hoax
70 http://www.youtube.com/watch?v=5v_BQAiwREI
71 http://beirutspring.com/blog/2011/06/12/thank-you-tom-macmaster/

Raw Footage

1 http://www.youtube.com/watch?v=Ej84d7OAJzw. Given its extremely graphic nature, please think carefully before watching the video.
2 http://www.time.com/time/magazine/article/0,9171,921108,00.html
3 http://www.theage.com.au/opinion/politics/syrian-situation-is-complex-and-unpredictable-20120216-1tbs2.html
4 http://www.aljazeera.com/indepth/features/2011/05/201153185927813389.html
5 http://en.wikipedia.org/wiki/File:Hamza_Al-Khateeb.jpg
6 http://aje.me/mzrK5m
7 http://tumblr.com/xto2w417nh
8 http://www.thestar.com/news/world/article/1001070--syria-s-sad-revolutionary-symbol
9 http://twitpic.com/5894zl
10 https://www.facebook.com/hamza.alshaheed
11 http://www.youtube.com/user/SHAMSNN
12 http://www.youtube.com/user/UgaritNews
13 http://www.lccsyria.org/en/
14 http://twitter.com/iyad_elbaghdadi/status/97611455255429120
15 http://twitter.com/rulaamin/status/97612603093815296
16 http://www.youtube.com/watch?feature=player_embedded&v=QcRNdf0hnvw#!
17 http://www.youtube.com/watch?v=W2MVOuKRc_I
18 http://www.youtube.com/watch?v=qt9dpvfvqmM
19 http://www.youtube.com/watch?v=gr0yHej9sLM EXTREMELY graphic.
20 http://www.youtube.com/watch?v=rjOp42Mk_7E Also graphic
21 https://twitter.com/acarvin/status/97741890161618944
22 https://twitter.com/acarvin/status/97743130337619968
23 https://twitter.com/acarvin/status/97743130337619968
24 https://twitter.com/acarvin/status/97730716498014208
25 https://twitter.com/acarvin/status/98018720500301824
26 https://twitter.com/acarvin/status/98106496772079616
27 https://twitter.com/acarvin/status/98108944182030336
28 https://twitter.com/acarvin/status/98109225808572416

29 https://twitter.com/acarvin/status/98109893717925888
30 https://twitter.com/acarvin/status/98111078659141632
31 https://twitter.com/acarvin/status/98111212105105408
32 https://twitter.com/acarvin/status/98111684845125632
33 https://twitter.com/acarvin/status/98112621080887296
34 https://twitter.com/acarvin/status/98112950287609857
35 https://twitter.com/acarvin/status/98113590900424704
36 https://twitter.com/acarvin/status/98114031512059904
37 https://twitter.com/acarvin/status/98114125330259968
38 https://twitter.com/acarvin/status/98114319149043712
39 https://twitter.com/acarvin/status/98114818766155776
40 https://twitter.com/acarvin/status/98118405453914112
41 https://twitter.com/acarvin/status/98118485237968896
42 https://twitter.com/acarvin/status/98119026613563392
43 https://twitter.com/acarvin/status/98120306505420800
44 https://twitter.com/acarvin/status/98491845553823744
45 https://twitter.com/acarvin/status/98492412325937154
46 https://twitter.com/acarvin/status/98492472379981824
47 https://twitter.com/acarvin/status/98492749745094657
48 https://twitter.com/acarvin/status/98493011327074304
49 https://twitter.com/acarvin/status/98493558956376064
50 https://twitter.com/acarvin/status/98498380359139328
51 https://twitter.com/acarvin/status/98498620776648704
52 https://twitter.com/acarvin/status/98498947995275264
53 https://twitter.com/acarvin/status/98495166947659776
54 https://twitter.com/acarvin/status/98498088553033728
55 https://twitter.com/acarvin/status/98498136825274368
56 https://twitter.com/acarvin/status/98499128530702336
57 https://twitter.com/acarvin/status/98501721449435136
58 https://twitter.com/acarvin/status/98504613090701312
59 https://twitter.com/acarvin/status/98499949767032832
60 http://twitter.com/hamzamu/status/101309714473816064
61 https://twitter.com/acarvin/status/101309870472564736
62 https://twitter.com/acarvin/status/101310722297962498
63 https://twitter.com/acarvin/status/101311350940237826
64 http://www.npr.org/2011/10/21/141568827/prominent-syrian-activist-flees-reveals-identity
65 Baba Amr is sometimes spelled Baba Amro, Bab Amro, etc., making hashtags a difficult way of following the discussion on Twitter. Generally it was easier to use the tag #homs instead, even thought it wasn't as geographically specific.
66 http://twitter.com/AlexanderPageSY/status/152185852779433985
67 https://twitter.com/acarvin/status/152186926596751360
68 http://youtu.be/Wr7865hS8LM
69 https://twitter.com/acarvin/status/152187586612428800
70 http://twitter.com/acarvin/status/152188485535666176
71 https://twitter.com/acarvin/status/152195755489243136
72 https://twitter.com/acarvin/status/152187921724751872
73 https://twitter.com/acarvin/status/152797709542244352
74 http://blog.bambuser.com/2012/02/we-mourn-loss-of-very-brave-syrian.html
75 https://twitter.com/syrianintegrity/status/166173367194488834

76 http://twitter.com/homsi_news/status/166172252440756224/photo/1pic.twitter.com/6ncjhARH
77 http://twitter.com/acarvin/statuses/166173629573382144
78 http://www.youtube.com/watch?v=eaOZICNlmxo Extremely graphic and upsetting.
79 https://twitter.com/acarvin/status/166184816692305921
80 The YouTube video that was originally circulated that day was later deleted. An exact copy of it is still available here: http://www.youtube.com/watch?v=eaOZICNlmxo Please consider the emotional impact of the video before you watch it; it will indeed haunt you for life.
81 http://twitter.com/acarvin/statuses/166186889009823744
82 https://twitter.com/Steven_Maclean/status/166185140291256320
83 http://twitter.com/acarvin/statuses/166186110794473472
84 http://twitter.com/AliAbunimah/status/166187299418292224
85 http://twitter.com/acarvin/statuses/166187943302672384
86 http://twitter.com/acarvin/statuses/166189004738408448
87 http://twitter.com/acarvin/statuses/166189186423062529
88 http://twitter.com/Mou2amara/status/166190822075793408
89 http://twitter.com/acarvin/statuses/166191195482112000
90 http://twitter.com/itsEnas/status/166191493055389696
91 http://twitter.com/acarvin/statuses/166191895633080323
92 http://twitter.com/acarvin/statuses/166193242428276736
93 http://twitter.com/acarvin/statuses/166195204896985088
94 http://twitter.com/acarvin/statuses/166195204896985088
95 http://twitter.com/acarvin/statuses/166243427388882947
96 http://twitter.com/acarvin/statuses/166245712898686976
97 http://twitter.com/acarvin/statuses/166245863998504960
98 http://twitter.com/itsEnas/status/166260786455515136
99 http://twitter.com/acarvin/statuses/166261136935747584
100 http://twitter.com/BigAlBrand/status/166263995668512768
101 http://twitter.com/acarvin/statuses/166264465011122177
102 http://twitter.com/acarvin/statuses/166273393765785601
103 http://twitter.com/acarvin/statuses/166257904884789249
104 http://twitter.com/acarvin/statuses/166280730471694338
105 http://twitter.com/acarvin/statuses/166310847147278336
106 http://twitter.com/acarvin/statuses/166329695137316865
107 http://twitter.com/acarvin/statuses/166333454802362369
108 https://twitter.com/acarvin/statuses/166329531156795393
109 https://twitter.com/acarvin/statuses/166329531156795393
110 http://twitter.com/acarvin/statuses/166330877947817984
111 http://twitter.com/acarvin/statuses/166333077889613824
112 http://twitter.com/acarvin/statuses/166334318334062592
113 http://twitter.com/acarvin/statuses/166343406375809025
114 http://twitter.com/acarvin/statuses/166334780168880128
115 http://twitter.com/acarvin/statuses/166339702981525504
116 http://twitter.com/acarvin/statuses/166339574979768320
117 http://twitter.com/acarvin/statuses/166341378169774080
118 http://twitter.com/acarvin/statuses/166341636245295104
119 http://twitter.com/acarvin/statuses/166344592617259008
120 http://twitter.com/acarvin/statuses/166358427457683456
121 https://twitter.com/apk222/status/166504605746855936

122 http://twitter.com/acarvin/statuses/166507482678697984
123 https://twitter.com/acarvin/status/166514603759636480
124 https://twitter.com/acarvin/status/166514810094231552
125 https://twitter.com/acarvin/status/166514918999339008
126 https://twitter.com/acarvin/status/166515127712092160
127 https://twitter.com/acarvin/status/166515537361387520

The Tear gas Club

1 Frogger was an arcade game in which you would navigate a frog across a highway dense with traffic. It came out in the early 1980s, well before most of these Egyptian revolutionaries were born. http://en.wikipedia.org/wiki/Frogger
2 https://twitter.com/acarvin/status/857806323404144640
3 One of the very first things I published on the Internet was a travel journal about my 1995 visit to the Middle East. I briefly reference Tahrir in one of the journal entries: http://www.edwebproject.org/mideast/journal.1029.html
4 @travellerW later changed his Twitter name to @eldahshan.
5 https://twitter.com/acarvin/status/85821413252014080
6 https://twitter.com/acarvin/status/85824404008865792
7 https://twitter.com/acarvin/status/85824806452342784
8 https://twitter.com/acarvin/status/85825176629018624
9 https://twitter.com/acarvin/status/85825313250082816
10 https://twitter.com/acarvin/status/85826215931428864
11 https://twitter.com/acarvin/status/85826429027233792
12 https://twitter.com/acarvin/status/85829223809425409
13 https://twitter.com/acarvin/status/85829680304881664
14 https://twitter.com/acarvin/status/85830271110348800
15 https://twitter.com/acarvin/status/85831937951936512
16 https://twitter.com/acarvin/status/85832192894312448
17 https://twitter.com/acarvin/status/85834032054673408
18 https://twitter.com/acarvin/status/85835094358634496
19 https://twitter.com/acarvin/status/85837747578875904
20 https://twitter.com/acarvin/status/85838190241517568
21 https://twitter.com/acarvin/status/85845871618555904
22 https://twitter.com/acarvin/status/85848335541473280
23 https://twitter.com/acarvin/status/85851400965337089
24 https://twitter.com/acarvin/status/85846136790855680
25 https://twitter.com/acarvin/status/85845921195229184
26 https://twitter.com/acarvin/status/85846187919425536
27 https://twitter.com/acarvin/status/85846055366828032
28 https://twitter.com/acarvin/status/85846847482105856
29 https://twitter.com/acarvin/status/85847047248416768
30 https://twitter.com/acarvin/status/85847207890255872
31 https://twitter.com/acarvin/status/85847291193331713
32 https://twitter.com/acarvin/status/85846804402413568
33 https://twitter.com/acarvin/status/85848220294578177
34 https://twitter.com/acarvin/status/85848220294578177

A Revolution's Legacy

1 After my visit, @libyasupreme changed his twitter handle to @MalikLofficial.